Democracy under stress

Ursula J. van Beek
Edmund Wnuk-Lipinski (eds.)

Democracy under stress
The global crisis and beyond

Barbara Budrich Publishers
Opladen • Berlin • Farmington Hills, MI 2012

A CIP catalogue record for this book is available from
Die Deutsche Bibliothek (The German Library)

© 2012 by Barbara Budrich Publishers, Opladen, Berlin & Farmington Hills, MI
            www.barbara-budrich.net
    ISBN   978-3-86649-453-4

Die Deutsche Bibliothek – CIP-Einheitsaufnahme
Ein Titeldatensatz für die Publikation ist bei Der Deutschen Bibliothek erhältlich.

Verlag Barbara Budrich (B) Barbara Budrich Publishers
Stauffenbergstr. 7. D-51379 Leverkusen Opladen, Germany

28347 Ridgebrook. Farmington Hills, MI 48334. USA
www.barbara-budrich.net

Jacket illustration by disegno, Wuppertal, Germany – www.disenjo.de
Typesetting by Susanne Albrecht-Rosenkranz, Leverkusen, Germany
Printed in Europe on acid-free paper by
paper&tinta, Warsaw

Table of contents

PART III: An authoritarian response

PART IV: Towards a new global configuration

Foreword and acknowledgments

This book is the third in a series produced by the Transformation Research Initiative (TRI) team based at Stellenbosch University in South Africa, www.sun.ac.za/tri. It differs sharply from its two predecessors in that it has no common theoretical framework or shared empirical data. In fact, the authors do not necessarily all agree with each other and they sometimes even offer differing viewpoints. This is because what follows is an initial exploration and conceptualisation of a complex global phenomenon whose origins are as yet poorly understood and whose outcomes and long-term consequences cannot at this point be more than speculation.

The TRI team members are greatly indebted to the Stellenbosch Institute for Advanced Study (STIAS) for initiating and supporting the project institutionally, and to the Tercentenary Bank of Sweden Foundation in Stockholm for providing seed funding.

List of contributors

Dirk Berg-Schlosser
Professor, Institute of Political Science, Philipps-University
Marburg, **Germany**

Stan du Plessis
Professor, Department of Economy, Stellenbosch University
Stellenbosch, **South Africa**

Pierre du Toit
Professor, Department of Political Science, Stellenbosch University,
Stellenbosch, **South Africa**

Sang-Jin Han
Professor, Department of Sociology, Seoul National University,
Seoul, **South Korea**

Ursula Hoffmann-Lange
Professor (Political Science), Faculty of Social Sciences, Economics and
Business Administration, University of Bamberg
Bamberg, **Germany**

Christer Jönsson
Professor: Department of Political Science, Lund University,
Lund, **Sweden**

Bernard Lategan
Professor (Theology) Stellenbosch Institute for Advanced Study (STIAS)
Stellenbosch, **South Africa**

Peng Lü
Doctor. Research Fellow: Institute of Sociology, Chinese Academy of Social
Sciences (CASS), Beijing, **China**

Philip Mohr
Professor: Department of Economics, University of South Africa (Unisa)
Pretoria, **South Africa**

Ursula J. van Beek
Professor, (History) Department of Political Science, Stellenbosch University,
Stellenbosch, **South Africa**

Edmund Wnuk-Lipinski
Professor (Sociology), Collegium Civitas,
Warsaw, **Poland**

Laurence Whitehead
Professor (Political Science and Economy), Nuffield College, Oxford University, Oxford, **United Kingdom**

The crisis that shook the world

Ursula J. van Beek

> Two things are infinite: the universe and human stupidity;
> And I am not sure about the universe.
>
> *Albert Einstein*

Introduction

This book is a cautionary tale about the September 2008 financial 'earthquake' and the global tsunami that followed. The worst of the panic might be over, but does this mean it is back to business as usual? Hardly. The earthquake exposed fault lines we can afford to ignore only at our own peril. In fact, the need to understand what happened, why it happened and what the possible long-term consequences could be, have turned into the most burning questions of our time, and certainly not only for economists.

The earthquake

At the epicentre of the global earthquake was the bankruptcy of Lehman Brothers in September 2008. This initial seismic event sent out shockwaves that triggered the global financial and economic crisis and plunged the world into the turmoil of the Great Recession. Since the originating event, unemployment rates in all the major liberal democracies, which were affected the most, are higher now than they were before 2008, and the level of their public debt has risen dramatically. Coupled with unwieldy budget deficits and poor growth prospects, the economies of these countries could well be weakened for years to come. The bleak reality is that the prospects for global economic growth predicted by most pundits in the midst of the short-lived burst in the market upswing in 2010 are very unlikely to be realised. The optimism that lulled governments, and the public, into believing the worst was over is now giving way to the realisation that the crisis is in fact not over, but has merely been delayed by stimulus packages and debt-shuffling from the private to the public sector on an unprecedented scale.

The world is now seen as more unstable in many key areas than it has been for many decades. At the time of writing, in the US a state budget crisis is looming; in the Middle East the Arab Spring is breaking up calcified autocratic orders, but the direction of political change is far from certain; and in Europe the profoundly serious situation in Greece and the shaky state of economic affairs in other peripheral, especially Southern European, countries raises the likelihood that the euro might not survive in its current form. There is even the possibility that the European Union project as a whole could be undermined and a more fragmented Europe will be less able to deal with the mounting global challenges.

The drama unfolding since 2008 ended the unquestioned supremacy of the model adopted by the rich developed democracies and firmly embedded after the Cold War; their seemingly ever-progressing economic development, which was the envy of the rest of the word, has now lost its shine. Economic progress has given way to a sustained decline in the trajectory of affluence, ending thereby the strong popular conviction that democracy and robust economic development necessarily go hand in hand. And there is also the risk that confidence in democracy itself might start to erode.

Against this trend, the economic strength of the more crisis-resistant emerging countries has been bolstered and has begun to crystallise into political power, as illustrated, among other things, by the upgrading in the course of the crisis of the G20 to a venue for heads of state. The global earthquake tilted the political axis of the globe away from the centre, with the result that established liberal democracies lost their monopoly on influence in global affairs. The question now is who will wield influence and in what way. The even more pertinent question is whether democratic principles can and will be applied, or whether different criteria will be used when deciding the fate of the world.

So far the crisis has not proved to be the earth-shattering event that was feared originally. The experience of the Great Depression in the wake of the 1929 stock market crash has not been repeated, nor has there been a similar degree of political upheaval: no young democracies have failed as yet, as was the case with many such fledgling democracies in the interwar period; nor has the economic downturn proved to be as deep as it had been in the 1930s.

Nevertheless, the crisis has taken a heavy economic toll on most countries and has profoundly changed the world in ways we have yet to understand. For one thing, a strong state is now believed to be better equipped than a weak one to sustain a fragile recovery, even as fiscal pressures force governments to unwind their stimulus packages. But are all states, or even most of them, up to the task? Not according to the 2010 state capability index compiled by the *Economist Intelligence Unit* (EIU) and based on 12 indicators that were thought to capture the main conditions likely to show whether or not a particular state has the ability to deliver. Of the 163 countries surveyed only 34 were classified as having highly capable states, and another 38 were classed as moderately capable; more than half of the countries were found to have either weak or very weak states.

At the same time polls show falling public support for capitalism, especially in the USA, the country that used to be the very epitome of free enterprise. And significantly, this is in sharp contrast to China, which has now emerged as one of the strongest supporters of capitalism. These sentiments suggest a shifting relationship between political systems and the free market in a context in which the success of China's state-capitalist model is becoming an advertisement for many developing countries.

Why and how?

The search for answers to the question as to why a calamity occurred starts with an attempt to identify and understand its causes, with a view to hopefully help avoid similar such occurrences in the future. But the causes of far-reaching events are inevitably multiple and hard to untangle. What triggered the downturn following the Wall Street crash on that fateful 'Black Thursday' on 24 October 1929, for example, still remains a matter of much controversy. Among many other specialist opinions, historians tend to emphasise structural factors such as massive bank failures and the crash itself, while economists point more often to monetary policies, especially the contraction of money reserves that resulted from policies adopted by the US Federal Reserve, or the decision by Britain to return to the Gold Standard at pre-World War I levels. While there will undoubtedly be prolonged and detailed future debates, it is already becoming quite clear that the most recent crisis, like the one before it, had many points of origin. The US Bipartisan Commission created in 2009 and the US Congressional Research Service between them identified no fewer than 26 different causes of the crisis, while according to the CEO of the ill-fated Bear Sterns 'everybody messed up': the government, the rating agencies, Wall Street, the commercial banks and the regulators.

At a superficial level the common denominator of the two periods preceding the onset of both the 1929 and the 2008 financial meltdowns was a sense of 'the good times', especially in the United States, where both the crises originated. Rapid industrial/economic growth along with high consumer demand and elevated aspirations characterised both the 'Roaring Twenties' and the two 'feel good' decades of growing prosperity associated with the progress of globalisation after the end of the Cold War. There was ample evidence of enormous wealth, excess, expanding credit and recklessness in speculation on the soaring stock markets in both instances when the world came tumbling down.

But the devil, of course, is in the detail, as the respective chapters by Stan du Plessis and Dirk Berg-Schlosser aptly illustrate. While excess and greed played a role, so did the incentives that created the credit-fuelled bubble, in the US property markets in particular, and the concurrent gearing in the US financial sector that led highly geared banks first into a position of weakness and then into failure on so massive a scale that policy intervention became indispensable. The reason why the problem was not contained locally but spread to the rest of the world was that the modern banking system relies on globally interlinked financial markets and that the world economy has become tightly integrated not only into the financial system across the world but also into the flow of goods and services across boundaries.

Some instructive comparisons have been made in this volume between the current crisis and the one that triggered the Great Depression. For example, in contrast to the present situation, of the 15 European countries in the inter-war period that could be described, albeit in some cases at a stretch, as parliamentary democracies only eight survived; the other seven fell victim to circumstance and turned to more authoritarian forms of rule, especially to fascism that set them on the slippery slope towards World War II. Reminiscent of the more current woes, international trade fell sharply during the Great Depression along with all major economic indicators, while unemployment rose steeply. The severe budget cuts and other austerity measures, which most of the hapless governments of the day had implemented, did not prevent the crisis situation from deteriorating even further. Instead the measures were met with strong social and political responses as large numbers of people took to the streets in often peaceful, but sometimes also violent, protest – a situation not dissimilar to the developments witnessed lately in Greece.

The most significant positive difference between then and now has been the avoidance of the 'beggar thy neighbour' policy implemented by nearly all central banks in the 1930s. This policy, which put short-term domestic interests above longer-term considerations of international cooperation and stability, can be contrasted with the current efforts to coordinate, at the regional and global levels, policies meant to counter the adverse effects of the crisis, even if the efficacy of these efforts is sometimes doubtful. There is also a major difference between the young democracies of the inter-war period and the well established liberal democracies of today. In the 1930s other political alternatives were at hand in the form of 'anti-system parties' spread across the political spectrum from left to right. They posed a real threat to the democracies that were as yet not fully consolidated, because they carried the considerable potential for non-democratic or anti-democratic alternatives to emerge, and emerge they did. In contrast, no coherent extremist social and political forces or reactions have so far materialised in the developed democracies of today, while the general structural and political-cultural conditions continue to favour the persistence of democracy. But the situation is less clear in the case of the younger 'Third Wave' democracies. As Berg-Schlosser notes, their continuing democratic future could be more dependent on policy and actor effects, and this makes them more comparable to the unconsolidated democracies of the 1930s.

For this very reason the democracies of the Third Wave are of particular interest in this book as its aim is not only to come to grips with how the crisis happened and how it was handled in the short term, but also to hypothesise about its possible long-term consequences, especially with regards to the future of democracy. One of the speculative questions posed in this volume is therefore whether the global crisis and its aftermath might bring on the reversal or further expansion of the Third Wave of democracy.

Political systems and the economy

The Great Recession accentuated the emerging global division into democratic and authoritarian capitalisms. China's economic success, in particular, started to undermine the once almost unshakable belief in political science that democracy and economic progress went together, whereas an autocratic regime was more likely to show poor economic performance. It is now also far less clear whether democracy increases the probability of economic success, or rather – and this is more likely – produces an improvement in the living standards of broad segments of a society, but only when good economic performance is already in place. And this leads to the question of whether the model of authoritarian capitalism might become a more attractive alternative to liberal democracy of the Western type, which is combined with a market economy, but is also 'encumbered' by the whole package of civic values such as human rights, the role of an individual in society, etc.

The first answers to the various questions emerge from the chapters by Ursula Hofmann-Lange and Philip Mohr. They both pursue the topic of the complex relationship between political systems and the economy, but look at this through the different lenses of their respective disciplines of political science and economics. What becomes evident from the political science perspective is that the democratic system requires a careful balancing of the concepts of liberty and equality. The in-built tension springs from the model's essential need for a market economy, which per se implies inequalities of wealth, and the concurrent necessity to ensure the equality of its citizens not only in terms of political rights, but also in terms of the responsibility of democratic governments to reduce socioeconomic disparities. This contradiction is democracy's inherent weakness. The strength of a democratic dispensation is greater political flexibility, whereby inefficient governments can be voted out of power without the threat of a decline in regime legitimacy and the possible consequent risks of political instability. In that sense democracies are generally better equipped than authoritarian political systems to weather economic crises.

But are democracies also better at guaranteeing economic success? The recent revolutions in Tunisia, Egypt and Libya showed once again how authoritarian leaders tend to exploit their political power to amass private fortunes in collusion with large private enterprises. Since neither side of the pact has an interest in ending the mutually profitable relationship, the ousting of the old leadership alone will not suffice. And if the old networks are left in place, while there is no legal framework of market regulation needed for a properly functioning market economy and the tradition of the rule of law is weak, then there can be no development of a competitive and successful market economy, despite democratisation. On the other hand, some authoritarian governments, notably China, promote the liberalisation of their national markets and stimulate economic success without democratising their political system. Market liberalisation and the consequent improvement of living conditions may in turn contribute to stabilising authoritarian political systems, at least in the short run.

Seen through the eyes of an economist, further complexities emerge. First, there is the fact that all economic systems are mixed systems, even if a particular form of ownership (collective: socialism or private: capitalism) usually dominates, or particular coordinating mechanisms such as tradition, command and the market prevail. Each type of ownership and each mechanism has its strengths and weaknesses, and each form of economic system has its adherents among economists. The dividing line lies between those who believe, as John Maynard Keynes did, that market economies are inherently unstable as they are subject to business cycles in the form of booms and recessions, and therefore governments have a role to play. Classical economists, conversely, are of the opinion that markets are inherently stable and that it is in fact governments that are responsible for creating business cycles. They advocate a hands-off approach. The recent crisis gave Keynesianism a massive boost when, after two decades of market fundamentalism, the urgent need for discretionary monetary and fiscal intervention became essential.

The two schools of economic thought are only part of the story. The other part deals with the specifics that impact on economic performance and can determine its success or failure, such as factor endowment, politics, history, geography, culture and attitudes of people in a particular country. Although some economists think that universal economic laws cut through time and space, there are others, such as Mohr, who devote attention to path dependence, recognising that a country's current and expected performance is shaped by the route it had followed to arrive where it is today. The Chinese economic success, for example, which confounds many economists, would be hard to understand without taking into account the salient features of the Chinese people and their history. Equally, there is a wider range of developing countries, particularly the BRIC countries (Brazil, Russia, India and China) from whose perceived success one can also distil lessons to look for guidelines.

Responses to crisis

At the core of the global crisis has been finance. The trigger was the liberalisation of the capital market that opened the door to a free flow of speculative money as from the 1990s. This dynamic has been unfolding largely beyond the effective control of national governments, which nevertheless had little option but to step in when the inevitable crunch came. Ironically, while the measures governments instituted staved off the worst scenarios, the faulty global financial architecture remained essentially unchanged, and in time much of critical popular sentiment turned from global to local: from hostility towards banks and speculators to apportioning blame to individual governments.

The financial 'earthquake' of September 2008 sent flood waves first and foremost across the most developed democracies, so much so that some have dubbed the problem a crisis of the rich nations. But the troubled waters did not stop there as the ripple effects spilled over to the rest of the globe. Given the uneven stages and severity of the contagion, responses varied widely over time, space and political systems, while counter-measures have been sought at both national and international levels. The wide variation of measures trying to cope with the crisis as well as an assessment of the results this has produced have been captured in this volume by Laurence Whitehead and the co-authors Sang-jin Han and Peng Lü. They unveil, respectively, the democratic mechanism employed by the leading old democracies, and the responsive policies deployed by the authoritarian Chinese regime.

At the national level democracies have an in-built safety-valve mechanism to address citizen discontent in the form of democratic alternation. This allows for a peaceful change of leadership that helps both renew public authority and bolster political responsiveness to economic challenges at a time of economic stress. In the United States and the United Kingdom, the two countries most accountable for the crisis, democratic alternation did take place and proved to be a powerful mechanism of political accountability. But in both cases the alteration had limited effectiveness as an error-correcting mechanism to help redress past errors by holding failed officeholders to account, or to institute improvements to economic policy-making to guard against similar relapses in the future. This is because the concentration of political energies on a corrective agenda is harder to sustain in the long run. Once the worst of a crisis is over, other issues distract the attention, while competing parties and lobbyists are likely to dilute the initially strong reform impulse by highjacking it to suit their own particular interests.

In the absence of the safety-valve mechanism democracies have at their disposal, the immediate response to the crisis by the authoritarian Chinese regime was to implement a policy of extreme Keynesianism. Even though the Chinese economy was far less affected by the crisis than were the economies of the developed countries, in November 2008 the Chinese government launched the rollout of the largest (as a share of GDP) stimulus package in the world, amounting to some US$586 billion; six months later well over half of the budget was already allocated. The giant scope of the project along with its swift implementation showed the strong capacity of a state unrestrained by electoral considerations. While the main aim of the package was to make up for the fall in exports by spurring domestic demand, the selective preferential targeting of recipients suggested a concurrent political aim, which was to mollify workers in the major sector of the Chinese economy to forestall any labour challenge to the regime.

The tentative conclusion one could draw from the two analyses is that in the longer run China, its multiple internal problems notwithstanding, is likely to be much less affected by the crisis and might even benefit from it – not only because of the softer impact that the financial and economic crisis has had on its economy, but also because of the response policy, which might have initiated a correction of the hitherto unhealthy imbalance of the Chinese economy in favour of exports. It is as yet hard to see if any long-term benefits might accrue to the developed liberal democracies in the wake of the crisis, given that much of the initial impetus to institute corrective reform has been lost.

In the international arena, similarly, major global decision makers did what they thought was best to stabilise the immediate crisis situation. But, as Whitehead notes in this volume, "established interests in many countries had regained their confidence and veto power, and any potential coalition that might have existed in favour of major curbs to the dynamics of financial globalisation had begun to splinter." And so the concerted response to the crisis, so robust to begin with, has been left unfinished. Little wonder then that another international banking crisis is now moving to the fore of the international agenda. And the insolvency of Greek banks is merely the tip of the iceberg as many banks in other euro zone countries are not only overly indebted, but have the transparency of their declared assets questioned. This situation gives rise to serious concerns about a new contagion spreading not only to more countries in the euro zone but also to areas well beyond the European common currency.

Quo vadis democracy?

A financial crisis has much wider ramifications than just precipitating the need to put one's fiscal house in order. The heavy impact on the economy and economic actors comes to mind first, but harmful knock-on effects put at risk social protection, public health, education programmes and food security, as well as affecting individual households; all these factors hold the potential to set off destabilising social reactions. And then there is the feedback loop. This is because a financial crisis is not only a causative factor that sets off a damaging chain reaction, but it is also a symptom. It is a symptom of poor-quality governance and regulation, and of profligacy, although this issue goes to the much deeper level of underlying values, attitudes and beliefs. These crucial elements are highlighted in this volume by Pierre du Toit.

At the heart of the matter is the social and physical context within which the modern Western consumer-oriented lifestyle and liberal culture have evolved. The origins of this culture can be traced back to the post-World War II 'baby boom' generation, whose values were formed during – and found expression in – the counterculture movement of the 1960s, which coalesced around the issue of the US involvement in the Vietnam War. The denunciation of war was the particular focus, but with it came the rebellion against an established cultural code and the rejection of many norms of restraint. Tolerance became the hallmark; equality was extended from political rights to such areas as sexual orientation and gender relations, and progress came to be viewed as an increasing 'quality of life' trend.

The wave of prosperity enjoyed by Western societies in the last 50 years served to entrench these values. A crisis-induced reversal of the trajectory of affluence could have far-reaching effects, not least in that it could undermine the liberal values of trust and tolerance that guard against ethnic nationalism with its concurrent attitudes of prejudice, racism and xenophobia. This applies especially to the integration of migrant populations into existing societies, which was already a problem prior to the crisis and not only in multi-cultural societies, but even in such mono-cultural environments such as Germany or the Netherlands. The deeply shocking images of the carnage perpetrated in Norway in the summer of 2011 is an uneasy illustration of the problem of waning tolerance, which could give rise to the emergence of illiberal democracies, and not just at the edges but at the very core of the liberal democratic zone.

At the global level the subject that warrants most attention is the rise of China. The phenomenon of this rise, already remarkable for its dynamic nature before the crisis, moved to the centre of the world stage as the Great Recession unfolded. One of the authors in this book and its co-editor, Edmund Wnuk-Lipinski, goes as far as to consider the possibility of a new global bipolarisation in the making, with China in one of the two key positions and the world divided into democratic and authoritarian capitalisms. When the earlier, ideologically defined, bipolar order ended in 1989 with the collapse of the Soviet bloc, liberal democracy was declared the ultimate winner set to conquer the whole world. But this was not to be. Looking at the world today, as Edmund Wnuk-Lipinski noted in this volume, it is safe to say that it was capitalism rather than liberal democracy that has won the day, as the whole of the global market economy is now capitalist, distinguished only by different

solutions to the various local economic problems, from liberal in the US, to
welfare state capitalism in the EU, to a mixture of state and private capitalism
in China. In this context the growing economic clout of the latter is being
watched with increasing concern by some countries, especially the United
States. But China's evident prosperity is also being watched, and most likely
with growing hope, by some formally democratic or authoritarian peripheral
countries whose development paths have not been success stories either in
economic or political terms. And China might become an example to follow
not only for them, but also for some liberal democracies, particularly those
that are relatively young and perform poorly economically. This possible
adoption of the 'Chinese model' is the more pessimistic of the two scenarios
offered in the conclusions to this volume.

The question is whether China is part of the problem or part of the solution to the problem. A recent BBC survey revealed that China becoming
more powerful is viewed with apprehension in all of the 27 countries surveyed, and especially in the G7 countries. Also, negative popular perceptions
in 2011 were up from 2005, when the last poll was conducted. The attitudes
of European leaders belied these popular sentiments in June 2011, when red
carpets were rolled out in European capitals to receive China's Prime Minister, Wen Jiabao. This is in contrast to American leaders, who view China
much more warily, but in the midst of the euro zone financial woes European
leaders undoubtedly have a greater vested interest in Chinese investments
than do their American counterparts. It could also be that they are better informed about China and are thus less uneasy about letting China in.

Bogeyman or saviour, China is here to stay and needs to be studied ob-
jectively to be understood better. In this volume a deeper knowledge of the
country is sought via its history. China's journey from being a proud ancient
Empire, through colonial exploitation and the later ravages of revolutions and
chaos, to a poor Third World country and then back to a position of power
tells its own story: the story of survivors who adapt to changing circumstances. Therein lie many lessons, but two are particularly pertinent to the discussion in this book. The one is that there is much to be learnt from the Chinese practice-based epistemology, which calls for distilling lessons from experimentation to feed innovation as the basis of progress. The other lesson is
that learning selectively from China is very different from trying to imitate
wholesale a culturally peculiar authoritarian form of governance. And among
the countries most likely to try this would be those with the most to lose:
poor defective democracies that would be unlikely to replicate China's economic success, but would be sure to destroy the last vestiges of democracy
their citizens still have as their meagre means by which to keep some kind of
check on their governments.

The last, but certainly not least, important topic in this book focuses on
the need and the possible ways in which we might begin to search for a dem-

ocratic approach to a new world order. The global crisis has taken this urgent need to a new level. It has shown that it will not suffice to patch up the shaky financial architecture or to ride out the Great Recession with all its economic, political and social consequences, as pressing as all these issues are. It will also be necessary to take the much more difficult step and go beyond these immediate tasks to a change in mindset in at least two vital respects. The one is the idea that progress is boundlessly incremental and is not only possible but will occur as a matter of course. This misconception does not take into account the rapidly growing population of the planet or the ecocidal depletion of the earth's natural resources by the economy. The other mindset that needs to change is the popular belief that values are defined by culture and we are therefore doomed to eternal miscommunication.

The contributions by Christer Jönsson and Bernard Lategan consider these issues. The one shows the incredible obstacles that stand in the way of global democracy; the other offers some hope for communication across cultural boundaries. Whether or not we will be able to muster the imagination and the necessary tenacity to institute change in managing global affairs in a new way remains an open question. What is beyond doubt is that in the long run there is no other alternative if we are to survive as a species. Only then we will be able to put to rest one of Einstein's 'infinite' worries, that about human stupidity.

Sources

BBC World Service, GlobScan (2011) survey. Accessible online: http://www.bbc.co.uk/pressoffice/pressreleases/stories/2011/03_march/28/china.shtml

The Economist Intelligence Unit (EIU) (2010). The state of the state. Accessible online: http://www.economist.com/node/17493405

Huntington, S.P. (1991). Democracy's Third Wave. Journal of Democracy. 2 (2): 12-34.

PART I
Global economic crises and their political impact

The bankruptcy of Lehman Brothers marked a new phase of globalisation. Risk and uncertainty about the future were, of course, not unknown before that event; they were part and parcel of the combination of Third Wave democratisation and the emergence of the global financial market. But after the Lehman Brothers collapse the element of uncertainty left the exclusive domain of academic inquiry and expert knowledge and became the experience of ordinary people the world over. People have learnt that nothing lasts forever, that a steady improvement of life conditions may suddenly be reversed, and that a lot depends less on their individual efforts or on local decisions and more on decisions taken by anonymous bodies in remote centres of the global financial game.

Global and local media offered countless and often shallow and mutually contradictory analyses on how we should understand the financial catastrophe. How serious is the crisis? What caused it? Who should be held responsible? Can we avoid similar turmoil in the future? Very quickly the Great Depression of the 1930s became a reference point but, while some insights have been gained, the most important question in fact remained unanswered: how could it happen again? Was it a human factor, such as greed, miscalculation, mismanagement? Is there perhaps a systemic feature built into modern global capitalism that is to blame? Or is it both of these?

In our view tentative answers to these fundamental questions should be the starting point for any serious inquiry into the possible influence of the Great Recession on the course of the Third Wave of democratisation. This is why in the first part of our book we offer our interpretation of what has happen and to what extent the events of the Great Recession coincide with or differ from those of the Great Depression.

Collapse.
The story of the international financial crisis, its causes and policy consequences

Stan du Plessis

Introduction

The logic of the industrial revolution is specialisation with cooperation. Increased specialisation raises productivity, but requires a high degree of cooperation from the level of local firms and the local economy to national and international levels. Adam Smith, the 18th-century moral philosopher and pioneer of political economy, realised at the outset that specialisation is held back by the scale and cost of cooperation, or in his words, by the "extent of the market" (Smith, 1776[1981], Book 1, Chapter 3). As the industrial revolution gathered momentum over the following centuries, entrepreneurs discovered new ways to specialise in an environment in which international trade was pushing the market outwards, while financiers were creating ever more efficient ways for savers and investors to cooperate profitably internationally.

By the first decade of this century this cooperation reached the highest level and was accompanied by the fastest rise in prosperity ever known to humankind. But this would not last. During 2008 the financial side of this process collapsed with alarming speed as markets failed on a grand scale. The force of the collapse was such that not only the financial markets but also international trade and the production of industrial goods and services suffered severe contractions, leading to what is now known as the Great Recession. Policy makers found themselves under immense pressure to act decisively. Despite some blunders, many successful policies have been implemented, but even those contributed to renewed pressure on international economic and political cooperation. By October 2010 this tension erupted in what has been called the 'currency wars'

This chapter is the story of success and failure in the financial markets, the markets for goods and services, and in politics. It is a difficult story to tell because the crisis had many causes. The US Bipartisan Commission created in 2009 to study the crisis identified 22 causes, while the US Congressional Research Service found four more (Roberts, 2010). But probably the most concise summary of events was offered by the CEO of the ill-fated Bear Sterns who said: "We all [messed] up". He meant government, rating agencies, Wall Street, commercial banks, regulators, in short, everybody (Roberts, 2010: 5).

To untangle the knot of causes in one short chapter means one can point out only the most important markers on the road to the crisis. This possibly controversial selection will focus on three main factors:

- First, the incentives that contributed to a credit-fuelled bubble, especially in property markets;
- Second, because the housing bubble alone cannot explain the subsequent events, the gearing in the financial sector which affected asset markets unrelated to sub-prime mortgages will be examined;
- Finally, an answer will be sought to the question of how highly geared banks first became fragile and then failed with such dire consequences for the economy that massive policy intervention became essential.

When incentives go astray

The sub-prime market

The story of the international financial crisis of 2008/09 starts with the issue of credit. The two principal actors involved in credit transactions are the lenders, who provide finance on profitable terms but subject to various risks, and the borrowers, who acquire finance at the cost of interest. To understand how the credit-fuelled housing bubble emerged, giving rise to the crisis, it is necessary to mention the incentives and opportunities available both to the financial institutions that provide credit and to the borrowers who obtain mortgages.

Since the Great Depression mortgages on residential property in the United States have been supported by a set of state-owned institutions known as Fannie Mae and Freddie Mac.[1] These institutions do not originate mortgages, but buy them from financial institutions who deal directly with potential home owners, such as local savings and loans corporations and local banks. The mortgages Fannie Mae and Freddie Mac acquire in this way are then packaged and sold as portfolios of property investment.[2] This has been a useful service in a country where, for historical reasons, there is no single bank with a national branch network and where geographically uneven growth places severe limits on the ability of financial institutions to allocate savings efficiently to investments.

Generally speaking, there are two types of mortgages. The one is the more traditional originate-and-hold model; the other is the originate-and-distribute model. In the originate-and-hold model a bank that grants the

---

1   Fannie Mae is short for the 'Federal National Mortgage Association' and Freddie Mac is short for the 'Federal Home Loan Mortgage Corporation'.
2   Such a portfolio is called a Mortgage Backed Security (MBS) and is an example of a broader class of Asset Backed Securities (ABS).

mortgage retains it as an asset on its balance sheet and is thus strongly motivated to control the credit quality of the mortgages. Paying close attention to the size of the mortgage, the income and credit record of the applicant and the value of the property is the traditional way to control the credit risk associated with the originate-and-hold model.

In the originate-and-distribute model the incentives are different, because the object here is to persuade others that the assets are of suitably high quality. As is often the case in the financial sector, the prospective home owner and the financial institution have different information, a discrepancy that makes co-operation between lenders and borrowers difficult. Mortgage originators have to convince potential investors of the credit quality of the mortgages they are selling, a problem alleviated somewhat since the 1970s, when mortgage institutions started to use credit-rating agencies to close the information gap (White, 2010).

In the USA government-backed Fannie Mae and Freddie Mac offered a special version of the credit-rating solution. They were willing to buy mortgages from mortgage originators and would then resell portfolios to other investors with the assurance that these investors would face no credit risk: both Fannie Mae and Freddie Mac would buy back any mortgages should these default in the future. This process of securitisation – that is, creating Mortgage-Backed Securities (MBS) – transformed risky mortgages into risk-free portfolios and played the double role of providing a subsidy to home ownership in the USA as well as serving an important political goal[3] (Roberts, 2010). But it left Fannie Mae and Freddie Mac exposed to credit risk, a risk they controlled by using a set of strict guidelines for the mortgages they would be willing to securitise. Mortgages that satisfied these guidelines were known as standard conforming loans.

Needless to say, insisting on 'standard conforming loans' restricted the class of potential home owners, a restriction politically unpopular because of its social cost. To sidestep this problem a series of reforms was instituted making possible a class of 'sub-prime' mortgages that did not adhere to these strict criteria either by size, credit record, income or wealth of the applicant. The first step was to allow market-related and adjustable interest rates on mortgages.[4] With greater flexibility to reflect the increased credit risk of customers whose credit scores were below the standard requirements, mortgage originators were now able to deal in what became known as the sub-prime market.

The second step was the Tax Reform Act of 1986 that pushed sub-prime to the fore by disallowing tax deductions for consumer credit, but retaining it

---

3   Private sector banks can also buy mortgages from originators to form MBS for later resale to investors and did so on a large scale.

4   This was achieved by the combined effect of the Depository Institutions Deregulation and Monetary Control Act (DIDMCA) in 1980 and Alternative Mortgage Transaction Parity Act (AMTPA) two years later.

for mortgage debt on a primary and one additional home. Mortgage finance in general, including the sub-prime component, expanded substantially in the wake of this decision (Chomsisengphet and Pennington-Cross, 2006). Other factors, such as the long economic upswing of the 1990s and the stable macroeconomic environment since the mid-1980s as well as political and social pressures, contributed to a dramatic expansion of mortgage lending in the USA over the last twenty years. In 1995 sub-prime mortgage originations amounted to $65 billion in a market of $639.4 billion mortgages. By 2003 these numbers grew to $332 billion and $3.76 trillion respectively (Chomsisengphet and Pennington-Cross, 2006, Table 3). Easy credit financed a dramatic expansion in residential property, driving up prices on existing homes and fuelling new developments. During the height of the 2004 property boom in Las Vegas, for example, a new house went up on average every twenty minutes (Kunzig, 2011). Too much of this was financed with sub-prime mortgages, the cumulative total of which exceeded a trillion dollars by 2007, the year in which the sub-prime boom turned to bust (Lockhart, 2008).

The rapid growth in the sub-prime market could only occur once the high costs associated with lending to this market had been overcome. Sub-prime mortgages are more expensive for both the lender and the mortgage originator, since the information asymmetry is more serious in this market segment and the likelihood of default is much greater. The application and appraisal fees are higher, as are interest rates and default insurance. Despite the inherently high costs three factors combined to make sub-prime mortgages relatively attractive over this period: monetary policy, financial regulation and politics.

Monetary policy and the 'great deviation'

What role, if any, did monetary policy play in creating the environment for the crisis and allowing it to unfold? Starting with the housing market, there seemed to have been acts of omission and commission especially by the Federal Reserve Board (Fed) and other central banks that either encouraged the housing boom or allowed it to run unchecked. Starting with acts of omission, there is little evidence that monetary authorities used policy instruments directly to contain the boom in residential property. In this the policy makers had implemented the modern consensus of responding to asset prices only to the extent that they affect general inflation or risk overheating the economy, leaving scope for strong policy action (or mopping-up) should an asset boom turn to bust (Bernanke and Gertler, 1999). But the severity of the episode has encouraged revision of this 'mop-up-afterwards' approach to asset bubbles and a finer distinction is now being drawn between types of asset price bubbles. The old consensus is still applicable for bubbles on the stock market, where bank credit plays a small part, but not for 'credit bubbles', where the provision of cheap credit by banks plays a central role (Mishkin, 2008).

Central banks are financial regulators and are therefore far better informed about lending by banks, and potentially also about the prudence of that lending, than about fundamental support for stock market prices. And central banks have a range of regulatory powers that can be used to rein in credit lending that is fuelling an asset bubble. In other words, they have instruments at their disposal that can influence the behaviour of banks. But to act against credit bubbles requires an ex ante reading and there is not much evidence that either the Fed, or other major central banks, were able to do that with respect to the recent crisis. In fact, the former Fed Deputy Governor, Alan Blinder, when assessing the risks to various dimensions of US monetary policy in August 2005 while the credit bubble was well under way, stated there were moderate risks to inflation, employment and aggregate demand and only a high risk of a supply-side shock. Crucially, he identified the level of risk for both the banking sector and credit risk to be low, stable and covered by strong risk management (Blinder, 2005: Table 1).

The Fed did not use policy measures to prevent either the housing boom or the associated development in the derivative markets from accelerating, despite the Bernanke-Gertler consensus that requires monetary authorities to care about asset prices to the extent they affect the outlook for price stability and the business cycle. In fact, between 2002 and 2006 the policy interest rate in the United State deviated further from the benchmark 'Taylor rule' than at any point since the 1970s. The 'Taylor rule' is fundamentally a normative instrument used to calculate the appropriate level of the policy interest rate. It also describes the actual Federal Reserve Board policy since 1980 with a high degree of accuracy, and in a modified version it is comparably accurate for other developed countries (Clarida, Gali and Gertler, 1997). At the same time, deviations from the rule can be interpreted as a measure of the discretion exercised by the Fed. In this sense the path that US monetary policy took between 2002 and 2006 can be interpreted as a substantial discretionary departure from normal practice; Taylor has called it the 'great deviation' and his argument is that the Federal Reserve board fuelled the housing boom, and the associated financial market gearing, by keeping interest rates too low for too long.

There is empirical evidence (Leamer, 2007; Taylor, 2007; Ahrend, Cournède and Price, 2008) to support the thesis that monetary policy decisions, whether reasonable or not, contributed to the credit-financed housing bubble in the US and elsewhere. But low interest rates had an additional unfortunate effect on the credit bubble that ultimately led to the collapse of key banks and financial institutions and the near collapse of many more internationally. In addition to encouraging lending, low interest rates also tend to change the incentives for banks as they tempt them into relatively more risky behaviour in the form of higher gearing on their balance sheets, which means expanding a bank's balance sheets without a corresponding expansion of its capital base.

Theoretically there are two ways in which low interest rates could promote higher gearing at banks (Borio and Zhu, 2008; Adrian and Shin, 2009). First, the low nominal returns on cash might encourage financial firms to pursue higher-yielding but more risky investments, especially if they are contracted to deliver a given nominal return. Second, the effect of low interest rates on asset prices and cash flows might allow financial firms to carry a greater proportion of unsafe investments, while their balance sheets will appear sound. Leonardo Gambacorta (2009) recently added empirical plausibility to these theoretical results by investigating the hypotheses for the current crisis with a database of 600 listed banks in the USA and Europe.

Financial regulation and moral hazard

The centrality of prices in market co-operation means that low interest rates typically play a large role in explaining asset bubbles, but low interest rates are not the only factor. Institutions, or 'rules of the game', as they are also called in economics (for example, North 1990) make it harder or easier to specialise and co-operate. These institutions affect a vast range of decisions and played a critical role in the financial decisions that led to the international financial crisis. This refers in particular to the rules of financial regulation.

Traditionally there are three justifications for formal financial sector regulation (Goodhart, 2010). The first is to prevent the abuse of potential monopoly power by very large institutions; the second is to protect consumers from the asymmetrical distribution of information in many financial transactions. But neither of these two roles had much impact in the run-up to the financial crisis. Instead, it was the third role, the containment of spill-over effects from one institution to others that played a key role. These spill-over effects (or externalities) are caused by the interconnected nature of the modern financial system, where the value of the assets of one firm is closely linked to the assets of other financial firms. Stress on a large firm that results in downward pressure on asset prices can quickly spill over to other firms in this kind of network. Economists call this an externality, because individual banks do not typically factor in the risk they pose to the rest of the financial system in which they operate.

The one way to contain potential spill-over effects is via changes to formal institutions; the other ways include financial innovation and amendments to regulatory practice. While some important changes to financial regulation had indeed been introduced during the last forty years, these often followed in the wake of financial innovation and regulatory practice. Perhaps the most famous single decision that had a bearing on the crisis was the enactment of the Graham-Leach-Bliley Act in the USA at the end of the 1990s, which formally removed the separation between commercial banks funded by insured deposits, and investment banks funded on the capital markets. The separation had been upheld since the 1930s by the Glass-Steagall and Bank Holding

Company Acts. Following the Act, larger financial groups emerged providing a wider array of financial services in an increasingly complex corporate structure.

The boundaries between commercial and investment banks had long since become blurred because financial innovations, such as money market mutual funds, allowed investment banks to compete with the formerly most profitable part of commercial banking (Kling, 2010), i.e. funding their investment activities by taking deposits on which they paid low interest rates. This, in turn, forced commercial banks to change their own behaviour. They became less dependent on deposits and started funding their investments on the capital markets, especially on the inter-bank and repo markets; since the 1970s, to expand their balance sheets, commercial banks supplemented their intake of deposits by using wholesale money markets such as the eurodollar market (Goodhart, 2010). With commercial banks adopting the balance sheet operations of investment banks, while the latter offered products that competed directly with commercial banks, the line between these two sectors had become blurred giving rise to a 'shadow banking system'.

The 'shadow banking system' is a term now used to describe a part of the non-commercial bank financial sector that competes with commercial banks to offer financial services, such as credit, to business enterprises. In the USA the shadow banking system became so large that by 2007 its lending exceeded that of the traditional banking system (Geithner, 2008). Although the shadow banking system operates outside the conventional system of bank regulation, it is deeply interconnected with the traditional banking system. Indeed, it is through the shadow banking system that the conventional banking system is now largely funded (Gorton, 2010; Goodhart, 2010).

Loans extended by banks to their customers are typically long-term and are profitable assets for banks. But to conduct this business, banks need to finance the assets. Traditionally commercial banks obtained their funding by accepting retail deposits, which are potentially short-term liabilities for banks. The mismatch between the highly liquid but potentially short-term character of the liabilities and the longer-term but less liquid character of the assets exposed traditional banks to the risk of a bank run. This occurs when a large proportion of a bank's depositors turn up to demand their deposits, which even a fundamentally solvent bank would be unable to satisfy because of the illiquidity of its assets.

Modern banks by contrast extend credit and fund lending by combining loans in securitised portfolios (ABS) in which the portfolios of assets have been rearranged using structured finance.[5] This is a set of techniques used to

---

5   An example of structured finance that played an important role during the crisis are so-called Collateralized Debt Obligations (CDOs), which are portfolios constructed by arranging the underlying portfolio into different 'tranches', each with a different priority claim on the income stream of the underlying assets. In this way the senior tranche of a CDO is much

combine and arrange portfolios of assets in such a way as to create portfolios of asset backed securities that have different risk profiles from the original assets. Not all ABSs were sold, though: during the crisis it emerged that banks held substantial portfolios of ABSs, which harmed their balance sheets once the underlying asset prices declined. There were two reasons for holding the risky ABSs on a bank's balance sheet:

- First, to satisfy the demand for another product that has become very important in the modern banking system, i.e. the wish to make risk-free highly-liquid deposits by institutional investors and other non-financial firms in the repo market (Gorton, 2010);
- Second, the Basel II accord incentivised banks to use the highly rated senior tranches of ABS to fulfil their capital adequacy requirements.

The shadow banking system emerged when the traditional funding mechanism of banks via deposits became unprofitable. Since then securitisation of assets came to play a central role in the modern funding of banks, while securitised asset portfolios became critical collateral in the repo market. In this way the balance sheets of banks, non-bank financial firms and other large non-financial firms became closely intertwined. Large insurance companies also formed part of the same system; American International Group (AIG) in the USA, for example, offered insurance called Credit Default Swaps (CDS) on the securitised portfolios that allowed the portfolios to obtain attractive credit ratings.

The modern banking system has become very dependent on extensive cooperation on globally interlinked financial markets. Banks need to finance their balance sheets on a daily basis (Blanchard, 2009), and a healthy capital ratio is the traditional method used by banks to show that they are creditworthy counterparties in such agreements.

The Basel I and II accords on prudential bank regulation aimed to help banks ensure adequate capital ratios, though they did so in a fundamentally flawed manner. For example, the Basel I accord differentiated between assets on a risk-adjusted basis, but the design was faulty and ended up requiring banks to hold higher capital requirements for good loans. The regulation merely enticed banks to either sell the better loans or move them to their shadow banking counterparts. "Basel I", as Goodhart (2010: 15) observed, "was threatening to turn 'good' banks into 'bad' banks".

---

less risky than the underlying assets, though the risk attached to the senior tranche is greatly affected by the degree to which the risks of the underlying assets are correlated. The more risky junior tranches of different CDOs can in turn be combined in a new portfolio which can be re-arranged to yield new senior tranches with apparently low risk. When CDOs are combined in this way to create a second generation of CDOs (CDO2), their value is even more sensitive to the underlying assumptions than a CDO. Coval, Jurek and Stafford (2009) provide an accessible introduction to the role of structured finance in the financial crisis.

Basel II was meant to correct this unhappy feature and did so by giving much greater importance to the internal risk assessment of banks. It attempted to extend regulation to assets and liabilities not on the bank's own balance sheet. But Basel II's capital requirements would become more accommodating when asset prices were rising, thus fuelling a buoyant asset market. The opposite would happen when asset prices declined, at which point capital requirements would tighten, putting further downward pressure on an already fragile market (Goodhart, 2010). Put another way, under Basel II less capital was required when risks appeared small and more capital was needed when risks appeared larger. The unintended consequence of the regulation was that banks were able to expand their balance sheets relative to their capital base in good times and still pass regulatory scrutiny, while they would be required to raise more capital precisely when they were under stress and least able to do so.

For these reasons both banks and non-bank financial institutions became inclined to hold insufficient capital: commercial banks held too little to cover potential losses from bad loans; investment banks held too little to cover potential losses on securitised and other risky financial products; Fannie Mae and Freddie Mac held too little to cover the guarantees they had issued on MBS; and large insurance companies, such as AIG, held too little to cover guarantees they had issued to banks under Credit Default Swaps (Kling, 2009).

In addition to the inadvertent incentives for risk taking created by financial regulation, governments introduced a moral hazard that strengthened this tendency. Governments and central banks have supported distressed financial institutions since the 19th century to avoid the spill-over effects of individual failures from disrupting the rest of the financial sector. It was the famous second editor of *The Economist* magazine, Walter Bagehot, who formulated the principle that a central bank should extend liquidity to distressed but fundamentally solvent financial firms that were experiencing difficulties with their short-term obligations.

The underlying principle claiming that an appropriate and limited intervention by a central bank could prevent larger social losses by forestalling the demise of otherwise solvent financial institutions has since been extended to protect the financial sector from losses that would undermine the firms in that sector collectively. In the extended form the Bagehot principle requires central banks to support any financial firm regarded as systemically important, that is, a firm so large or important that its failure might cause the collapse of other solvent financial firms. The wave of bank defaults during the Great Depression, which saw the demise of thousands of banks in the US, demonstrated the apparent worth of this principle. Central banks resolved not to make the same mistake again.

In 1984 a large American bank, Continental Illinois, found itself in financial distress. The Fed reasoned that this was a case fitting Bagehot's expanded principle, since Continental Illinois was judged to be systemically important; banks such as Continental Illinois had become 'too big to fail', the title of a now famous book by Stern and Felman (2004). The subsequent bailout returned the full value of loans extended to Continental Illinois. To put it differently, the US government lowered dramatically the credit risk associated with loans to large banks such as Continental Illinois. This practice guided subsequent bailouts in the USA, with creditors hardly ever out of pocket, even when the financial firms they had lent to were insolvent: for example, 99.7% of all deposits in the 1100 commercial banks that failed in the US during the 1980s were bailed out by government (Roberts, 2010: 10).

Not everyone was bailed out though: shareholders often suffered substantial losses when the share price of a distressed financial firm crashed. But these shareholders were still working in an institutional setting which had both the profit and loss aspects necessary for effective market allocation. Creditors in the financial sector were operating under a different set of rules, though. There profit and loss had been replaced by a system of profits and bailout, undermining the need to manage risk through prudent screening and expensive monitoring on the part of creditors or the retention of substantial capital in banks to guard against unexpected losses.

Not just large banks, but countries too were perceived to be 'too big to fail'. During the 1990s Mexico was the most notable case of a US government bailout, which protected lenders to the Wall Street creditors of the Mexican government (Roberts, 2010). This bailout and the IMF bailouts of East Asian governments in 1997 created the impression that creditors to large emerging market economies with substantial international debt would enjoy the same protection from credit risk as did the creditors of large banks in the developed world. Many investors in Russian debt acted on this belief in 1998 by holding the debt of a state at the point of fiscal collapse.

The decision not to bail out the Russian government in August of 1998 sent shockwaves through the international system and worked to encourage more bailouts. At this point the bailout principle was expanded to cover hedge funds, a highly risky financial institution. A prominent hedge fund, Long Term Capital Management (LTCM), suffered massive losses during the crisis and the Fed was concerned about other hedge funds and investment banks that had large investments with LTCM. An insolvent LTCM would cause substantial losses for these creditors and in the heat of the crisis the Fed organised a private sector bailout of LTCM (Roberts, 2010). Once more the creditors who had enjoyed considerable up side from their investments in LTCM were protected from a credit risk associated with their investments.

While the bailouts mentioned above created a moral hazard that made banks less prudent and creditors less concerned with the imprudence of the banks they were lending to, there were also other incentives working in the same direction. One of these, the culture of high salaries and bonuses on Wall

Street, has been widely discussed. The other, a change in the nature of modern banks' finance via a shadow banking system based on the securitised assets and repurchase agreements, has received much less attention.

The salaries and especially large bonuses tied to short-run performance led to a public outcry in the wake of the bailouts. While it is true that the executives lost capital as the share prices of their firms and others declined during the crisis, they did not, by any stretch of the imagination, face symmetrical risks. The structure of their salaries and bonuses with rewards for short-term profits and share options was such that they gained enormously from good results, while their downside risk was considerably smaller (Roberts, 2010). Given this asymmetry, it is not really surprising the executives were keen to expand the more risky business which brought them handsome returns while the boom lasted.

Public incentives and the role of politics

Politicians played a role in the run-up to the crisis especially through their support for bailouts. But their involvement in the housing market bears closer scrutiny. The account here focuses on the United States and concerns the specific ways in which home ownership was encouraged, creating incentives that ultimately fuelled the property bubble. Similar incentives were created elsewhere, but the particular policies differed from those in the US.

After many decades of encouraging home ownership through tax breaks on mortgage interest and the sponsorship of Fannie Mae and Freddie Mac mortgage associations, the US government became much more aggressive in its promotion of home ownership during the 1990s. To give practical effect to the desire for expanded home ownership in the USA, politicians enacted new regulations for Fannie Mae and Freddie Mac in 1993. The regulation not only weakened the prudential safeguards that prevented these companies from doing business at the risky end of the mortgage market, but also required them to raise the proportion of loans they supported to families with incomes below the medium for their areas to 40% by 1996 (from 30% for Freddie and 34% for Fannie in 1993). This requirement was pushed up to 42% in 1999 and 55% in 2007, as both firms expanded their business in these market segments in step with the rising targets (Roberts, 2010: 25).

At the same time Fannie Mae and Freddie Mac expanded their business in mortgages with small down payments of less than 5% and eventually with no down payment at all. In the mid-1990s such mortgages accounted for a small fraction (4% or less) of the loans they purchased, but by 2007 almost a quarter of their loans had down payments of 5% or less[6] (Roberts, 2010: Figure 8). In this way political pressure pushed mortgage associations to sup-

---

6   Fannie and Freddie bought a quarter of the 272 billion dollars worth of MBS sold in the first half of 2006 (Roberts, 2010: 23.

port a housing bubble that was becoming dangerously overheated and in a market segment where risks were poorly assessed. This is not to suggest that the housing bubble in the US and elsewhere was exclusively or even largely due to incentives of the kind created by politicians. It was not. The private financial sector financed the bulk of the credit-fuelled property bubble and it is the private financial sector that increased its gearing dramatically over the last 20 years, thereby amplifying the potential consequences of mistakes in their investment strategies. But the political incentives meant that public officials had little interest in scrutinising an industry that had become not just wonderfully profitable but also politically expedient.

Financial collapse

The housing bubble fizzled out during the course of 2007 as balance sheets in the household and financial sectors became ever more stretched. An important factor in this loss of momentum for the market was the reversal of the 'great deviation' in US monetary policy, with the policy interest rate rising from a level of 1% in 2004 to 5.35% in 2006. Other central banks followed suit, leading to tighter monetary conditions internationally.

The highly geared property market, where the worst-quality loans were predicated on the assumption of an uninterrupted rise in property prices, was vulnerable even to stagnation, let alone price declines. When house prices started to decline by early 2007, these loans were soon and predictably under water, though few at the time anticipated the force of the process that started to gather pace.

Large banks, including investment banks and other financial institutions, started to report sub-prime mortgage-related losses during the first quarter of 2007. At this time the US-based New Century Financial, a mortgage lending specialist of the sub-prime market, filed for bankruptcy. More disturbingly, the prominent investment bank Bear Sterns announced in June 2007 that two of its large hedge funds had suffered massive sub-prime-related losses; it became clear that the losses would not be confined to one or even a few banks. Losses started to appear also in large European banks, such as BNP Paribas and the German Sachsen Landesbank in August 2007, and in the UK where in September of that year Northern Rock suffered the most serious traditional run on a British bank since the 19th century. Worse was to come.

By late 2007 insurance companies providing bond insurance for Collateral Debt Obligations (CDOs) were also suffering massive losses. The troubled Bear Stearns finally succumbed in March 2008, though it was supported by the Fed until bought by the rival investment bank JP Morgan. This did not restore stability as the housing market continued to decline, causing the failure of another mortgage lender, IndyMac, in the USA by June 2007 in what was the second largest bank failure in US history. While the US government had to support Fannie Mae and Freddie Mac to prevent their collapse, the UK government nationalised another bank, Bradford and Bingly, to prevent its collapse.

The financial market turmoil deteriorated further during September 2008: Lehman Brothers, a famous Wall Street investment bank, collapsed and, critically, was not bailed-out by the authorities.[7] Instead it was purchased by its rival Merrill Lynch, which was also heading for collapse and would be bought by Bank of America by the end of the year. The crisis was no less acute in Europe. While Northern Rock had suffered from a traditional run on the bank a year earlier, large continental investment banks faced a modern bank run in the third quarter of 2008 (Blanchard, 2009). At the same time the Belgian government bailed out the insurance and banking giant Fortis, and large Icelandic banks were nearing collapse.

As already mentioned, modern banks are not mainly financed by retail deposits and hence are not greatly exposed to the risk of a traditional bank run. Instead they are financed on the interbank and repo markets on a daily basis. These highly efficient markets allow banks to co-operate to an unprecedented degree, as long as both parties to each transaction feel secure in the value of the assets traded. This trust collapsed in the third quarter of 2008, with banks unable to use their securities as collateral in the interbank market, because other banks could no longer judge their value. Banks were now forced to sell other assets, such as shares, corporate bonds and so on, in an attempt to restore liquidity to their balance sheets and to meet the capital requirements of Basel II.

The result was a fire sale in many asset markets unrelated to the housing market. Globally, stock market wealth was halved during the first year of the crisis, a rate of decline steeper than at the onset of the Great Depression (Almunia, Bénétrix, Eichengree, O'Rourke and Rua, 2009). As asset markets declined the financial sector and corporate balance sheets deteriorated even further and companies were pushed towards bankruptcy.

By the second half of 2008 much of the developed world had declined into recession and with a downward trajectory that suggested disquieting comparisons with the Great Depression of the 1930s. The economic historian

---

7   From a risk perspective Lehman Brothers closely resembled Bear Sterns in early 2008: its highly leveraged balance sheet had a similar composition to that of Bear Sterns, though Lehman's was many times the larger of the two. The failure of Bear Sterns in March 2008 therefore raised the specter of similar trouble at Lehman's and a declining Lehman's share price reflected these concerns (Roberts, 2010). But the subsequent bailout of Bear Sterns put these fears to bed and five months later it was discovered that Lehman's had done little to strengthen its precarious balance sheet. Only this time the expected bailout did not come. Credit risk, which commanded little attention after 20 years of bailouts, returned dramatically, for the creditors (mainly other banks) and for insurance companies involved in securitising the debt contracts.

Barry Eichengreen and his co-authors showed these parallels empirically, both for the USA and for the world economy (Almunia, Bénétrix, Eichengree, O'Rourke and Rua, 2009). For the sake of comparison they identified the peak of economic activity that preceded the Great Depression and the Great Recession as June 1929 and April 2008 respectively.

While US industrial production in the recent crisis did not decline as fast as it did in 1929, at the global level the international economy was more fragile and the decline in industrial output was as steep during the first year of the Great Recession as during the comparable period of the Great Depression. As production declined, unemployment rose to levels not seen in the developed world in many decades.

Despite strong policy intervention financial conditions became much more restrictive in the private sectors of developed economies from this point onwards. While policy interest rate declined, the interest rates demanded on corporate debt were pushed higher, while other credit requirements such as higher down payments and increased credit-rating requirements also pushed up the cost of borrowing. The higher cost of credit reflects the kind of friction that emerges in financial markets during distress when monitoring costs and uncertainty rise sharply (Hall, 2010). More expensive credit and the massive shocks to aggregate demand were the main factors lowering output during the first months of the crisis.

The world economy is extensively integrated not just financially but also in the flow of goods and services across boundaries. These transactions are another barometer of the extensive co-operation upon which modern economies are based. Each of these transactions requires a financial transaction, which is often a credit transaction. The turmoil on international financial markets, especially the tighter credit conditions in combination with the collapse of demand for imported goods and services, and the fact that 70% of international trade was in manufactured goods[8] (compared with 44% in 1929) created a precipitous decline in international trade. Indeed, Almunia *et al.* (2009) showed that the contraction of international trade was notably steeper during the first year of the Great Contraction than at the start of the Great Depression.

Policy makers to the rescue

The trauma of the Great Depression lay not just in the rapidity of the economic collapse, but in its persistence throughout the 1930s in countries such as the USA. During the first months of the Great Recession, though the

---

8   Manufacturing production is a volatile component of total production and was particularly adversely affected in the Great Depression and the Great Recession (Almunia et al., 2009).

downward trajectory of production in the developed world resembled that of the Great Depression, the policy response was dramatically different. Although policy makers did not stand idly by during the early years of the Great Depression, there was far greater policy activism at the macroeconomic level in response to the Great Recession. The activism has been most evident in the monetary and fiscal policies pursued during the current crisis and the considerable efforts to prevent the fragmentation of the global economy through beggar-thy-neighbour policy responses of the 1930s.

There were undoubtedly many factors that pushed policy makers towards greater activism this time around, including the nature of the political system, a topic explored elsewhere in this book. But the two major economic factors were, first, the lessons learnt from the Great Depression, especially the role economists attributed to policy failures of that era and, second, the flexibility of the modern international financial system, which allowed policy makers to respond more dynamically to the pressures that emerged in their own economies.

Since the early 1990s a durable and flexible international financial system emerged in which most developed and emerging market economies have become integrated with global co-operation in the production of goods, services and the investment of capital. By combining largely free capital flows with market-determined exchange rates, this system created scope for considerable domestic discretion in monetary policy, which has mainly been exercised in the direction of pursuing low and stable inflation and output stability. Explicit inflation targeting is the exemplar of this system, but many countries, including the USA, followed an implicit inflation targeting system that can hardly be distinguished in operational terms from explicit inflation targeting (Greenspan, 2004).

At the start of the Great Depression the international financial system was ordered by the gold standard, a system with little scope for the kind of monetary activism seen in response to the Great Recession (Almunia et al., 2009). The post-War Bretton Woods system was an explicit attempt to design an international financial order that served both the ends of stability and policy flexibility. But it was inherently unstable and collapsed barely 13 years after the European economies joined it (Rose, 2006; Reinhart and Rogoff, 2004).

The system that emerged after the collapse of Bretton Woods is unplanned and is not maintained by any central direction, authority, or a reference point such as gold convertibility. It is a spontaneous order resulting from a rules-based system of international trade and investment with flexible currency markets. The system proved durable and flexible (Rose, 2006), though the aftermath of the Great Recession has put it under unexpected pressure. Yet its flexibility created scope for policy makers to intervene as the extent of the crisis became obvious in the course of 2008.

In the light of the unnerving parallels with the early months of the Great
Depression, monetary authorities were unlikely to repeat the inadvertent error
of their predecessors by tightening monetary policy in the midst of a financial
crisis; according to the standard interpretation of those unhappy events by
Friedman and Schwartz (1963), the monetary contraction between 1929 and
1932 in the United States was to a large extent to blame for the depth and
persistence of the Great Depression.

The Fed and the Bank of England reduced their policy interest rate ag-
gressively as the crisis became more serious in late 2008. Money supply data
also testify to the accommodating stance of monetary authorities as the crisis
deepened, with the narrow stock of money expanding briskly despite the financial crisis, because of the introduction by central banks of large quantities
of liquidity to prevent a repetition of the monetary contraction that exacerbated the Great Depression (Almunia *et al.*, 2009: Figures 9 and 10). In conventional terms, then, that is, using a policy interest rate to measure the
stance of monetary policy, monetary authorities responded quickly and
sharply to the unfolding crisis. But there is a limit to interest policy, as it is
not possible to implement a negative nominal interest rate.

Despite the prominence of interest rate policy, central banks have other
policy instruments at their disposal. They can alter broader monetary or other
asset market conditions directly by changing the size, composition and risk
profile of their balance sheet. These policy actions are collectively called
'balance sheet operations' and have been an important part of the policy response to the Great Recession (Borio and Disyatat, 2009). To give an indication of the size of these balance sheet operations, it will suffice to say that the
total assets on the Fed's balance sheet expanded from $880 billion to $2.3
trillion between July 2007 and December 2010, including $1 trillion of mort-
gage-backed securities bought from the financial sector by the Fed to shore
up private sector balance sheets. In late 2010 Fed Chairman, Ben S. Bernanke, announced that there would be a further round of balance sheets questions, which has become known as Quantitative Easing 2 (QE2) and would
amount to a further $600 billion expansion of the Fed's balance sheet. In ad-
dition, fiscal authorities responded vigorously to the crisis with highly accommodating discretionary policies, including bailouts for large financial and
non-financial firms, tax rebates and tax cuts for households.

Have these policies been a success? It is difficult to say. For a start, the
question is not whether the policies have been successful in some ultimate
sense, but whether they have been better than the alternatives. For each country the appropriate evaluation is a comparison with the outcomes of particular
forms of monetary and fiscal interventions with counterfactual outcomes under alternative policy regimes. Those counterfactuals, however, can never observed. Two additional problems contribute to the difficulty of evaluating the
policy initiatives. First, outcomes cannot be associated on a one-to-one basis

with policy decisions given the complex and dynamic interactions in the economy; and, secondly, 'other', that is non-policy, factors impact continuously on the economy with far-reaching effects on the outcomes generated under any policy regime.

Because of such evaluation difficulties, there is still no consensus on what role policy played in the eventual recovery from the Great Depression. In an influential paper Romer (1992) claimed that the reversal of monetary policy from contractionary to expansionary in the 1930s did far more to turn the economic corner than did fiscal policy. But behind this claim lies the observation that fiscal deficits were not very large during the 1930s; the historical record cannot tell us what would have happened had the fiscal authorities adopted policies during the Great Depression as expansionary as their successors did in 2009.

There are two reasons for expecting policies of recent years to have been more important than during the Great Depression. First, the power of fiscal policy rises relative to conventional monetary policy, when the latter nears zero bound on nominal interest rates (see, for example, IMF (2009), but also Keynes (1936)). Second, there is evidence that the fiscal policies of the 1930s, modest though they were, still had a positive impact on the recovery (Almunia *et al.*, 2009). This time around the fiscal authorities have been much more active, and if the transmission mechanism has remained approximately the same, the impact on output has been powerfully enhanced.

The evaluation of monetary policy is no less difficult. The rapid interest rate response by monetary authorities avoided the inadvertent mistakes of the 1930s and after some months the various credit markets returned to stability. But it is very difficult to determine whether stability returned because of or in spite of the extensive balance sheet operations used by central banks. A further complication emerged in the course of 2010, with the inadvertent but unwelcome impact of expansionary monetary policies, especially in the USA, on the exchange rates of developing countries such as Brazil just as these economies were starting to recover from the recession.

Consequences of policy activism

Policy makers around the world, as well as the IMF, supported the active monetary and fiscal policy interventions of 2008 and 2009, and committed themselves to maintaining an open and integrated global economy. They were going to avoid the beggar-they-neighbour policies that featured so prominently and cost the world so dearly in the 1930s. On the whole they succeeded. There were only sporadic protectionist responses to the crisis and international co-operation was sustained.

But in the course of 2010 the spill-over effects in developing countries of the policies pursued by developed countries cast a shadow over continued international co-operation. The Fed's move towards a further large round of quantitative easing in September and October 2010 pushed the issue to breaking point. "We're in the midst of an international currency war, a general weakening of currency," claimed an alarmed Guido Mantega, the Brazilian Finance Minister in September 2010. This war, he continued, "threatens us because it takes away our competitiveness". The problem, according to Minister Mantega, was the influence of US monetary policy on the international value of the dollar, which implied appreciating currencies for developing countries like Brazil and South Africa. According to Minister Mantega, the US monetary policy had, in effect, become another example of the beggar-they-neighbour policies by which a government tries to gain an economic advantage by manipulating the international price of goods and services.

Minister Mantega is not right. The depreciation of the dollar has not been the intention of the US monetary authorities, nor it is not inappropriate given the imbalances in trade and capital flows internationally. A substantial depreciation of the dollar had long been expected because of the said imbalances (Obstfeld and Rogoff, 2005). But Minister Mantega was not wrong to argue that beggar-they-neighbour policies have been disrupting the global economy; it is the Chinese government that has manipulated currency market outcomes in its favour on an unprecedented scale over the last decade (Wolf, 2010a).

The accumulation of approximately $2.5 trillion in foreign currency reserves, a third of all such reserves internationally and equal to half the annual size of the Chinese economy, is major evidence of currency manipulation. It is the combination of reserve accumulation with tight controls on the inflow of capital into China that creates the scope for this kind of market distortion. By preventing a rise in domestic demand and a real appreciation of the Chinese currency, its government is subsidising Chinese exports internationally. Since the Chinese economy is now the largest exporter in the world, this kind of distortion matters (Wolf, 2010b).

While the Chinese government had, in the past, denied that its currency was undervalued, it has lately offered a different explanation: a rapid appreciation of the Chinese currency would undermine the profitability of Chinese exporters and risk social unrest which would, in the words of Premier Wen Jiabao, "be a disaster for the world" (Beattie, Chaffin and Brown, 2010). This argument is not very persuasive outside China; it merely suggests that Chinese export firms might be competitive only on account of the undervalued currency.

While international trade has the potential to leave all parties better off, that will only happen if the goods and services are produced internationally where there is comparative (cost) advantage to do so. The rules-based system for international trade, maintained by the World Trade Organisation (WTO), has been designed to ensure open international co-operation that is beneficial for all parties concerned. The asymmetrical manner in which the Chinese economy has entered this system over the last decade, exporting capital on an unprecedented scale while restricting capital inflows to China and maintaining an undervalued Chinese currency, has put tremendous strain on international co-operation.

The strain became visible with the retreat from co-operation by countries such as Brazil, Russia, Thailand and others as they re-imposed various capital controls. Consequently the currency war was high on the agenda when the G20 heads of state met in South Korea in November 2010. In Seoul the American delegation proposed a three-point plan to untangle the currency wars by, first, putting numerical limits on current account imbalances with policy commitments to keep them effective; second, a stronger role for the IMF to monitor behaviour relative to these limits; and, third, sufficient exchange rate flexibility and openness to ensure an orderly rebalancing of the world economy. These suggestions along with that of World Bank chief Robert Zoellick (2010), who recommended a return to a form of a gold standard, are meant to reduce the tensions in international economic co-operation by designing a new and more co-operative international order. But the inflexibility of the former gold standard and the instability of the Bretton Woods system suggest that these are not promising ideas. Nor did the G20 heads of state find them attractive in Seoul, preferring the much watered-down 'indicative guidelines' on international balances. At the time of writing the pressures created by the policy responses during the Great Recession remain a substantial threat to the open rules-based international order.

Another, and potentially more disruptive, consequence of the policy response to the financial crisis has since emerged in the form of fiscal crises in Europe (and potentially in the United States and Japan). Concerns about the solvency of these governments have disrupted financial markets, caused policy anxiety and later policy action, followed by public protest (in Greece, but also the United Kingdom), where the fiscal adjustments asked too much from the public.

Greece is the most afflicted of the countries currently in distress because the roots of its fiscal demise lie much deeper than the financial crisis. Years of fiscal mismanagement, an inefficient tax structure and revenue service as well as a bloated public sector, left the government, by mid-2011, unable to finance current expenditure and service existing debt, while investors were charging ever higher interest rates to buy new debt. In contrast, Ireland, Portugal and Spain (as well as the UK and USA) are facing the fiscal consequences of the financial crisis and the policy responses described above. It is not just that activist fiscal measures added to government debt; implicit fiscal guarantees emerge during a crisis and the loss of government revenue due to the economic contraction contributed even more to the fiscal strain. International experience since 1800 shows an average rise of 85% in public debt during or immediately following a systemic financial crisis (Reinhardt and Rogoff, 2010) and the current experience seems consistent with the historical average.

These fiscal pressures raise fundamental challenges in democratic societies. We have already seen the public resistance to fiscal consolidation in Greece (and even the UK), and the democracies of Europe are finding it profoundly difficult to assist Greece to the extent now evidently required. In the United States, too, politicians have to date proved unable to find a sustainable outcome to the deteriorating fiscal position. While the Americans have time on their side, the Europeans do not. At the time of writing the continued existence of the euro zone with its present membership is in serious doubt. The history of a century does not suggest that fiscal consolidation is a major strength of democracy, but it is precisely what many established democracies will face in the decades to come.

Sources

Adrian, T. and H. S. Shin (2009). Financial intermediaries and monetary economics. New York, Federal Reserve Bank of New York Staff Report number 398.

Ahrend, R., et al. (2008). Monetary policy, market excesses and financial turmoil. Paris, OECD Economics Department working paper No. 597.

Almunia, M. et al. (2009). From Great Depression to great credit crisis: similarities, differences and lessons. Cambridge (Ma). NBER working paper, 15524.

Beattie, A., J. Chaffin, et al. (2010). China defends its currency policy. Financial Times. London. 7 October 2010: 1.

Bernanke, B. and Gertler, M. (1999). Monetary policy and asset price volatility. Federal Reserve Bank of Kansas City Economic Review (4th quarter): 17-51.

Blanchard, O. J. (2009). The Crisis: basic mechanisms and appropriate policies. Washington, IMF. Working paper, WP/09/80.

Blinder, A. S. (2008). Two bubbles, two paths. New York Times, 15 June 2008.

Blinder, A. S. (2005). Understanding the Greenspan standard. Paper presented at the Federal Reserve Bank of Kansan City symposium, The Greenspan era: lessons for the future, Jackson Hole, Wyoming, 25-27 August, 2005.

Board of Governors of the Federal Reserve System (2003). Minutes of the Federal Open Market Committee. June 24-25, 2003, Washington.

Borio, C. and Disyatat, P. (2009). Unconventional monetary policies: an appraisal. Basel, BIc Working paper No. 292.

Borio, C. and Zhu, H. (2008). Capital regulation, risk-taking and monetary policy: a missing link in the transmission mechanism. Basel, BIS. Working Paper No 268.

Cecchetti, S. G. (2009). Crisis and responses: The Federal Reserve in the early stages of the Financial Crisis. Journal of Economic Perspectives. 23(1): 51-75.

Cecchetti, S. G., Mohanty, M.S. and F. Zampolli (2010). The future of public debt: prospects and implications. Basel, BIS. Working papers, No. 300.

Coase, R. H. (1991 [1994]). The Institutional Structure of Production. Essays on Economics and Economists. R. H. Coase. Chicago, Chicago University Press.

Coase, R. H. (1937). The Nature of the Firm. *Economica*. 4: 386-405.

Coval, J., Jurek, J. and Stafford, E. (2009). The Economics of Structured Finance. *Journal of Economic Perspectives*. 23(1): 3-25.

Clarida, R. *et al.* (1997). Monetary policy rules in practice: some international evidence. New York, New York University, C.V. Starr Centre for Applied Economics. Economic research report No. 97-32.

Chomsisengphet, S. and Pennington-Cross, A. (2006). The evolution of the subprime mortgage market. Federal Reserve Bank of St Louis Economic Review January/February: 31-56.

Friedman, M. and Schwartz, A.J. (1963). *A monetary history of the United States 1867 to 1960*. Princeton, Princeton University Press.

Gambacorta, L. (2009). Monetary policy and the risk-taking channel. *BIS Quarterly Review* (December): 43-53.

Geithner, T. F. (2008). Reducing systemic risk in a dynamic financial system. New York, Remarks at the Economic Club of New York, New York City.

Goodfriend, M. (2005). The monetary policy debate since October 1979: lessons for theory and practice. Federal Reserve Bank of St Louis Economic Review 2005(March/April): 243-261.

Goodhart, C. A. E. (2010). The emerging new architecture of financial regulation. Paper prepared for the conference: Monetary policy and financial stability in the post-crisis era. Pretoria. South African Reserve Bank (SARB). 4-5 November 2010.

Gorton, G. B. (2010). Questions and answers about the financial crisis. Cambridge (Ma). NBER. Working paper, No. 15787.

Greenspan, A. (2004). Risk and uncertainty in monetary policy. *American Economic Review* (papers and proceedings). 94(2): 33-40.

Hall, R. E. (2010). Why does the economy fall to pieces after a financial crisis? *Journal of Economic Perspectives*. 24(4): 3-20.

IMF (2009). World economic outlook. Washington, DC. IMF, April 2009.

Kasper, W. and M. E. Streit (1998). *Institutional economics: social order and public policy*. Cheltenham: Edward Elgar.

Keynes, J. M. (1936). *The general theory of employment, interest and money*. Cambridge: Cambridge University Press.

Kling, A. (2009). *Not what they had in mind: a history of policies that produced the Financial Crisis of 2008*. Arlington (VA). Mercatus Centre: George Mason University.

Kunzig, R. (2011). Population 7 billion. *National Geographic*. 219(1): 32-69.

Leamer, E. E. (2007). Housing ii the business cycle. Paper presented at the Federal Reserve Bank of Kansas City. Jackson Hole symposium : Housing, housing finance, monetary policy. Wyoming, 30 August to 1 September 2007.

Lockhart, D. P. (2008). Thoughts on the subprime mortgage crisis. Paper presented at the Atlanta Commerce Club in a panel discussion entitled: The subprime crisis: Is it contagious? February 29, 2008.

Mishkin, F. S. (2008). How should we respond to asset price bubbles? Speech at the Wharton Financial Institutions Centre and Oliver Wyman Institute's Annual Financial Risk Roundtable, Philadelphia, Pennsylvania, 15 May 2008.

Mishkin, F. S. (2007). *Monetary policy strategy*. Cambridge (Ma): MIT Press.

North, D. C. (1990). *Institutions, institutional change, and economic performance*. Cambridge (Ma): Harvard University Press.

Poole, W. (2007). Understanding the Fed. Federal Reserve Bank of St. Louis Economic Review 2007(January/February): 3-13.

Obstfeld, M. and K. Rogoff (2005). Global current account imbalances and exchange rate adjustments. Brookings papers on economic activity. 1: 67-122.

Reinhart, C. and Rogoff, K. (2010). From financial crash to debt crisis. Boston(Ma). NBER Working paper No. 15795.

Reinhart, C. and K. Rogoff (2004). The modern history of exchange rate arrangements: a reinterpretation. *Quarterly Journal of Economics* (February). 119: 1-48.

Roberts, R. (2010). *Gambling with other people's money. How perverted incentives caused the financial crisis.* Arlington, (Va). Mercatus Centre: George Mason University.

Romer, C. D. (1992). What ended the Great Depression? *Journal of Economic History.* 52: 757-784.

Rose, A. K. (2006). A stable international monetary system emerges: inflation targeting is Bretton Woods reversed. *Journal of International Money and Finance.* 26: 663-681.

Smith, A. (1776 [1981]). *An inquiry into the nature and causes of the wealth of nations.* Vol. 1. Indianapolis: Liberty Fund.

Stern, G. and Felman, R. (2004). Too big to fail: the hazards of bank bailouts. Washington (DC): Brookings Institution.

Svensson, L. E. O. (2009). Flexible inflation targeting: lessons from the financial crisis. Speech given at the workshop: Towards a new framework for monetary policy? De Nederlandsche Bank, Amsterdam, 21 September 2009.

Taylor, J. B. (1993). Discretion versus policy rules in practice. Carnegie-Rochester conference series on public policy. 39(2): 195-214.

Taylor, J. B. (1998). Applying academic research on monetary policy rules: an exercise in translational economics. Stanford, The Harry G. Johnson Lecture, Stanford University.

Taylor, J. B. (2007). Housing and monetary policy. Federal Reserve Bank of Kansas City's 2007 symposium : Housing, housing finance, monetary policy. Jackson Hole, Wyoming, 30 August to 1 September 2007.

Taylor, J. B. (2009). *Getting off track.* Stanford: Hoover Institution Press.

White, L. J. (2010). The credit rating agencies. *Journal of Economic Perspectives.* 24(2): 211-226.

Wolf, M. (2010a). Currencies clash in the new age of beggar-thy-neighbour. *Financial Times.* London. 29 September.

Wolf, M. (2010b). How to fight the currency wars with a stubborn China. *Financial Times.* London. 6 October.

Zoellick, R. (2010). The G20 must look beyond Bretton Woods. *Financial Times.* London. 8 November.

The impact of the Great Depression on democracy

Dirk Berg-Schlosser

Should the Western world experience a major crisis, it is likely that national politics will vary along lines that stem from the past, much as they did during the 1930s. Political scientists of the future, who seek to explain events in the last quarter of the century, will undoubtedly find important explanatory variables in earlier variations in the behaviour of the major political actors.

S. M. Lipset

Introduction

In the aftermath of the greatest global financial and economic crisis since the 1930s political actors today are still haunted by the spectre of events that followed the 1929 crash, which led to civil wars, a breakdown of democratic systems and the rule of law, and the opening of the door to World War II and the Holocaust. This chapter examines the conditions and factors that shaped events and outcomes then with a view to learning from those experiences today. The analysis draws largely on the results of an international and inter-disciplinary research project[1] which examined closely a number of European countries during the inter-war years in Europe. Among them were eight democratic survivor cases, which included Belgium, Czechoslovakia, Finland, France, Ireland, the Netherlands, Sweden and the UK, as well as seven major cases of democratic breakdown, such as occurred in Austria, Estonia, Germany, Greece, Hungary, Romania and Spain. Although the starting hypothesis contained in the statement above by S.M. Lipset refers to the behaviour of major political actors, of interest here are also the wider historical, social, political and cultural background conditions in each of the countries mentioned.

The inter-war experience

The countries studied here shared many socio-economic and political-cultural characteristics during the period clearly demarcated by the two World Wars, which significantly altered the internal and external political landscape and set this period apart from earlier and later developments. All of the countries could be described as parliamentary democracies, although some were democratic more in form than in substance. All were affected by a common exter-

---

1   The project involved more than 20 historians, economists, sociologists and political scientists from almost as many countries and has been fully documented in two comprehensive volumes (Berg-Schlosser/Mitchell 2000, 2002).

nal factor, the world economic crisis of the late 1920s and early 1930s. Some survived as democracies, others turned to more authoritarian forms of rule, in particular, to fascism.

Only five (Belgium, France, the Netherlands, Sweden and the United Kingdom) were already well-established democracies before the First World War. Out of the ashes of the former Habsburg and Tsarist empires seven new countries emerged and in six others new democratic systems had been installed immediately after (as in Germany) or shortly before the war (as, for example, in Italy and Spain). The Great War had left its mark on daily economic and political life in large parts of Europe, leading to a critical period of readjustment. But in spite of the considerable economic and political turmoil of the immediate post-war years, parliamentary democracy survived for a time in many of the countries, even if it was rather fragile in some cases. The exceptions were the 'legal' fascist takeover by Mussolini in Italy in 1923 and the more conventional military coups d'état by Primo de Rivera in Spain in 1923, by Josef Pilsudski in Poland in 1926 and by Gomes da Costa in Portugal in 1926.

Following the immediate turbulence of the post-war period and the first democratic breakdowns in Italy, Poland and Portugal, things settled down somewhat in the majority of cases. In Germany hyperinflation had been brought to an end by the successful currency reform of November 1923. In April 1924, thanks to the Dawes Plan, more favourable terms were agreed upon for the German reparation payments imposed by the Treaty of Versailles and to pay French war debts. At the same time the treaty of Locarno in 1925 initiated a period of détente in French-German relations. In 1926 the League of Nations, of which Germany became a member, facilitated the ratification of the newly-drawn post-war boundaries and the establishment of a collective international security system (Bracher 1953). Economically things also improved with an increase in industrial production and per capita income, and inflation and unemployment held at manageable levels. One ominous sign, however, was the negative balance of trade for most countries considered here, which to some extent was compensated for by the influx of American capital, mostly in the form of loans. The level of external debt also remained extremely high in a number of cases, for example, in France and Portugal.

The political situation remained relatively calm, but the newly established and surviving democracies could not yet be considered as having become consolidated, especially in the case of Germany, Greece, Czechoslovakia and Finland, where the existence of relatively strong 'anti-system parties' from the right and left posed a threat. But even in the case of some of the older democracies, such as Belgium and France, there was considerable potential for non-democratic or anti-democratic forces to emerge.

This is the background against which the impact of the Great Depression as the common external denominator has to be seen. On 24 October 1929, later referred to as 'Black Thursday', panic set in on the New York stock exchange. Shares were sold in record numbers and similar frantic sales followed during the next weeks. The Dow Jones industrial average reached a low of 198 on 13 November, nearly half the value of 381 which had been noted as recently as 3 September. The crash, however, was not merely a financial matter affecting banks and speculators. The ensuing liquidity panic quickly extended to mortgages, with the result that many homeowners who could not renew their due loans or mortgages faced foreclosure. The price of housing dropped sharply. Other commodity prices and imports similarly fell to record lows, while industrial production dropped by 10% within a mere two months (for a detailed account of the economic crisis see Kindleberger 1973).

Other countries quickly felt the crunch, too. By the end of December 1929 share prices declined by one third in Canada and Belgium, and by 16% in Germany and Austria. However, the effects that were to be felt during the coming years proved to be even more devastating. International trade was reduced considerably, national products and per capita incomes declined, industrial production fell and unemployment rose sharply. This process generated its own internal dynamic and was further reinforced by severe budget cuts and other restrictive policies on the part of most governments. Similar effects were produced by the 'beggar-thy-neighbour' policies implemented by nearly all central banks, which put short-term domestic interests ahead of longer-term considerations of international cooperation and stability.

It is not possible to discuss in detail here the economic and political causes of these events and the interactions between them. What will be attempted instead is, first, to assess the overall economic impact of the crisis as it affected the cases under consideration and, second, to indicate the respective social and political reactions and their link to the final regime outcomes. In order to assess the overall impact of the world economic crisis in each case, the year 1928, i.e. the year before its sudden outbreak, is taken as a basis against which to note the percentage changes in each of the major economic indicators (National Domestic Product, industrial production, employment, external trade and the cost of living) until its peak or bottom before the beginning of a recovery.

There are data to show that the fall in per capita income at constant prices was steepest in Romania, Germany and Austria. Industrial production declined by more than half in Czechoslovakia, Austria and Belgium. Unemployment rose most dramatically in Ireland, the Netherlands and Czechoslovakia. It reached its highest absolute peaks of more than 30% of the working population (including the level of unemployment prevailing before 1928) in Ireland, Austria, the Netherlands and Germany. Exports fell most sharply in Germany (to 16%(!) of the figure for the reference year) and levelled out at around one third in countries such as the Netherlands, France, Czechoslovakia, Austria and Estonia. Since both survivor and breakdown cases can be found among the most seriously affected countries, it follows that the final regime outcome cannot be explained in terms of the impact of the economic crisis alone, but must be seen in its broader social and political context. In particular, the simplistic notion, still held by many, that it was the high level of unemployment that brought Hitler to power in Germany has to be refuted as a mono-causal explanation; the fact is that the increase in unemployment was higher in countries such as Czechoslovakia and the Netherlands, where democracy nevertheless survived.

The sobering economic figures just cited indicate severe suffering and outright misery for millions of families and individuals affected by the crisis. Even in the more highly industrialised countries, publicly supported social security systems were often weak. In countries where unemployment benefits and similar measures were guaranteed by legislation, the respective institutions and their budgets were quickly stretched to their limits as the crisis lasted much longer than anyone had originally expected. Falling incomes and rising unemployment also led to strong social and political reactions in the face of what seemed to be a continuously deteriorating situation, which those in political office appeared to be unable to cope with. Large numbers of people took to the streets in what were often peaceful but sometimes also violent demonstrations in which participants clashed with either the forces of law and order or with the militants of opposing political camps. Strikes, however, generally decreased in number, since those who were still gainfully employed did not want to put their employment at further risk. The organisational power of the unions also declined as a result of their losing a considerable percentage of their membership.

Public violence was often reinforced by uniformed armed militias of the extreme right and left, or by the so-called 'veterans' movements, as in Estonia, for example. These groups sought to achieve their political ends by non-democratic means and increasingly called into question the existing parliamentary system. At the electoral level growing polarisation could be observed in many cases, which strengthened the anti-system parties on both the right and the left. Depending on the type of electoral system and the timing and frequency of elections, this often brought strong and sometimes even majoritarian, albeit not united, anti-system forces into parliament. The consensus of those in favour of parliamentary procedures and democratic values was put to a severe test. In some cases it cracked, for example in Germany, where the last democratically elected grand coalition government consisting of the liberal and centrist parties and the social democrats fell apart in March 1930 over the issue of maintaining social security benefits.

The overall anti-system reactions were strongest in Germany and Spain, followed by Greece, Austria, Estonia and Finland. In Germany in the last free elections in 1932 the anti-system parties on the left (communists) increased their share of the vote by 6%, while the party on the extreme right (National Socialists) reached a peak of 37.3%, an increase of 26%. In total, the anti-system forces reached a (disunited!) majority of 60.5% of the electorate. Among the cases with the strongest social reactions, only Finland emerged as a democratic survivor, albeit with some restrictions.

Economic policy and the impact of some of the major actors and their respective moves also warrant attention. The principal measures adopted by most governments to combat the crisis consisted of conventional austerity policies. The main task of such policies was to attempt to balance the public budget at times of shrinking revenues by cutting down public employment, social welfare benefits and other expenditures as much as possible. At the monetary level many countries pursued high-interest and tight credit policies in order to maintain international credit and the convertibility of their currency at fixed exchange rates. With the advantage of hindsight it is obvious that most of these measures were counterproductive and served only to aggravate the crisis even further.

But these social and political background conditions in the context of the post-war crisis, the impact of the Great Depression, the social and electoral reactions to the crisis and the economic policies pursued were in themselves not enough to determine whether or not democracy survived or broke down in a given country. In addition, there were many real actors whose decisive moves at critical turning points must also be considered. Persons such as Hindenburg, von Papen and Hitler in Germany, Masaryk in Czechoslovakia, Svinhufvud in Finland and Päts in Estonia, to name but a few, obviously had a hand in what finally transpired in their respective countries.

It is helpful to visualise the interrelationship between the structure- and the actor-oriented perspective as a coastline threatened by a tsunami. The existing topography of the seashore shaped by geology, the elements and by man-made structures such as dykes plays a crucial role when disaster strikes. The landscape can be conceived of as the respective historical and structural conditions determining the situation in each case prior to the onslaught of the tsunami and other secondary consequences triggered by a quake with their potential to further exacerbate the devastating impact. In this scenario the shape of the coastline as well as individual groups and actors who man the dykes and the specific actions they take come into play in a crisis situation and determine the success or failure of their efforts. All these factors are shown graphically in Figure 1 below.

Figure 1:   Survival cases

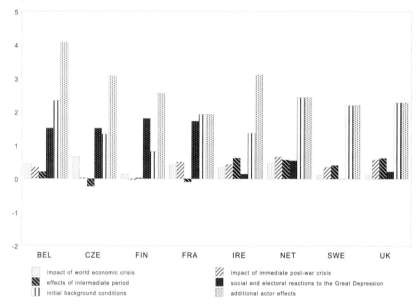

▒ impact of world economic crisis	▨ impact of immediate post-war crisis
▩ effects of intermediate period	▦ social and electoral reactions to the Great Depression
‖ initial background conditions	▥ additional actor effects

The strength of the initial quake, in this case the impact of the Great Depression, is represented by the first (dotted) bar. The topography of the seashore shaped by the two previous periods, that is, the immediate post-war crisis and the intermediate period before the Great Depression, is shown by the next two (shaded) bars. The impact of these forces is measured against the strength and the height of the existing dikes as an expression of the basic background conditions that are either favourable or unfavourable for democracy and are represented here by vertically lined bars. The actual tidal wave reflecting the social and electoral reactions in each country is indicated by the fourth (dark) bar. Finally, the figure shows the impact of particular actors who either improved the efficiency of the embankments or weakened them against the flood; this is indicated by the last darkly shaded bar for each case. The positive values in the figure can be conceived of as a reef that had withstood previous floods and continues to serve as a protection for the coast, while negative values indicate the existence of a trough created by earlier floods that now facilitates the onslaught of the new force.

Looking at the survivor cases, and in particular at the patterns exhibited in the right-hand side of Figure 1 above representing the solid democracies of the Netherlands, Sweden and the United Kingdom, one can conclude that in these three countries the impact of the various crisis factors over time did not much affect the final outcome; the dykes remained consistently high and stable, and did not require any specific intervention by any relevant actor. In Ireland the crises factors were also relatively insignificant, although the dyke in this rather poor Catholic country with no previous experience of independent statehood and democracy was somewhat lower. In this case, though, it was significantly reinforced by the supportive actions of Prime Minister de Valera and his Fianna Fáil followers after their election victory in 1932; this victory united the previous anti-Treaty forces on the issue that was the cause of the Irish civil war in 1922/23 between those who established the Free State in December 1922 and supported the Anglo-Irish Treaty and the Republican opposition for whom the Treaty represented a betrayal of the Irish Republic.

The situation in Belgium and France, in contrast, was much more critical. In Belgium the anti-democratic forces represented mainly by the (francophone) Rexists and the Vlaamsch Nationaal Verband and Verdinaso on the Flemish side gained considerable strength. Even though the dyke in this highly industrialised early democracy was very high, the crisis situation in 1937 when Rexist leader Degrelle put forward his major challenge was serious. But the tension was considerably relieved by the positive intervention of Cardinal van Roey and by the formation of a broader-based democratic coalition under Prime Minister van Zeeland. In France, similarly, the anti-system forces represented by right-wing groups, such as Action Française, the Ligues and in particular the Croix-de-Feux headed by Colonel de la Rogue, gained considerable strength and reached almost the top of the dyke. But following the failed coup attempt in February 1934 and the formation of a Popular Front government under Léon Blum in 1936, which included for the first time the Communist Party as part of a democratic coalition, the situation became somewhat more consolidated. Yet the parliamentary governments remained shaky until the German invasion and the establishment of the Vichy regime in 1940.

The Czech and, especially, the Finnish cases exhibit a pattern where the ultimate flood wave reinforced by the post-war and intermediate periods would have gone over the dike had it not been for the determined pro-democratic interventions by President Masaryk in Czechoslovakia and President Svinhufvud in Finland. The latter first outlawed the Communist Party, whose strong links with Moscow posed a threat from the extreme left, and two years later, in 1932, put down the revolt by the fascist 'Lapua' movement at Mäntsälä by making use of the military. The establishment in 1936 of a broad-based red-green socialist-agrarian coalition consolidated the situation.

Figure 2: Breakdown cases

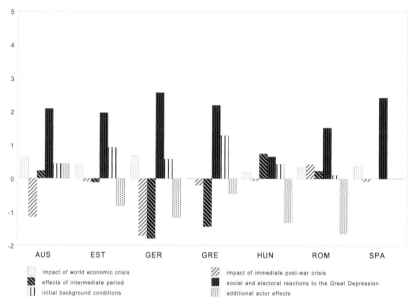

Legend:
- impact of world economic crisis
- effects of intermediate period
- initial background conditions
- impact of immediate post-war crisis
- social and electoral reactions to the Great Depression
- additional actor effects

The discernible patterns among the observed breakdown cases represented in Figure 2 are equally revealing. In countries such as Hungary, Romania and Spain the democratic dykes were very low or practically non-existent from the very beginning, while the anti-system forces maintained or regained their strength. In Hungary, in the quasi-monarchy or façade of democracy under the governorship of Admiral Horthy, certain variations of the conservative-authoritarian forces maintained the upper hand until the regime finally gave way to the external pressures of fascist Germany during World War II. In Romania King Carol II himself established a royal dictatorship in 1938, which then paved the way for the Iron Guard and the dictatorship of Marshall Antonescu, who formed an alliance with Adolf Hitler in 1941. In Spain the civil war after 1936 sealed the fate of the second democratic republic and brought to power Generalissimo Franco and his authoritarian and Falange supporters.

In Austria, Greece and Estonia the strength of anti-system forces was also overwhelming and clearly too much for the existing dykes to withstand. In these cases the post-war crisis and, to some extent, the lack of political stabilisation in the intermediate period also left their mark. Considerable internal turmoil undermined the democratic systems in Austria and Greece, giving way to authoritarian regimes under Dollfuss in 1934 in the former, and under Metaxas in 1936 in the latter. In Estonia the incumbent president, Konstantin

Päts, pre-empted a perceived fascist threat by the Veterans' movement, abolishing parliament and establishing an authoritarian regime in 1934.

Germany remains the most intriguing case with by far the most wide-ranging and, it seems, to some extent never-ending, repercussions. Within the set of cases discussed here, Germany was the one racked by the most turbulent events throughout the entire inter-war period. The effects of the post-war crisis in the form of army mutinies, local left-wing rebellions, right-wing coup attempts and a period of hyperinflation were particularly strong and were not significantly alleviated during the intermediate period; the depth of the remaining troughs is indicated by the second and third bars in the above diagram. The overwhelming effect of the Great Depression (as shown by the first bar) led to the collapse of an already very fragile democratic system, an unsurprising outcome given that more than 60% of the electorate gave their active support to anti-system forces. This doubly reinforced wave ran with ease over the existing dyke. In fact, the presidential cabinets, which no longer enjoyed a parliamentary majority but were appointed by Hindenburg since 1930, can already be seen as representing the beginning of the end of the first experience of democracy in Germany (see also Winkler 1993; Bracher 1953). The tsunami merely pushed events in an anti-democratic, and ultimately fascist, direction when President Hindenburg and the former German Nationalist Chancellor von Papen handed over power to Hitler and his Nationalist Socialist Party on 30 January 1933. It is an open question whether any other intervention could still have saved the regime. At best, an authoritarian intervention, perhaps with strong support from the military along the lines of the Austrian and Estonian cases in 1934, might have still succeeded. The world might have then been spared one of its worst experiences, but the Weimar democracy would not have survived.

Lessons for the present world economic crisis

The above is just an outline of a systematic comparative political analysis and indicates the potential such a study holds for an understanding of similar crisis situations. It highlights the fact that a comprehensive and meaningful analysis has to take into account longer-term structural conditions together with the varying impacts of the crisis, specific social and political reactions, and finally, the concrete moves, policies and speed of the reactions by major political actors.

For the crisis of 2008-2009 we do not as yet have the necessary data to conduct such an analysis. Nevertheless some general conclusions can be drawn to at least outline the similarities and important differences between these two major crises.

1. Even though the overall magnitude of the latest crisis and its fallout are considerable, the decline of GDP, industrial production and exports, as

well as the rise in unemployment, are all lower when compared with the figures for the 1930s.

2. The 2008-2009 crisis has been truly global and not confined mostly to the Western world.

3. The new important centres of the emerging markets of China, India, Brazil and South Africa have been less affected by the crisis than were the countries of the developed world.

4. The OECD countries and, in particular, the European Union member states are today much more intertwined. The 1930s policy of 'beggar-thy-neighbour', the aim of which was to save one's own country at the expense of other countries, is no longer feasible for them.

5. There has been much greater coordination in devising counter-measures to the crisis within the EU, but also at the global level through the G8 and G20 summits. And while individual national measures differ, they affect all of the closely linked economies. The German car wreck subsidy (cash for clunkers), for example, was used to buy not only German-made cars but also those produced in Italy, France, Portugal, etc.

6. There are now better informed insights into the causes and mechanisms of the crisis; neo-Keynesianism has been accepted again on a much greater international scale. Nevertheless, there are still no effective international controls to avoid similar bubbles and excesses.

7. The political effects of the 2008-2009 crisis have been far less severe, at least in the longer-established democracies. There have been no strong extremist social and political reactions in those countries and the general structural and political-cultural conditions favouring the persistence of democracy clearly prevail. The reasons for political disaffection in some of those countries have other roots that are mostly not related to the crisis.

8. The modern welfare states now have built-in buffer effects, which cushion the social and political impact of the crisis, at least for a while.

9. The situation in the younger Third Wave democracies is shakier. There things depend more on policy and actor effects comparable to the inter-war crisis. But the international situation and the political climate have also changed. External factors and international assistance, for example, the EU in Eastern Europe, now play a much greater role.

10. So far there has been no sizeable reverse wave of democratisation. The few individual cases, such as Guinea, Honduras or Niger, for example, are not related to the world economic crisis.

11. Oil- and mineral-exporting authoritarian rentier states have seemingly remained politically stable, but their exports have been affected by lower world market prices. This has been in part compensated by a greater demand from the emerging markets.

12. Capitalist democracies may no longer be the 'only game in town' for others to follow. For some countries China might possibly serve as a new

model combining a controlled market economy with authoritarian rule. This also provides more leeway for other authoritarian or rogue states, such as Angola or Sudan. Similarly, a new national-authoritarian model in Russia and in the other Commonwealth of Independent States (CIS) and neighbouring countries may follow this route.

In the final analysis the epigraph by S.M. Lipset needs to be modified for to-day's conditions. We certainly can (and should!) learn from the past, but we also have to take into account in a coherent and systematic way the factors that have changed. What we know so far is that the global and financial crisis of 2008-2009 did *not* have any serious political repercussions. But we also know that in the age of globalisation things have become far more complex and that in this context we are still far from having established international regulations that would be able to avert similar crises in the future.

Sources

Berg-Schlosser, D. and Mitchell, J. (eds) (2000). *Conditions of Democracy in Europe, 1919-39*: Systematic Case-Studies. London: MacMillan.

Berg-Schlosser, D and Mitchell, J. (eds) (2002). *Authoritarianism and Democracy in Europe, 1919-39: Comparative Analyses*. London: Palgrave.

Bracher, K. D. (1953). Die Auflösung der Weimarer Republik. Villingen: Ring Ver-lag.

Kindleberger, C. P. (1973). *The world in depression 1929-1939*. London: Allan Lane.

Lipset, S. M. (1960). *Political man –the social bases of politics*. New York: Double-day.

Winkler, H. A. (1993). *Weimar 1918 – 1933*. München: Beck.

PART II
The economy and democracy

The free market can function without democracy, but democracy cannot do without the free market. This is because a free civil society forms the foundation of a democratic system and as such needs economic resources independent from the state to create the economic bases for unrestricted civic initiatives. And so far the marriage of democracy and capitalism has proved to be a peaceful and relatively efficient mode of economic development.

However, the Great Recession put various models of democracy on trial. The violent social unrest in Greece in the summer of 2011 revealed that during times of serious economic troubles the range of counter-measures available to a democratic system is more limited than the measures open to an authoritarian system. What is more, a free civil society may reject even a rational reform package, because it usually calls for a painful adjustment to a given habituated standard of living of the citizens. The democratic system must take into account the expected social responses to the implementation of counter-measures and ruling politicians are well aware that implementation of such measures under democratic conditions results more often than not in a withdrawal of political support and a subsequent loss of their power.

Nevertheless, the following review of democratic responses to the Great Recession shows that, for the time being at least, democracies have proven to be stronger than the latest crisis. Even young democracies do not seem to have lost legitimacy, which may be interpreted as the efficient functioning of intra-systemic shock-absorbers such as alternation of power, the reorientation of economic policies as a result of public discourse and organised protests, etc. This, of course, does not mean that all democracies are equally successful in coping with recession, but that generally there has as yet not been a serious threat to the democratic system that could be linked to the Great Recession. In fact, the Arab Spring suggests the Great Recession undermined the stability of authoritarian capitalisms more than it has destabilised democratic capitalisms.

The crisis: possible impacts on economic systems and policy

Philip Mohr

Introduction

In the wake of the 2008-2009 global crisis there has been much speculation about its possible impact on the politico-economic systems and broad economic policy strategies, particularly in developing countries. A widely-held view is that since China has apparently been affected less by the crisis than the major Western economies, there will be a tendency for developing countries to adopt all or part of the 'Chinese model' of market authoritarianism, instead of pursuing market fundamentalism in a democratic political environment. Some observers prefer to focus on a broader range of developing countries, particularly the BRIC countries (Brazil, Russia, India and China), and to try to distil lessons and guidelines from their perceived success.

In discussing the possible demonstration effect of the variable impact of the crisis it is necessary to first look at some key aspects of economic systems and economic performance to avoid the danger of becoming embroiled in peripheral issues, while neglecting or overlooking the fundamental ones. Also, a distinction should always be drawn between the impact of sustained high economic growth and the possible impact of the crisis as such. It could be argued, for example, that China already warranted extraordinary attention on account of its sustained growth performance irrespective of the crisis, which probably had only a marginal impact on the attractiveness of the Chinese model. In addition, there is also a need to differentiate between the impact of the crisis on advanced and developing countries. In contrast to other recent international economic crises, the latest crisis had its origin in the advanced economies. Moreover, the level of financial development and integration in the more advanced economies made them much more vulnerable to the crisis than developing countries with less developed financial sectors. As a result, the crisis has been labelled a rich world's crisis. The focus in this chapter, however, is on developing rather than developed countries.

Economic growth in recent years

Table 1 shows the annual rates of economic growth in selected countries prior to and during the crisis. The first two columns indicate average annual growth rates over a decade or so and the last two show the rates for 2008 and 2009 respectively, with the latter reflecting the impact of the recession.

Table 1: Economic growth in selected countries prior to and during the crisis

Country	Annual percentage change in real GDP			
	1990 – 2000	2000 – 2008	2008	2009
Germany	1,8	1,2	1,3	-4,9
Japan	1,1	1,6	-1,2	-5,2
United Kingdom	2,8	2,5	0,5	-4,9
United States	3,5	2,4	0,4	-2,4
Australia	3,6	3,3	3,7	1,3
South Korea	5,8	4,5	2,3	0,2
Brazil	2,7	3,6	5.1	-0,2
Russia	-4,7	6,7	5,6	-7,9
India	5,9	7,9	5,1	7,7
China	10,6	10,4	9,6	9,1
Greece	2,2	4,2	2,0	-2,0
Ireland	7,4	5,0	-3,0	-6,0
Poland	4,7	4,4	5,0	1,7
Angola	1,6	13,5	13,2	0,2
Mozambique	6,1	8,0	6,7	6,3
Uganda	7,1	7,5	8,7	7,1
Venezuela	1,6	5,2	4,8	-3,3
South Africa	2,1	4,3	3,7	-1,8

Sources: IMF, OECD, World Bank

The first four countries in the Table are well established developed economies. Like most other advanced economies, each country in this group experienced significant economic decline in 2009. Note that all four, especially Germany and Japan, had not fared particularly well (on average) during the two decades prior to the crisis. Germany was struggling with the economic impact of unification, while Japan had become a mature economy with an ageing population after decades of comparatively rapid economic growth. In the 1960s the Japanese economy grew at an average annual rate of 10%, much like China today and South Korea in the 1970s and 1980s, but by the end of the 1980s growth had become lacklustre. Numerous subsequent efforts to revive the Japanese economy have proved singularly unsuccessful. Nowadays many observers regard the 'Japanese model' of stagnation and deflation as highly relevant for other advanced economies. They analyse the Japanese experience in detail in an attempt to ascertain what to do to avoid a similar experience. A fundamental question, however, is whether or not the mature advanced economies still have the potential to grow at rates approaching those experienced in the past. It may be argued, for example, that Japan's demographics, especially its ageing population and declining labour force, is the main cause of the country's economic woes.

The next two countries in the Table are the only advanced economies in which positive, albeit low, real GDP growth was recorded in 2009. After decades of rapid growth, South Korea joined the ranks of the advanced economies in 1997, ironically at just about the time of the Asian economic crisis. Following Japan, South Korea also became a more mature economy in recent years and the average annual growth rates of 9% in the 1970s and 8% in the 1980s will not be repeated in coming decades. Australia fared the best of all the advanced economies, largely because of its mineral wealth and close economic ties with China and other Asian countries.

The next four cases, the BRIC nations, are large countries that potentially constitute an important bloc in international economic and political affairs. Brazil, Russia, India and China all rank among the top nine countries in the world as far as land area, population and GDP are concerned, the latter on a purchasing power parity (PPP) basis. As a group they accounted for more than 25% of world territory, more than 40% of world population and about 25% of world GDP in 2009 (World Bank, 2009). In 2011 South Africa was invited to join BRIC, which would then become BRICS, but for the purpose of this chapter the focus is on the original BRIC group, as identified by Jim O'Neill of Goldman Sachs in 2001. South Africa was probably invited to join to obtain a foothold in Africa, but from an economic point of view the country is a minnow compared to the other four countries. Moreover, there is nothing particularly interesting about South Africa's economic performance prior to, during and after the crisis.

Although the BRIC countries are undoubtedly the most important emerging market economies because of their size, they have not all performed particularly well economically. Following the collapse of communism, the Russian economy declined during the 1990s, particularly during the crisis of 1998. It subsequently recovered, mainly due to the country's oil and gas resources, but collapsed again during the latest crisis. Brazil performed reasonably steadily albeit not spectacularly, stagnated during the recession and has grown rapidly since then (not indicated in the Table). China and India, however, recorded consistently high economic growth prior to and during the crisis and are therefore often regarded as role models for other developing countries to emulate.

It should be emphasised, however, that the BRIC countries are still developing countries, with average living standards and levels of development that are substantially below those in the advanced economies. For example, in the 2010 *Human Development Report* (UNDP, 2010) Russia was ranked 65th, Brazil 73rd, China 89th and India 119th of the 169 countries for which human development indices were estimated. A similar picture emerges when PPP-adjusted per capita income data are used. The BRIC countries also perform badly in international rankings of economic freedom, international competitiveness (except China) and corruption. There are also some serious reservations about the quality of economic data in the BRIC countries, especially China.

In the next group in the Table are three European countries. The first two, Greece and Ireland, both members of the euro zone, are under severe fiscal strain and had to be bailed out during 2010. In contrast to most of the other countries in the Table, their economic decline continued into 2010. Ireland, in particular, suffered a severe economic collapse from 2008 onwards. After two decades of high growth during which Ireland was labelled the 'Celtic Tiger' and was often mooted as an example for other countries to follow, the Irish economy imploded quite spectacularly. The 'Irish model' of social pacts, wage moderation, tax cuts, the promotion of foreign direct investment and financial sector development has definitely lost its sheen. Some observers argue that the Irish boom was driven by special circumstances, such as the advantages (including massive subsidies) deriving from the country's membership of the European Union, rather than by a particular approach to economic policy. The third country, Poland, is the only European country that did not experience negative growth during the crisis. This former communist bloc country implemented a big-bang 'move to the market' in the 1990s and, although it is still classified as a developing country, its performance, especially relative to other former command economies, appears to indicate that the market system is not as inherently flawed as supporters of greater government intervention tend to suggest.

Of the four African countries in the Table, the first three serve to remind us that some quite significant growth rates have been recorded in Africa, albeit off very low bases. In fact, most African countries recorded positive real GDP growth during the crisis, although the reliability of their data can also often be questioned. If the data are taken at face value, the Angolan figures illustrate what can be achieved in a resource-rich country once a degree of political stability has been established. South Africa is included since it is by far the most important and influential economy in Africa, a major commodity-exporting country and a prospective member of BRICS. Although South Africa escaped most of the direct consequences of the financial collapse, its exports suffered as a result of the international meltdown, dragging the economy into its own recession.

Venezuela is included since the 'Venezuelan model' of nationalisation and other forms of government intervention is often propagated by politicians in developing countries. The country was, however, hit quite hard by the crisis. Venezuela's economic decline continued into 2010 despite the recovery in the oil market, and at the time of writing the decline was projected to continue into 2011. The Venezuelan model has lost most of its appeal, except for economically uninformed, power-hungry politicians in some developing countries.

Fundamentals

Economic systems can be classified on the basis of the predominant form of ownership (i.e. according to property rights) or on the basis of the predominant coordinating mechanism. Property can be owned collectively or publically (as in socialism) or privately (as in capitalism) and there are fundamentally three types of coordinating mechanism: tradition, command and the market. All economic systems are mixed systems, but a particular form of ownership and a particular coordinating mechanism usually dominate (as in market capitalism).

Each form of ownership and each coordinating mechanism has its own particular strengths and weaknesses. There is consensus, for example, that the market system allocates scarce resources efficiently, but tends to generate or exacerbate inequality. Economists of a Keynesian persuasion also believe that market economies tend to be inherently cyclically unstable. In other words, they believe that business cycles (booms and recessions) are part and parcel of the way in which capitalist market economies operate, and that government should try to smooth these fluctuations as far as possible. Economists of a Classical persuasion, on the other hand, believe that a private market economy is inherently stable and that business cycles are caused by inappropriate government intervention (e.g. to stimulate economic growth). They see no role for anti-cyclical policy and propagate a hands-off approach. The age-old ideological debate between these competing schools of thought is unlikely to ever be settled and should always be borne in mind when considering different views on, or examining different analyses of, the Great Recession.

Economic performance is shaped by a variety of determinants including factor endowment, economic systems, institutions, economic policy and various non-economic factors (such as politics, history, geography, culture and attitudes). The first thing to consider when examining the performance of a particular country is its factor endowment. Many differences in economic performance can be explained by considering the quantity and quality (productivity) of each country's factors of production (land, labour, capital, entrepreneurship, technology). But other aspects can also be very important. For example, although certain schools of economic thought believe there are universal economic laws that cut through time and space, each country has its own geography, history, institutions and culture that impact on its economic system and performance. These influences are captured in the term 'path dependence', which refers to the notion that a country's current and expected performance is shaped by the path it followed to arrive where it is today. Analysts who emphasise path dependence sometimes trace the roots of current institutions and performance to ancient history (e.g. Beattie, 2009).

Economic policy can also be very important, but the first priority should be to avoid policy mistakes rather than to try to significantly improve economic performance. Policy mistakes can be disastrous, while good policies will probably at best only generate marginal improvements in economic performance. Classic examples are the populist economic policies implemented from time to time in developing countries and which resulted in harming the very groups whose interests the policies were supposed to serve. Policy makers should always be cognisant that their policies may have unintended consequences.

Experiences

China

The most notable feature of Table 1 is the sustained high rates of economic growth in China prior to and during the crisis. One of the themes of this book is that China's high recorded growth rate during the recession may result in a strong demonstration effect on other developing countries, who may try to emulate the 'Chinese model' of authoritarian capitalism. However, to the extent that such a demonstration effect exists, it probably preceded the crisis and the latter possibly only had a marginal impact on the attractiveness of the 'Chinese model'. Long before the crisis many developing countries were probably already in awe of China's continued high growth and contemplating ways and means of emulating that performance. The Chinese experience is particularly attractive to those leaders who believe that they too can create a dynamic economy without easing their grip on economic power.

But is there a 'Chinese model'? What are the real causes of the rapid economic growth in China? Do they lie in the Chinese economic system, the political system, the country's factor endowment, its stage of economic development, Chinese culture, specific policy strategies or something else? And if there is such a model, is all or part of it for export? For background information on these and similar issues, see the chapters by van Beek and by Han and Lü in this book.

Some observers distinguish between the Washington Consensus, which is often regarded as the policy package emanating from market fundamentalism, and the Beijing Consensus, a more pragmatic approach to economic development that is more appropriate to developing countries. The original Washington Consensus was formulated in 1989 by John Williamson to encapsulate the broad economic policies prescribed to developing countries by the IMF, the World Bank and the US government. The great irony, of course, is that the US itself did not adhere to a number of these policies.

According to Williamson (1989), the Washington Consensus consists of ten elements or policy prescriptions: fiscal discipline, reprioritisation of public expenditure, tax reform, market-determined positive real interest rates, stable competitive exchange rates, privatisation, deregulation, measures to secure property rights, promotion of trade and promotion of foreign direct investment. On closer examination, these measures do not amount to radical free-market fundamentalism. On the contrary, they would generally be regarded as necessary elements of any prudent economic policy strategy. The main problem with the Washington Consensus did not lie in its contents, but in the way in which it was thrust upon the developing countries that had been forced to approach one or more of the Washington institutions for financial support. In fact, many elements of the Consensus have been key elements of economic policy in successful developing countries. However, where the free-market approach does feature strongly in the Washington Consensus is in its ahistorical, apolitical, 'one-size-fits-all' nature. Not all the elements necessarily apply to the same extent in every situation or at each point in time, and those that do apply need not always have to be implemented to the same degree. In other words, a pragmatic approach is called for.

This is precisely what the Beijing Consensus purports to be. The term was coined by Joshua Cooper Ramo, a former foreign editor of *Time*. He described it as a pragmatic commitment to innovation and constant experimentation, or "crossing the river by feeling the stones", as the old Chinese saying goes. In contrast to the Washington Consensus, the Beijing Consensus thus does not consist of a set of rules. The key features are mixed ownership, basic property rights and heavy government intervention. However, in contrast to most other countries, government intervention in China is not primarily aimed at correcting potential market failure (e.g. rising inequality or environmental problems), providing social security or serving the interests of groups other than the Central Committee of the Chinese Communist Party (CCCCP). Government spending is devoted largely to investment spending to stimulate economic growth, with the ultimate aim of ensuring the legitimacy of the regime. The pursuit of economic growth is also the goal of local governments, who behave like private corporations, rather than being involved in matters of redistribution and social development.

An examination of the evolution of economic policy in China since 1978 yields evidence of most, if not all, the elements of the Washington Consensus. In fact, if one compares China with the United States there is more evidence of it being applied in the former than in the latter. But there was no 'big bang'. China started from its existing institutional base (unlike the former communist countries in Europe, who started with radically new institutions) and applied the various measures in a piecemeal fashion, without an ideological commitment to any of them. This lack of ideology is arguably the main feature of the Beijing Consensus, or the Chinese approach to economic policy. The Chinese are notorious for their lack of respect for patents and copyright. Likewise, they will 'import' any element of Western economic policy and adapt it to Chinese circumstances, if necessary. By the same token they are not loath to discard certain elements, or to change direction as conditions change. The Chinese approach may therefore perhaps be labelled an eclectic approach to free markets. In 1998, for example, China embarked on one of the largest privatisation drives in history by privatising much of the country's housing stock. This housing reform has been described as "the largest one-time transfer of wealth in the history of the world" (*The Economist*, 29 May 2010: 76).

But what have been the main drivers of Chinese economic growth? In attempting to answer this question, one must always remember that China was an extremely poor country before 1978 and that it is still a poor country (on a per capita basis). On a PPP basis per capita gross national income in China was only two thirds of the world average, less than 15% of that in the US and about 20% of that in Japan in 2009. To a large extent, therefore, China was and still is in the process of catching up with the developed world. It is always easier to grow fast off a very low base during the catch-up phase, but as the economy matures growth will inevitably decline. Some observers believe that to put things in the right perspective present-day China should be compared with Europe at the time of the industrial revolution, the United States towards the end of the nineteenth century and Japan in the 1960s.

There is also the questionable quality of Chinese data to be taken into account. China has a reputation for publishing dubious statistics about its economy. Even top Chinese leaders acknowledge that there are problems with the integrity of the data. One of the basic problems is an antiquated data-collection system (Baumohl, 2009: 358-359). The National Bureau of Statistics still collect data from local managers who have an incentive to lie to promote their own interests. The degree of fabrication and falsification is believed to have diminished, but question marks remain. While there is no doubt that the Chinese economy has grown spectacularly during the past three decades, the level and, particularly, the steadiness of the growth rate are simply too good to be true. This has led one cynical observer to comment that China's present is almost as murky as its future. One of the recent mysteries, for example, is how economic growth could have remained fairly steady during the crisis despite millions upon millions of Chinese workers becoming unemployed. Perhaps the answer lies in the fact that reliable quarterly GDP data are not published, along with the success of the massive stimulation package. Nevertheless, some lags between stimulation and job creation are inevitable and should have been reflected in the data.

A key factor in Chinese economic growth has been, and remains, the massive amount of unemployed, underemployed or unproductive labour in the rural areas available for productive employment at low wages in the cities. In the 1950s W Arthur Lewis formulated a theory of economic development for which he was awarded a Nobel Prize for Economics in 1979. In this theory of "economic development with unlimited supplies of labour" Lewis argued that development occurs when non-productive workers from the agricultural or traditional sector are shifted to the manufacturing or capitalist sector, where they are more productive. This is exactly what has happened in China and what is expected to continue to happen for quite some time since there are still tens, if not hundreds, of millions of unproductive Chinese in subsistence agriculture in the traditional interior regions available for transfer to the capitalist sector at low wages. The Chinese miracle is first and foremost a labour story. Without the availability of unlimited supplies of labour, it would not have occurred.

However, while an adequate supply of labour may be regarded as a necessary condition for economic development to occur, it is by no means a sufficient condition. China has long had millions upon millions of unproductive citizens, but it did not experience extraordinary economic growth or development prior to the 1980s. Other necessary conditions included the changes to the Chinese economic system introduced from 1978 onwards. Much attention is focused nowadays on the authoritarian nature of the Chinese regime and on the possible advantages of authoritarianism for economic growth. But without the introduction and expansion of markets, property rights and most of the other elements of the Washington Consensus, the growth process would not have been set in motion or sustained at such high levels. In modern history there have been a few classic examples of the superiority of a market system over a command system, including West versus East Germany, South versus North Korea and Taiwan versus China (prior to 1978). The recent experience of China (in contrast to the situation prior to 1978) can definitely be added to this list. Without adopting key elements of a free enterprise economy, the Chinese miracle would not have occurred.

The command element of the Chinese variety of a mixed economy has, however, also been a significant factor in Chinese economic growth. In this regard China was fortunate to have other Asian models to follow, including Taiwan, Singapore and South Korea, which all achieved economic development under autocratic regimes. The important prerequisite, of course, is that economic growth should be at the top of the political agenda. In China economic growth serves as the tool that the Communist Party uses to entrench its legitimacy and power. There are many complicating factors, including corruption, environmental destruction and, especially, growing inequality. The latter is particularly serious, since the government does not address income disparities through redistributive policies. There are no safety nets, no social security measures and in such a situation social and political stability hinges on a continuous rise in living standards. This growth imperative is an important factor in the 'Chinese miracle'.

A key advantage of an authoritarian system is that economic policy can be formulated and implemented without having to consult an elected parliament. For example, when the recent crisis resulted in the loss of millions of jobs in the export sectors, the Chinese government immediately implemented a massive rescue package centred on the expansion of the country's infrastructure. This aspect is discussed in some detail in the chapter by Han and Lü.

Other drivers of economic growth in China include a good infrastructure, an educated workforce, the absence of independent trade unions (only one state-controlled trade union is allowed), flexible labour markets, a high rate of savings, massive natural resources (China has the third-largest proven mineral resources in the world) and the advantages of playing catch-up in a large and growing world economy. As far as policy is concerned, many mistakes have been made but the economy is so large and the government so powerful that high economic growth is maintained, despite the unavoidable policy errors.

From this brief discussion it should be clear that there is no simple 'Chinese model' of market authoritarianism. In many respects it is a unique combination of state control and rampant free-market capitalism. Anyone interested in learning from (or trying to emulate) the Chinese experience should also take note of Chinese culture and history.[1] For much of recorded history China had the largest economy in the world and many technological breakthroughs originated in China. As recently as 1820, the Chinese GDP accounted for 30 per cent of the world total. This was followed by a century of anarchy, rule by warlords, foreign suppression, civil war and conflict with Japan, By 1978, after three decades of communism, China was an extremely poor country. In many respects, however, the recent rise of the Chinese economy can be viewed as a move towards a return to a situation that existed centuries ago.

---

1   Discussed in detail in the chapter by van Beek in this volume.

Other BRIC countries

Brazil has almost traditionally been regarded as a large country with a huge but largely unrealised economic potential. *The Economist* has on occasion referred to the country's "infinite capacity to squander its obvious potential". Brazil's traditional drawbacks included a large and ineffective state and a high degree of political and economic instability, one of the symptoms of the latter being periodic bouts of high or hyperinflation. Matters have improved since the mid-1990s, but as indicated in Table 1 Brazil's rate of growth did not threaten to reach Chinese proportions in the 1990s and 2000s.

The Brazilian state is still large and by all accounts still tends to be ineffective, but a substantial degree of political and macroeconomic stability has been achieved. Among the most significant changes in the politico-economic sphere was the full or partial privatisation of the plethora of state-owned enterprises including Petrobras, the largest company in the Southern Hemisphere. Another was the pragmatic leadership of Lula, the popular former trade unionist who refrained from adopting a populist approach to economic policy.

In a more stable political and economic environment Brazil has experienced commodities-driven economic growth, including a massive increase in the contribution of oil to GDP. The country has also benefited greatly from China's industrialisation, particularly through exports of food and iron ore. This has boosted growth and eliminated the balance-of-payments problems that were often experienced in the past. Nevertheless, the country also experienced a recession (albeit brief) in 2009. As far as policy is concerned, there does not appear to be a unique 'Brazilian model' for other developing countries to follow. If anything, Brazil's experience seems to support the Washington Consensus rather than any alternative approach. In the context of the BRIC countries, Gideon Rachman described Brazil as "less scary than China, less authoritarian than Russia and less chaotic than India" (*Business Day*, 29 September 2010: 11).

Russia's membership of BRIC can be ascribed to its size, its massive natural resources and its international political influence. As far as economic systems, institutions and policies are concerned, there are no particular positive lessons for developing countries to be distilled from the Russian experience. What lessons there might be, relate to what to avoid rather than what to do. By and large the Russian economy has not fared particularly well and the booms that have been recorded were associated with its massive natural wealth, including gas and oil. Economic reforms have been limited and there are clear signs of a movement back towards an interventionist authoritarian state.

According to Beattie (2009: 250-261), Russia's politics and government have two specific characteristics that can be traced back to the medieval era: a dominant executive with little in the way of checks and balances, and the absence of a clear dividing line between power and poverty. As a result, Russia was an ideal candidate for both monarchical autocracy and communism and is not really amenable to a market economy. As Putin (quoted by Beattie 2009: 260) stated: "From the beginning, Russia was created as a supercentralised state. That's practically laid down in its genetic code, its traditions, and the mentality of its people". Other communist countries (e.g. Poland) had different political and economic histories before the communist takeover and therefore had different attitudes and experiences that resurfaced once they were freed from communism.

Another important aspect of recent Russian experience is that political reform (*glasnost*) preceded economic reform (*perestroika*). In contrast, China started with economic reform and instituted the reform in the existing institutional framework, without destroying the framework itself.

As indicated in Table 1, *India* recorded rapid economic growth during the past two decades. To a certain extent the economic rise of India and China represents a return to the situation prior to 1800, when these two populous countries together accounted for half of the world economy. Their recent growth paths have differed, however. In particular, the Indian experience provides little or no support for authoritarianism or greater government involvement in the economy.

India and China are different in other fundamental respects. India has an English-speaking population, a tradition of democracy, a transparent legal system, a decentralised economy, a healthier and better capitalised banking system and a younger population. Whereas China is focused on the manufacturing sector, in India it is the service sector that traditionally leads the way. The dominant role of services is the result of both India's factor endowment and a deliberate strategy to focus on its own unique comparative advantage, rather than compete head-on with China and other Asian countries. The comparative advantage includes a young educated English-speaking and often well-travelled labour force. As the largest English-speaking country in the world India has decisive advantages in areas such as telecommunication, business outsourcing, computer software, banking, insurance engineering, the media, film entertainment and medical diagnostics.

But why did India not fare particularly well prior to the 1990s? The following are among the reasons that have been advanced: an anti-capitalist culture, a fatalistic caste system, overpopulation, hot and humid climate, corruption, central planning, nationalisation, import substitution and various bureaucratic controls (inherited from the British), including rigid labour legislation.

The change came in 1991 when a serious balance of payments crisis gave rise to sweeping political and economic reforms. Economic isolation and central planning were abandoned, the economy was opened up to more imports, most price and exchange controls were eliminated, the rupee was allowed to float more freely, industries were deregulated, state-owned firms were privatised and taxes were cut. Many of the previous disadvantages remain, including inadequate infrastructure, but the economy is growing in leaps and bounds. As far as manufacturing is concerned, the focus is on establishing a sophisticated industry rather than to try to compete with other low-wage Asian countries.

As mentioned earlier, the Indian experience provides little or no support for authoritarianism or heavy government involvement in the economy. On the contrary, the Indian economy serves as an example of what can be achieved through market-related economic reforms.

From this brief discussion of the BRIC countries it should be clear that there is no such thing as a BRIC model. Each country has arrived where it is along a different path, each has different factor endowments, different political systems and different approaches to economic policy. Although all four have generally performed quite well economically, average living standards are still quite low and they all tend to rank poorly on a number of measures of institutional quality, including the rule of law, control of corruption and regulatory quality. All have implemented market-oriented reforms but in a gradual piecemeal fashion, rather than the full market liberalisation propagated by the Washington institutions. For example, all BRIC countries still have a complex set of onerous legal and regulatory regimes that make it difficult for foreign companies to invest in them.

Venezuela

When examining individual countries' experiences, one should try to identify both the positive and the negative aspects of these experiences. In matters of economic policy, for example, it is more important to know what to avoid than what to aim for. Venezuela is a case in point. Before the onset of the crisis, economic growth in Venezuela was quite impressive and the 'Venezuelan model' of nationalisation and other forms of government intervention had many admirers in developing countries. In 1999 Hugo Chavez came to power in the country with the largest oil reserves outside of the Middle East. He behaved like a typical Latin American populist leader (e.g. Peron in Argentina), succeeding in cloaking authoritarianism in outwardly democratic forms. *The Economist* (15 May 2010: 13) described his approach as "a post-cold-war model of authoritarian rule which combines a democratic mandate, populist socialism and anti-Americanism, as well as resource nationalism and carefully calibrated repression".

While oil prices were high and increasing, the Venezuelan economy grew quite rapidly as indicated in Table 1, but when oil prices plummeted the economy collapsed. Significantly, Venezuela's economic decline continued despite the subsequent recovery in the oil market and at the time of writing Chavez, who announced in January 2010 that he was now a Marxist, was very unpopular domestically. Prior to that Chavez had described his approach as "21st-century socialism" (The Economist, 2010) and regarded this as a viable alternative to liberal democracy, citing Iran, Russia, Zimbabwe and Sudan as examples of other countries following this approach.

The 'Venezuelan model', among others, involves the nationalisation of key natural resources, including the expropriation of land, price controls and exchange-rate controls. The state-owned oil company, Petroleos de Venezuela, was placed under direct government control in 2003. Oil production dropped and domestic petrol shortages ensued. Electricity generation was nationalised in 2007 and power outages became the norm. State-sanctioned land invasions led to the collapse of commercial agriculture, and price and exchange-rate controls gave rise to black markets. In short, Venezuela is paying the price for a decade of economic mismanagement. These events are, of course, also reminiscent of what happened in Zimbabwe, as well as in other Latin American countries under previous populist leaders.

The Venezuelan experience clearly underlines the point that populism should be avoided. Nevertheless, the 'Venezuelan model' is still popular among aspiring populist leaders. This should come as no surprise because, as Tim Cohen a prominent South African journalist, stated, "populist messages are not susceptible to logical argument" (Business Day, 10 February 2011: 11). One of the main traits of populists is that they tend to ignore the basic facts of economic life.

Theory

How has the crisis changed the way we think about the economy? At first blush, it should serve as a strong indictment of (if not death-knell for) classical, neo-classical, new classical, real business cycle and all other schools of thought that allow little or no scope for active macroeconomic stabilisation, apart from the adoption of rules for monetary and fiscal policy. Economics, however, is a faith-based discipline and much of economic theory is ideological. As a result, the different schools of economic thought always try to find ways and means to reconcile their views with the empirical evidence and they steadfastly refuse to adjust their respective basic ideological stances.[2] In this regard we need to look no further than the Great Depression of the 1930s. Eight decades later the disciples of the different schools (or religions) still ar-

---

2   Referring to market fundamentalism, Hector Torres has stated that it is "a faith that is difficult to dispel, because its priests can always claim that its failures result not from theological bankruptcy, but from insufficient orthodoxy" (Business Day, 22 April 2010: 11). In a similar vein, Gideon Rachman believes that "the Great Recession seems unlikely to dissuade many economists from the belief that there are predictive 'laws' out there, just waiting to be discovered" (Business Day, 8 September 2010: 9).

gue about the real causes of, and appropriate policy responses to, the depression and there is no reason to believe that the reaction to the Great Recession will be any different.

By and large, however, the recent crisis has given Keynesianism a massive boost. After having been effectively sidelined during the worldwide 'move to the market' and the prolonged cyclical upswings during most of the past two decades, the urgent need for discretionary monetary and fiscal intervention on an almost unprecedented scale reminded economists and policymakers of the basic tenets of Keynesian macroeconomics, as formulated by Keynes himself. The circumstances that developed from 2007 to 2009 left no scope for a laissez-faire approach and showed that the business cycle was still alive and kicking. Intervention was essential. The only real questions concerned the types of intervention that were required and how drastic the intervention had to be.[3]

Despite the ongoing ideological battles, the crisis undoubtedly did have a lasting impact on economic policy. Likewise, the Great Recession has already had an impact, although it is uncertain how lasting the impact will be.

The well-known economic commentator, Anatole Kaletsky, is one of those who believe that the financial crisis will have a lasting impact on economic systems at least in the developed world. He distinguishes three varieties of capitalism during the past two centuries. Capitalism 1.0 was the classical era of laissez-faire capitalism that originated during the Napoleonic wars. Capitalism 2.0 was the interventionist era that followed the Great Depression, and Capitalism 3.0 the free-market era following the stagflationary 1970s.

Kaletsky (2010) believes that the recent crisis will again alter the respective roles of government and the market, as well as the relationship between politics and economics. Capitalism 4.0 will differ significantly from Thatcherism, Reaganomics and pre-1970s Keynesianism. It will not be characterised by a fundamental faith in either the role of government (2.0) or the market (3.0), but by experimentation. In some areas of the economy government will become more involved, but in other areas it will retreat. In other words, he envisages a more pragmatic blend of market forces and government intervention, along the lines of the Beijing Consensus referred to earlier.

One of the areas in which government is set to retreat is the labour market, where the trend is towards more flexibility. In international trade there will probably be some tendency towards greater nationalism and protectionism, but in a globalised world economy there are definite checks and balances in this regard. Currencies will also tend to be managed, although again there is extremely little scope for this, except in a country like China. There

---

3   Nonetheless, there are economists who predict that the Great Recession will become the
     deathbed of Keynesian economics (Business Day, 24 February 2010: 6).

will tend to be greater regulation of financial markets, but care should be taken not to strangle this sector. Although unregulated financial innovation caused immense problems, the evolution of credit has been as important as any technical advance in history. It is important, however, that models of the real economy incorporate the financial sector. One of the most serious drawbacks of mainstream economic theory is a failure to account for the real economic effects of developments in the financial markets. As Kaletsky said: "The dirty little secret of modern economics is that the models created by central banks and governments to manage the economy say almost nothing about finance" (*Sunday Times*, 2009).

Concluding remarks

The crisis of 2008-2009 and the Great Recession forcefully reopened the age-old debate on the relative merits of the state and the market. According to Ecclesiastes 1:9, there is nothing new under the sun. This applies in economics as well. Over the years, the pendulum has swung forwards and backwards between state intervention and reliance on market forces. After two decades during which market fundamentalism generally prevailed, particularly in the advanced economies, a swing in the opposite direction was virtually inevitable. But the market has not lost its place. Thirty years ago Arthur Okun, a prominent American economist at the time, stated that the market always has a place, but he immediately added that the market always has to be kept in its place. In the aftermath of the crisis there will be a greater emphasis on the latter in the form of more domestic and international regulation of financial and economic affairs, and a greater appreciation of the role of the state in the pursuit of goals such as job creation, which will assume greater prominence than before. With inflation under control (for the time being at least) there is already pressure on central banks to accord a higher priority to economic growth and employment creation, and as a result they have lost a measure of the independence they enjoyed prior to the crisis.

The lure of free-market thinking will diminish somewhat, but it will not disappear. Market fundamentalists are still in charge in the advanced economies and the same models (incorporating notions such as rational expectations and efficient markets) are still used to analyse the economy and advise policymakers. Bad ideas die a slow death.

But what about the developing countries and the attractiveness of the 'Chinese model'? Will China continue to spurt ahead and will an increasing number of developing countries try to emulate the 'Chinese miracle'? High economic growth is set to continue in China, but it will not last forever. Whether or not the Chinese economy will eventually surpass that of the US, and whether or not it will become an advanced economy (on a per capita basis) are by no means certain. For the time being, however, the 'Chinese model' will remain an attractive option for developing countries. One can only hope that potential emulators of this model pay heed to the salient features of Chinese history and society, and recognise the pragmatic, eclectic nature of the model. In particular it is important to realise that the 'Chinese miracle' would not have occurred without greater reliance on private initiative and market forces.

Sources

Baumohl, B. (2008). *The secrets of economic indicators* (second edition). Upper Saddle River, NJ: Wharton School Publishing.

Beattie, A. (2009). *False economy. A surprising economic history of the world.* London: Viking.

Kaletsky, A. (2010). *Capitalism 4.0: The birth of a new economy in the aftermath of crisis.* London: Bloomsbury.

Sunday Times Business Times, 1 November 2009: 12.

The Economist, 15 May 2010: 13.

UNDP.2010. *Human Development Report.* New York: United Nations Development Programme.

Williamson, J. (1990). *What Washington means by policy reform. In Williamson, J. (ed). Latin American adjustment: How much has happened?* Washington (DC): Institute for International Economics: 5-35.

World Bank (2009). Available on-line at: http://data.worldbank.org

Democracy, error correction and the global economy

Laurence Whitehead

Introduction

The financial crisis of 2008 and the subsequent global 'sudden stop' to trade and investment briefly elicited a broad international consensus that severe errors in the management of the world economy required concerted correctives. But that moment soon passed. The worst scenarios of sustained and cumulative economic disruption never materialised, and a cautious normalisation was provisionally restored. The existing institutions of international economic governance re-established much of their authority and restored an adequate level of public and market confidence, implementing various partial reforms.

Even so, effects of the severe shock of 2008 linger on in various critical domains. Youth unemployment has ratcheted up in most of the world's old democracies, while many welfare provisions and pension funds have been severely affected. Fiscal deficits widened and sovereign indebtedness also rose, creating a mismatch between what the compensating policies of states could afford to finance over the medium to long term, and what existing entitlement programmes were likely to cost. At the same time efforts to restore a (lightly reformed) version of the previous growth model required regaining the confidence of the very market participants whose indiscipline had precipitated the original downturn.

This chapter reflects on the concept of democracy as an 'error-correction' mechanism as it relates to the management of the 2008 downturn in the international economy. At the national level democratic procedures can precipitate a change of leadership (perhaps also accompanied by a change of policy, although that is more uncertain) that renews public authority and so reinvigorates political responsiveness to economic challenges. At the international level democratic controls over policy choices are at best more diffuse. In hard times they may take the form of obstructions to needed international cooperation, rather than supports for constructive reform. On the assumption that the existing structure of international economic relationships is likely to remain intact for the time being, despite its failings, and that many leading states in the system will remain subject to the logic of democratic political competition, it becomes a matter of urgency to identify the conditions under which democracy can function more as an error-correcting, rather than as an error-compounding, procedure.

2008 in perspective

It is easy to forget how dire the international economy seemed in the immediate aftermath of the September 2008 Lehman Brothers bankruptcy. In a representative article published in July 2009 Randall Germain highlighted parallels with 1931 that seemed entirely plausible at the time, but that look far too negative two years later.[1] No doubt it remains possible that a second phase of the same crisis could still erupt and so justify the initial gloom. But from the perspective of early 2011 it seems far more likely that 2008 will be judged to have been an abrupt global shock, but not the onset of a world depression. Even if future developments are as negative as the most pessimistic analysts anticipate, the rebound of 2009-10 has driven a wedge between the first crisis and its potential sequels. It is easier to see parallels with 1982 (when the Latin American debt crisis seemed briefly threatening to the world as a whole, before it settled down into a 'lost decade' for a single large region); or 1998, when the Russian and East Asian 'sudden financial stops' may have paved the way for the global imbalances of ten years later, but assumed a classical U shape and were widely judged to have been successfully contained within a brief time-span.

Whether or not the post-2008 recovery subsequently falters, this two-year interval of apparent recovery makes a huge difference in political terms. Democratic time horizons are quite brief. When a financial or economic crisis proves sufficiently stark and severe, it can generate a concentrated demand for corrective action – typically involving some mixture of assigning blame, sanctioning those held responsible, and enacting reforms intended to prevent future relapses. But the momentum behind such responses is time limited. After a couple of years many of those initially singled out for criticism have often moved on, or stepped aside. Diagnosis of precisely who was to blame, and which failings require corrective action, becomes cloudier and the interested parties settle into their respective defences.

As time passes, then, the initial concentration of political energies around a corrective agenda becomes harder to sustain, in part because competing parties and rival lobbyists are likely to try to appropriate the reform impulse for their own selective purposes, but also because other issues arise over time

---

1   Germain, R. (2009). Financial order and world politics: crisis, change, and continuity. International Affairs. 85(4). The author refers to stock market losses of 30-70 percent in 2008, year-on-year falls in industrial production of as much as 38 percent (in Japan) and "in sector after sector, across almost all industrialized and emerging economies credit markets have quite simply seized up" (p. 673).

that distract attention from the original point of convergence. Thus, the 2011 resurgence of commodity prices (especially oil) and anxieties over energy security are tending to displace the hostility towards banks and financial speculators that was so prevalent in 2009-10. Finally, and of central importance for the analysis undertaken here, within two or three years of a financial crisis the conventional electoral calendars that govern democratic life bring about either a replacement or a renewal of national political leadership in many of the affected countries.

Since the 2008 crisis was global in impact, it is essential to examine the international as well as national levels of political responsiveness to such shocks. Here, too, the time lags are critical. In the initial phase of crisis management crucial decisions may be taken within days, or even hours, and therefore with very little opportunity for planning and coordination. The most powerful states and the most strategically placed institutions within them (typically central banks and finance ministries) will do what they consider necessary to stabilise the immediate situation, postponing consideration of the knock-on effects of their decisions. At this stage democratic accountability is liable to be viewed as a luxury.

But once emergency resources have been deployed and crucial commitments to key players undertaken, there comes a second, more reflective, phase. This may take some months, since in the heat of a financial crisis the information asymmetries tend to become even more severe than usual, and those in charge of the levers of power are too busy – and too uncertain of their control over the situation – to take time off for broader deliberations. But in due course it becomes necessary to rebuild international cohesion, address the concerns of those governments most adversely affected by the initial policy responses, and to sketch out an agenda for the restoration of international economic normality. Much of the international co-ordination involved at this stage is likely to be dominated by the need to transmit messages of confidence and reassurance to international markets. In the current global system policymakers, even in the most powerful and interventionist of states, are extremely keen to avoid adverse verdicts from private wealthholders and autonomous market participants, which may result in currency flight, bond market strikes and bank runs. Caught between the need to justify the emergency decisions taken at the height of the crisis, and the wish to present a confidence-enhancing united front to the financial markets, international economic policymakers have limited scope for deep analysis or root-and-branch reforms during the early post-panic months. At best they may recognise the case for commissions of enquiry and expert advisory reports, thus postponing for a year or so the more comprehensive re-thinking that the crisis is seen to demand from them.

At a third stage, as confidence returns and more precise evidence and analysis become available to guide further cooperative deliberations, the pressure for unified action is likely to dissipate. By then some of the key de-cision-makers at the heart of the crisis will have left office. In any case, as the various governments involved reflect on how the crisis has impacted on their national economies, and how post-crisis realignments might reassign the costs and benefits of reform, they are likely to arrive at divergent conclu-sions. In 2008, for example, an early assessment was that the prime source of the crisis was located within the USA, and that the main responsibility for tackling it rested with the Treasury and the Federal Reserve in Washington.

Many developing countries initially supposed that they could 'decouple' themselves from an upheaval not of their making. The governments of the Eurozone were at first inclined to respond along similar lines (although Lon-don could not escape its immediate involvement). However, by the time that the international community was ready for more in-depth analysis of what had hit them, it was already apparent that the crisis had much wider ramifica-tions, and that policies designed to counter it were likely to impose substan-tial further adjustment costs on all participants. The design of such policies, and the distribution of the associated costs, could not be farmed out to the ini-tial originators of the crisis alone; nor could the first mover be relied upon to spontaneously promote diagnoses and prescriptions of the kind favoured by policymakers in the rest of the world. To take one example, Chinese policy-makers generally considered that they were not responsible for the debacle of 2008, and that the debacle confirmed their belief in the wisdom of their own approach to economic policymaking. However, once international delibera-tions got underway concerning who was at fault, and what policy changes should be prioritised, the misalignment of China's exchange rate soon emerged as a high priority issue in Western capitals.

By the time the Group of Twenty, the Bank for International Settlements, the International Monetary Fund and a host of other intergovernmental bodies had buckled down to serious debate on how to respond to the crisis and even undertaken some significant policy coordination, the national priorities of most leading states had become strongly defined. It would be an overstate-ment to argue that this eliminated all margin of choice at the supra-national level, but it surely imposed heavy constraints. Arguably, the main benefit of these collective deliberations was to discourage the adoption of directly harmful single-country initiatives – especially trade protectionism but also 'beggar-thy-neighbour' financial innovations. Crafting positive collaborative responses to post-crisis economic dislocations was a more difficult, perhaps unattainable task.

To summarise the temporal rhythms of national and international res-ponses to the crisis, by the time it was possible to assess its overall contours and to reflect on appropriate longer-term remedies, much of the initial mo-mentum in favour of reform had been lost. Established interests in many countries had regained their confidence and veto power, and any potential coalition that might have existed in favour of major curbs to the dynamics of financial globalisation had begun to splinter. So long as the shock of the 'sudden stop' continues to retreat over the horizon, and on the assumption that there is no second round of financial collapse that can be proven to represent a direct continuation of the first, it seems that existing democratic systems of deliberation are apparently incapable of generating a root-and-branch policy response. This was also what we witnessed after 1982 and 1998. The best that one can say of this structure of decision-making is that it may buy time until emerging economic and financial problems either cure themselves or can be managed below the danger threshold. For all the modesty of this 'muddling through' claim, this has the merit of radically improving on the policy responses adopted internationally after 1929.

The first section of this chapter looks more closely at the process of democratic alternation as a 'shock absorber' of economic stress, examining the dynamics of political responses within the leading old democracies. The second section addresses the scope and limit of international co-ordination insofar as this can be assessed at this relatively early stage. Section three reviews some structural factors at work – on the assumption that if political management of the aftermath of the crisis is weak, then other deeper forces will shape the outcome and determine the prospects for longer-term economic stability. The conclusion returns to the theme of political control under broadly democratic conditions. How do our current democratic institutions measure up as 'error-correcting' rather than 'error-compounding' mechanisms? Is 'muddling through' an adequate remedy for the economic vulnerability revealed in 2008? Only the most preliminary of answers can be attempted here, but these are crucial questions for those concerned with the quality and effectiveness of current democratic political systems.

Crisis and alternation in the established democracies

Regular free and fair elections are the cornerstone of contemporary democratic politics. This rests on certain background assumptions that are, in fact, only quite recent and perhaps fairly contingent. The locus of modern democracy is assumed to be a territorially bounded and administratively integrated nation-state (or state-nation). But it was not until the decolonisation of the 1950s that such units became the norm in Western Europe; and by the 1990s many of these democracies were ceding a degree of national sovereignty to the European Community in Brussels, and the European Central Bank in Frankfurt. Elsewhere stable territorial boundaries and administrative integration are frequently no more than works in progress, and free and fair elections are often something of a novelty (if they exist at all). Even the more established old democracies do not always satisfy other background assumptions about national democracy. Regular elections empower voters mainly though offering real opportunities for choice between alternative parties (and perhaps alternative policy priorities); but for many decades the party systems of Italy and Japan, for instance, while meeting the institutional requirements for genuinely democratic elections, basically failed to offer genuine prospects for alternation (the same can be said of democratic South Africa).

However, the United Kingdom and the United States do meet all the required conditions for electoral alternation at the national level. So regardless of any reservations about essentialising and universalising this model of democracy, it was available after 2008 in the two long-established democracies that were most clearly responsible for promoting the economic and financial practices that went awry during that year. Consequently, in November 2008, when the crisis was still at its most acute and unsettling, the US electorate transferred executive and full legislative authority from the Republican to the Democratic Party. Similarly, in May 2010 (in an election that had been delayed until the very last moment by a Labour government still trying to postpone the inevitable) the British electorate ousted the party that had been in charge for the previous thirteen years and replaced it with a Conservative-Liberal 'coalition' that united around a five-year joint platform mainly concerned with economic rectification. In both cases the course and outcome of the electoral contest was heavily shaped by views concerning the locus of responsibility for the economic debacle and the need for a fresh team in office to manage its consequences. Thus, at least in the core established democracies most responsible for the crisis, democratic alternation intervened as a powerful mechanism of political accountability and (perhaps even) "error correction."

On a broader canvas, there were electoral alternations largely driven by the fall-out from the crisis in Greece, Ireland and Iceland. This list may not yet be complete, since several other severely affected democracies have elections pending. There are also some examples of competitive elections in countries affected by the crisis where alternation did not occur. In Brazil, for example, the PT retained the presidency in October 2010, at least in part because the voters judged that the outgoing administration had proved successful in managing the impact of the crisis on their country. There are, at least as yet, no cases of established democracies that have been institutionally destabilised by the socio-economic fallout from the crisis. This is in striking contrast with the experience of the 1930s, as shown by Dirk Berg-Schlosser in this volume, and also contradicts some fairly widespread expectations of political polarisation and even regime breakdown that were current in 2009.

Thus, on the evidence available so far, it could be concluded that democratic procedures have offered a safety valve for citizen discontent, an opportunity for the peaceful renewal of political authorities, and perhaps even some scope for the termination of failed strategies of economic management and their replacement by more promising approaches. National democracies seem to provide some structural opportunities for collective deliberation and lesson-learning that might be harder to achieve under alternative political dispensations. This is the basis for the assertion that they can work as a relatively effective 'error-correction' mechanism.

But it would be premature to close the discussion there. The longer-term political fall-out from the economic shocks of 2008 has yet to become clear. Moreover, it was the most established Anglo-Saxon democracies that allowed the conditions of crisis to develop before 2008, so we must also consider whether this form of electorally-driven short-term policymaking could be error compounding as much as error correcting. From that standpoint, it is important to keep in mind that not all the major states caught up in the crisis were governed according to the principles of electoral competition and alternation. There is at least one alternative political model (the Chinese) that may prove competitive, and there is a wide range of democratic possibilities, some more error compounding and others more error correcting. Some of this diversity has been more closely examined in the literature on 'varieties of capitalism'; for the purposes of this chapter it will suffice to mention some narrow political considerations drawn from the recent British and US experiences.

The precise timing of each election is highly significant when assessing its impact on political management of an economic crisis. By the time President Obama assumed office on 20 January 2009 the essential features of the US emergency response were firmly in place. From the very beginning of his term, therefore, he was heavily constrained by the situation and the policies he had inherited. At the same time, the ousted Republicans were immediately committed to shifting responsibility for the hardships that were bound to follow onto the incoming administration. Whatever the merits of strong electoral competition, this was not a situation conducive to reflective deliberation, nuanced attribution of responsibility, and broad-based consensus-building on how to rectify the policy deficiencies that had been uncovered. In the abstract, electoral alternation might seem relatively propitious for such purposes, but time matters a great deal here. If the outgoing administration had remained responsible for longer, it would have had to explain the realities more fully to its supporters. If control of the lower house of Congress (the crucial tax-and-spend branch under the Constitution) was not up for grabs every two years, a longer time horizon might have encouraged better debate. These details of the US democratic process may have damaged its potential as an error-correction mechanism.

In the UK electoral timing was also a material consideration. Here, the opposite problem arose. By mid-2009 the nature and origins of the economic crisis facing the nation were reasonably clear to all informed observers. The shape of the ensuing policy responses was also fairly narrowly prescribed, and economic and financial experts were generating something approaching a broad consensus on what needed – most urgently – to be done. But it turned out that there was no way of forcing a discredited administration into a prompt election it could be sure to lose. Instead, the logic of British democratic procedure dictated that something like a year must elapse between the recognition of the major issues to be tackled and the appointment of a new administration with a renovated mandate and a new parliamentary time horizon. Moreover, given the eccentricities of the British electoral system and its lack of recent experience with two-party coalition governments, even after the election had finally cleared away the debris from the past, there was no unified and coordinated alternative waiting in the wings. Despite the long year of advance notice and preparation, when the alternative came, the joint victors in the election had to improvise in great haste and to renegotiate the terms of their policy proposals in accordance with the new distribution of power that suddenly became apparent. The electoral process proved a lost opportunity to educate the British public about the problems that a new government would have to face, and many electoral statements (including formal pledges) given by the victorious parties had to be nullified once alternation had occurred.

In summary, therefore, although both US and the British post-crisis elections brought about clear-cut alternations of national political leadership, neither of these democratic processes unfolded in a manner favourable to the effective redress of past errors, of the holding to account of failed officeholders, or the subsequent improvement of economic policymaking to guard against further relapses of the same kind in the future.

International policy coordination and democratic error correction

If there is any democratic influence or accountability at the international level of economic governance, it is extremely indirect. The only channels of representation available to ordinary voters exist through their national governments and the (usually very thin) procedures by which they report back to their parliaments and express their public opinions on such issues. Since the end of the Cold War some academic analysts have waxed eloquent about the emergence of what they term an "international civil society," a network of experts, non-governmental organisations and special interest lobbyists that aim to shape policymaking at the supra-national level. Although many such activists can be criticised as being self-appointed and unaccountable to any well-groomed constituency, there may be some areas of international decision-making where their activities are beginning to acquire a little plausibility.

But international economic coordination in the face of severe financial instability is not yet one of those areas. Here the non-governmental pressures that are brought to bear on inter-ministerial gatherings have a quite different structure. Financial conglomerates, transnational corporations, professional macro-economic analysts, bureaucrats from the Bretton Woods institutions and the network of central bankers are the only ones with a voice. By common consent these gatherings operate on the assumption that guidance of the world economy is a topic too esoteric and unintelligible to be subject to open democratic deliberation. The experts and specialists must meet behind closed doors, exchanging position papers and insider knowledge in the hope of reaching some degree of shared understanding, and perhaps even agreement, to co-ordinate aspects of international policy. It is only after such closed deliberation that political leaders attempt to transmit sound-bites about what was discussed and agreed on to the wider public. (In parenthesis, it should be noted that international economic crisis management is not unique in this respect. Decisions to go to war may also be taken in a similarly opaque manner, even by long-established democracies, although in this case rather than consulting with economic technicians, the consultations would be with military security experts).

For the most part these simplified messages are designed to provide reassurance, deflect criticism and exaggerate the constructive achievements of the individual leaders presenting their reports. That leaves little scope for genuine clarification of the dilemmas and uncertainties under discussion. Not only do such communiqués generally fail to educate international public opinion about the real issues at stake; they also encourage busy politicians to deceive themselves about what has been achieved. It is politically more attractive to declare a victory over adversity than to confess to indecision or defeat. In short, there is little scope for democratic accountability or even honest reporting back from G20 summits and other such conclaves. This also limits their utility as error-correction mechanisms and renders them vulnerable to special interest pressure groups, and distortions arising from the insider bias of these deliberate processes.

This is clearly a sub-optional structure of decision-making from a democratic standpoint. But it is a reflection of genuine difficulties that limit the scope for direct democratic accountability at this level; and it may be less damaging then the available alternatives. So the two questions that are briefly considered here are whether somewhat more open and responsive procedures could serve to improve policy responsiveness; and, if so, what practical scope may exist for promoting such democratising reforms.

On the first question, the chapter by Christer Jönsson largely makes my case for me. As he concludes, "global governance arrangements in general, and those in global finance in particular, rate low on basic democratic criteria." Nevertheless, "the financial crisis has entailed a certain degree of democratisation," and there are some grounds to hope for small further incremental steps in that direction. These would be desirable, not only on the grounds of principle, but because under the present system "interest articulation is truncated, and there is a relative lack of interest aggregation.". I would only add that in view of the huge distributive consequences required by adjustment to the new global financial realities, it may be difficult to secure an adequate level of collective consent and cooperation in the absence of more solid and legitimate structures of decision-making. The present arrangements are quite vulnerable and precarious, because of the absence of public understanding and endorsement. They may be slightly better than in the past (they have at least kept the principles of international dialogue alive, in contrast to the 1930s), but they lack democratic authorisation and may not prove robust enough to cope with eventual backlashes.

Secondly, as Jönsson also says, the scope for further democratising measures in this area is highly constrained. Some of the principal obstacles are more or less insurmountable, at least in the near term. Not all the states participating in the G20 are democratic, and even those that are may have sharply clashing interests and perceptions. There is a deeply entrenched culture of closed expertise almost amounting to mystification among the insider professionals, which adds to the problems of communication between policymakers and the wider public. In reality, even the most well-informed and strategic of policymakers find themselves acting under conditions of extreme pressure and with imperfect and limited information at their disposal. The models and statistical tools they have been accustomed to relying on proved to be poor guidance at the time of the 'sudden stop', and may not work any better in its aftermath. The market forces unleashed by liberalisation and global economic integration are turning out to be almost as hard to track as they are to manage politically. Nevertheless, some incremental learning is possible, some broader deliberation could prove stabilising and democratic leaders will need the support of an informed public opinion if they are to contain the pressures from unaccountable concentrations of economic financial power.

Economic globalisation versus democratic political management

Whether one considers democratic accountability to be lodged at the level of national governments (as in the first section) or to be pooled at the intergovernmental level (as described in the second section), the underlying assumption remains that political authorities, answerable in some way to their electors and their societies, must be in a position to regulate, supervise and authorise the broad functioning of the economic system. After all, a market-related system of resource allocation requires voluntary cooperation and some degree of trust between buyers and sellers, and between producers, intermediaries and consumers. So there has to be a framework of rules – laws, regulations, structures and dispute-resolution mechanisms – to permit the non-coercive exchange of goods and services.

In a liberalised global economy these legitimate transactions *within* each national political unit have to be sealed up and harmonised so that they can also be conducted across state boundaries. The dividing line separating legitimate business from criminal transactions has to be clearly established and credibly patrolled, not only within but also *between* market economies. In summary, even on a narrowly 'neo-liberal' definition of the scope of political supervision, there is an indispensable role to be played by public authority in underpinning and promoting the market economy. Moreover, once voters begin to exercise influence over the choice of their political masters, they are almost certain to make further demands on them beyond the bare essentials required for legitimate commerce. In practice, of course, some electorates add extensive welfare requirements that have to be balanced against the claims of the legitimate market. Others may be more concerned about issues of security or collective identity. In summary, the political leaders required to stabilise and promote a dynamic commercial society will also need to process other citizen demands not directly geared to the smooth functioning of a liberalised market economy. For this they raise tax revenues, lead complex state bureaucracies, and enforce elaborate structures of law and social restraint. At least that is how democratic politics were believed to operate throughout the twentieth century, and this belief still shapes most democratic rhetoric and expectations at this time.

Nevertheless, there are good theoretical grounds for doubting how effectively public authorities can be in controlling or supervising a liberalised market economy – and the crisis of 2008 showed that such doubts are not purely theoretical. After all, even in a closed economy the same voters and citizens who demand market accountability from their public officials are also the consumers and borrowers who expect to enjoy the personal freedom and choice promised by deregulated markets. Furthermore, as liberalisation proceeds it transfers social and indeed market power to private producer interests and to financial conglomerates and their media spokesmen, all of which become lobbyists for greater liberalisation. At best they may have an interest in 'light touch' forms of regulation, but they can be expected to actively resist any serious democratic pressure to restore political controls over market transactions, however scandalous the abuses that may arise. This is not so much a case of myopia or ill-will, but rather a reflection of the skewed distribution of social power that arises as a consequence of liberalisation. This would almost certainly have been the case even if liberalisation had been confined within closed national economies.

The dilation of democratic counterweights to market pressure is all the more extensive and irreversible when liberalisation is driven by global economic integration. The successful private media conglomerates are no longer checked by effective public service broadcasting, so they have no incentive to exercise restraint in pursuit of their own interests. The civil servants, trade unionists, local authorities, cooperatives and mutual societies, etc. that may once have sustained a pluralist equilibrium restraining the excesses of private market power all lose traction as economic liberalisation rolls forward.

Such a context transforms the market for votes and reduces the scope for political control over corporate vested interests. It might be thought that, even so, in an extreme crisis of the type briefly witnessed in 2008, power would shift back to the more market-critical sections of the political class as a result of a public opinion alarmed at the fiscal transfers and other privileges demanded by corporations deemed 'too big to fail'. But as a broad and provisional generalisation, the aftermath of 2008 does not appear to bear out such expectations. Few market-critical political elites remained in play by that stage and the support they could muster is proving to be ephemeral.

Thus, even where left-of-centre governments did emerge from the crisis (as in the USA and Greece), the incoming administrations inherited such fiscal imbalances and such international economic vulnerabilities that any initial intentions they may have had to reassert democratic controls over the management of the economy were promptly countered by the importance of restoring 'market confidence'. Moreover, such incoming left-of-centre democratic administrations are caught in a cross-fire. In addition to opposition from powerful business interests opposed to any political reform that would curb their privileges, they are equally challenged by dissent from their own national constituencies of support, as these sectors discover that the main burden of post-crisis austerity and pro-market adjustment is likely to fall on their communities.

The underlying issue here is not which democratic electoral alternative is best placed to manage the political choices arising from the crisis (each option has its strengths as well as its limitations, and alternative experiments may be worth trying out in different national contexts). The broader issue is whether public authorities periodically selected through electoral contestation, whatever their initial programmes or bases of social support, possess the cohesion and leverage necessary to oversee and redirect the course of economic events in the wake of the latest crisis of financial globalisation. The alternative hypothesis would be that massive forces of economic and financial transformation will work their way through, under their own momentum, and with minimum guidance from the democratic authorities nominally in charge. Elected politicians and public authorities will still go through the motions of holding summits, writing budgets and appointing regulators, but most of this will be reactive or cosmetic, rather than directive.

A few illustrations appear to support this alternative view. Voters will want an early return to fairly full employment in all Western democracies. Is this something that their political leaders are in a position to deliver? Or, given that they need to maintain the illusion of authoritative leadership, will they not be driven to seek out scapegoats, or in others ways shift responsibility and disguise their relative impotence on this crucial matter? But if unemployment remains intractable and elected politicians are unable to explain why, or to admit their powerlessness, then discontented electorates are unlikely to welcome proposals for enhanced international cooperation that appear to place the interests of outsiders above the unheard voices of the nationally enfranchised. Thus, whatever politicians might hope to agree to in the international area, they will be constrained by their lack of domestic legitimacy.

There is no space here to elaborate on all the many possible variations on this theme. Consider politicians under pressure from ageing electorates who therefore cannot redress grave injustices in inter-generational equity (British tuition fees provide one illustration out of many); or consider huge resource transfers from welfare provision and local government infrastructure (key foundations of the social pact long established in most Western democracies) to insolvent financial institutions or deficit-ridden pension funds. Moreover, in an interdependent liberalised international economy many of these deep distributional conflicts and transfers also flow *between* nations as well as within them. Consequently, undocumented international migration, non-transparent money transfers, migration to tax-sheltered jurisdictions, among other phenomena, further complicate the picture and accentuate the contrast between illusions of effective economic management by elected politicians and the realities of market-determined *sauve-qui-peut*.

It is still too soon after the trauma of 2008 for a firm judgment to be made about the extent and limits of democratic political capacity to manage these forces in the aftermath of the crisis. Both on theoretical grounds and in the light of first-round indicators so far, it is reasonable to query whether the standard 20th-century model of democratic accountability will remain useable in the emerging globalised economy. Conventional theories about rational choice and institutional design may grossly over-estimate the precision and consistency of conventional top-down systems of public management of core economic variables. The alternative picture of market-determined economic forces overflowing the channels of restraint manned by weak and disoriented political authorities may be too drastic a corrective. But recent events crystallise what were in any case growing doubts about the over-confident liberal international consensus of the early post-Cold War years. It is in this insecure and uncertain context that we locate our concluding reflections on democracy as an 'error-correcting' system.

Tentative conclusions about democracy and the global economy

A central theme in democratic theory concerns whether democracy is to be commended as an 'end in itself' or for the benefits it delivers in other respects. When we study the history of why people join together and often at a personal cost, in order to promote broad processes of democratisation, it turns out that few political actors give much attention to this distinction. They pursue some roughly defined democratic objectives, such as dignity, equality, tolerance and cooperation all rolled into one, in the hope that these will both enhance societal cohesion and may also deliver other desired benefits, as suggested by democratic peace theory, democracy and development studies, and so on. If one variant of democracy seems a disappointment by some of these criteria, the response may well be to call for a further or different democratising reform rather than to relinquish the pursuit of the overall goal. Perhaps the essential intuition motivating such an outlook is that through appropriate cooperative political action ordinary people must surely be able both to have their voices heard *and* prod their rulers into improving their conditions.

The international 'sudden stop' to international financial flows of 2008 clearly raises new doubts about the reliability of that intuition in a globalised market economy, but falls far short of dispelling it. Even if all the problems outlined above prove truly intractable, that will not silence demands for democratic governance either at the national or the supra-national level –for both deontological and consequentialist reasons. Even if the results delivered by democratic politics prove a severe disappointment, it will remain possible to argue that more or better democracy is the remedy, and that dispensing with democracy would only aggravate the problem.

The focus of this chapter has been on democracy as an 'error-correction' mechanism. This is only one strand among the armoury of justifications that can be derived from democratic theory and experience. It is, however, one that merits more careful examination in the context of current international economic realities. In principle, democracy could be *either* error correcting *or* error compounding *or* not directly relevant to how well the world financial system is evolving. There is a wide spread of viewpoints about which of these positions is more convincing. While the evidence remains provisional and difficult to interpret, there remains plenty of scope for the contention that if one particular set of democratic arrangements turns out to be error compounding, then the remedy is a redesign or a renewed democratisation drive, rather than a loss of commitment to the broader enterprise.

Most Western democratic governments currently claim to be heavily focused on their 'error-correction' duties. They have by now nearly all settled
on their respective narratives to explain what their predecessors did wrong, or
failed to do, thus allowing the 2008 crisis to get out of hand. (Democratic
governments outside the core regions of Europe and North America have
emerged better placed, and therefore tend to highlight what they believe they
did right.) They are mostly engaged in combining fiscal consolidation with
monetary laxity at the democratic level, together with loose international coordination at the international level. Whether this will prove error correcting
or error compounding over the next decade remains very much an open question at this stage. Even if this turns out to be the correct 'technical' response,
and even if subsequent market 'normalisation' is managed smoothly, the political strains associated with this stance are likely to generate considerable
turbulence and eventual policy instability. This would not be such a problem
if the intellectual foundations for these corrective policies were robust and
consensual. But, in practice, after the shocks of 2008 many economic and financial analysts are no longer so much in agreement as before about how best
to respond to current policy dilemmas. It is in this context of uncertainty and
low self-confidence among the experts that democratic accountability, supervision and experimentation could achieve more leeway.

The purpose of these concluding reflections is therefore not to generate a
new set of prescriptions about how democratic leaders should take charge of,
or redirect, the course of the international economy. The question of which
prescriptions might make matters worse or better requires a different level of
analysis. Here the objective is more modest – to separate out some crucial
factors that help to determine how democratic responses to economic crises
are best analysed, and where to look when assessing whether such responses
are constructive, destructive, or simply irrelevant. The four interrelated and
extremely complex factors selected for brief examination here are the time-
scale; the feedback; the delicate balance between political and technical considerations; and the conditions under which democratic politics can remain
independent from, or absorb the failings of, economic mismanagement.

Timescales

There is almost invariably a substantial mismatch between the relatively
fixed calendar of political processes (annual budgets, periodic summits, and
multi-year election schedules) and the decision-making rhythms required in a
globalised economy. If all depositions in Northern Rock are not fully guaranteed by Monday morning the bank run will be unstoppable.... No matter
what that signifies for national budgets over future years. At the other end of
the scale, globalisation also sets in motion global tectonic shifts (of manufacturing in Asia, or of agro-industry in South America, for instance), and these

proceed relentlessly over decades almost regardless of intervening political minuets. Mismatches on this scale reveal limited scope for political direction over fundamental economic and financial developments. But some scope still remains. Democratic politicians and their expert advisers can, in principle, learn lessons from recent demonstrations of the severity of these mismatches. Left unchecked, they can be expected to further discredit the democratic process, but once this is understood there could be scope for adjusting the timetable and instruments of policy management to narrow the gap between the requirements of political deliberation and consultation, on the one hand, and the logic of the markets, on the other. It should be possible to improve the timing of political decision-making in order to render democratic procedures less error compounding, even if they can never be made fully effective as error-correcting mechanisms.

Feedback

That connects with feedback and the role of expertise pretending to steer a liberalised international economy with the help of overly rigid and scholastic models, relying on backward-looking data with large error terms and sharp discontinuities, which has proved to be a poor formula indeed. Expertise is certainly needed to identify which defects were most damaging, and what alternative forms of data collection and analysis might reduce the dangers of radical misdiagnosis. But this is not solely – or even mainly – a question of technical reform. Many democratic policymakers become too dependent on specialised bureaucratic procedures that promised more certainty and control than they could possibly be expected to deliver.

Another crucial dimension of improved feedback is therefore the need for elected politicians to develop a greater sense of realism about the deficiencies of the tools on which they rely. This is disquieting for busy and harassed decision-makers who need to maintain public confidence, and who like to shelter behind expert advice as a means of protecting their political reputations. Nevertheless, one clear lesson of the 2008 crisis is that politicians who rely uncritically on a narrow set of orthodox indicators and advisers will not escape blame when their errors are exposed.

Some useful lessons can be extracted from this experience. Since the costs of misplaced over-confidence have proved so high, a more cautious experimental and incremental approach to policymaking might help minimise the risks of gross error; since the most prestigious sources of expertise have proved so fallible, a wider and more diverse pool of advice could be worth considering; since the most powerful economic groups in a liberalised system can be expected to press their interests without restraint, good democratic leadership requires the encouragement of countervailing pressures and ultimate sources of expertise. Qualitative as well as quantitative considerations may merit respect, and feedback from civil society (including what ordinary citizens understand and will tolerate from their leaders) could be weighed more carefully against the certainties of the established elites.

The delicate balance between authority and responsiveness

This is to turn direct attention to the delicate balance that democratic politicians always need to maintain between the effective exercise of their delegated political authority, on the one hand, and their responsiveness to the larger society and its diverse constituencies, on the other. A simple approach to managing the tensions between these two logics is to cater to citizen's expectations at the moment of each election, and to govern in accordance with orthodox expert advice in between. Even in normal times the change of gear between these two periods can be very disruptive; in times of financial crisis and severe economic dislocation that is likely to prove short-sighted and destabilising as an electoral strategy, while also enhancing the risks of error-compounding behaviour between elections.

A sounder democratic strategy for handling this delicate balance would need to include more efforts to educate the electorate about the real choices they confront, and not just during but also between elections. The importance of a two-way dialogue with the political community as a whole should also be conveyed to the bureaucrats, the regulators and the economic managers. A more 'deliberative' approach to policymaking may not be easy to promote, especially not in the fraught and polarised context of the post-2008 crises, but there could be a high cost for persisting with a standard electoralist approach arising from its error-compounding and societally de-legitimising properties.

Democracy's absorptive and deflective capacities

Finally, then, the underlying question raised by these tentative conclusions is under what conditions the distribution stresses and policy failings generated by the 2008 crisis can be absorbed or deflected by democratic strategies of policy management. So far the evidence is mildly reassuring, but the absence of abrupt regime breakdowns, such as occurred in the 1930s, should not be over-interpreted.

This chapter has surveyed a succession of theoretical and practical concerns, and focused more on the risks of poor policymaking and of 'low-quality' democratic performance than on the probability of outright regime rupture. Over time democracies that compound economic management errors and that fail to address the fundamental concerns of large sectors of the electorate may become more vulnerable to downward spirals. This is all the more of a concern in an internationalised policy framework, where citizens fear that unaccountable decision-making in inter-governmental agencies is subverting the sovereignty of their parliaments, parties and national political systems. But this chapter does not regard any artificial index of 'probability of breakdown' as the crucial metric. Rather, it has been concerned to outline the scope for adjustments in the style and structure of democratic decision-making so that its error-correction potentialities can be enhanced, and its sources of social support reinforced. The aftermath of the 2008 crisis makes it clear that these are urgent issues and not easy problems to tackle. But some scope for creative responses can still be highlighted.

The model of liberal democracy and varieties of capitalism

Ursula Hoffmann-Lange

Introduction

As this book considers the possible impact of the Great Recession on global democracy, it is necessary to understand what democracy is and how it functions, what makes it desirable and preferable to other political systems, what its inherent strengths and weaknesses are, how it fares in various cultural contexts, and how it is linked to the market economy.

This contribution starts from the assumption that the model of liberal democracy is universally applicable and has the ability to ensure both social peace and political legitimacy. The model is by no means a prescription for a uniform set of political and economic institutions, as it can be adjusted to fit the specific cultural traditions of any country, but it suffers from an inherent tension between its two basic principles: liberty and equality. On the one hand, it requires the existence of a market economy, that is, a capitalist system, which necessarily implies inequalities of wealth. On the other hand, democracy has to ensure the equality of its citizens and this raises the question of whether equity should be limited only to political rights, such as equality of the vote etc., or whether it should also imply that democratic governments have a responsibility to reduce socioeconomic disparities. The topic remains highly controversial. Even so, the market economies of the consolidated liberal democracies are characterised by a good deal of government intervention into the market in favour of securing a basic standard of living for their citizens. Because liberal democracies are politically more flexible, ensure the existence of an open market of ideas and allow an electorate to vote inefficient governments out of power, they are also better equipped than authoritarian political systems to weather even deep economic crises without the threat of a decline in regime legitimacy and the consequent risk of political instability.

Democracy is inherently a continuous rather than a dichotomous concept. It is an ideal type of government in the sense that it can never be fully achieved in reality. In practice, even consolidated liberal democracies are in many respects deficient. They have biased systems of interest representation in public policymaking, low-level corruption is endemic (cf. *Transparency International*) and political parties frequently deceive citizens in electoral campaigns by making promises they will not be able to fulfil after they have come to power. Still, even critical observers would probably agree that such violations of democratic norms are much less severe in established liberal democracies than in authoritarian regimes.

The initial question to ask is whether liberal democracy is indeed the best system for securing "the greatest happiness of the greatest number" (Jeremy Bentham) in the course of championing "life, liberty and the pursuit or happiness" (United States Declaration of Independence). The first and most crucial distinction between democratic and non-democratic polities lies in the method by which political leaders are selected. In a democracy this happens by means of regular, competitive popular elections that ensure elected leaders can be held accountable to the wishes of the citizens.

While competitive elections are the central criterion for a liberal democracy, many theorists have argued that such a narrow definition is insufficient because electoral procedures may unfairly benefit some competitors. Electoral rules may, for instance, prevent certain parties or candidates from running for electoral office because of unduly high requirements for candidate registration; constituencies may be of grossly unequal size or their boundaries may be unfairly drawn; high electoral thresholds may effectively bar the representation of minorities, etc. Likewise, governments can use their resources to prevent effective campaigning by opposition parties, opposition candidates may be harassed or even thrown into prison, etc. Most political scientists therefore agree that the existence of several parties and their representation in the national legislature is only a minimal requirement liberal democracies have to fulfil.

Robert Dahl (1998), a well-known theorist of democracy added other criteria to the list besides meaningful competitive elections, among them, fundamental liberty rights and the rule of law. According to another theorist, Guillermo O'Donnell (2004), the rule of law is an essential pillar of democracy, because it is the precondition of effective political rights, civil liberties and mechanisms of accountability. This is why most scholars of democracy distinguish between merely electoral democracies in which the rule of law is not effectively realised, and 'embedded democracies' that guarantee and effectively protect the constitutional rights of citizens.

In Central and Western Europe the development of the rule of law started in the Middle Ages and was already established at the beginning of the period of democratisation in the 19th century. It was, in fact, an important precondition for democratisation in that part of the world because it allowed citizens to form voluntary associations and political parties, which then became the driving force in mobilising the people to demand an expansion of the suffrage to ever larger parts of the population.

According to a famous thesis by Samuel Huntington, there have been three waves of democratisation. The First Wave started in the 19th century in Western Europe and North America, and then lost momentum in the period between the two World Wars, as illuminated in this book by Dirk Berg-Schlosser. The Second Wave emerged in the wake of World War II and faded out between the 1960s and 1970s. The Third Wave was initiated in 1974 with the democratisation of Portugal, Spain and Greece. After the end of the Cold War, the Third Wave of democratisation spread to all regions of the world. While the First Wave was largely limited to countries that had achieved the rule of law before becoming democratic, the same has not been true for Second and Third Wave democracies. In many of those countries democracy was introduced without such a tradition and therefore lacked an effective and impartial public bureaucracy and an independent judiciary. This made the consolidation of democracy more difficult, because there were several challenges to be confronted at the same time. Moreover, many of the Second and Third Wave democracies have also been poor and lacked the financial resources to establish an effective bureaucracy and an independent judiciary.

A recent article by Nicholas Charron and Victor Lapuente (2010) argued that democratising countries that have already achieved higher levels of socio-economic development are better equipped to invest in the development of an effective public service, while democratic leaders in poor countries do not only have fewer resources at their disposal, but are also exposed to much stronger pressures to use the spoils of office for the benefit of their followers. New democracies in poor countries are therefore apt to experience a prolonged stage of poorly functioning institutions, high levels of corruption, intense social and political conflict as well as government instability. Such electoral democracies are frequently called *defective democracies* or *hybrid regimes*. According to Leonardo Morlino (2009), such hybrid regimes may persist for extended periods of time and can therefore not be considered as transitional regime types.

(Liberal) democracy as a universal value

Historians of non-European cultures, advocates of multiculturalism, but most of all autocrats of all sorts have frequently claimed that liberal democracy is a model of state organisation that was developed in Europe during the period of the Enlightenment and cannot easily be transferred to regions with different cultural backgrounds. They have therefore denounced attempts by democratic governments and NGOs (such as Freedom House or IDEA) to promote democracy in other world regions as cultural imperialism. This argument is not particularly compelling, however, because almost no one has ever raised similar objections to importing technical products such as automobiles or telephones, and most critics have also not criticised the adoption of modern medicine or new production technologies on the basis that these were not invented in their own country or culture. The rejection of liberal democracy on the basis that it is unsuitable for a particular country is mostly advocated by authoritarian political leaders intent on preserving their power, by orthodox religious leaders demanding a monopoly for their religious teachings, or by members of the well-to-do middle classes who fear that democracy will empower the lower classes and endanger their own privileged socio-economic status. Such criticism of democracy is thus primarily self-serving.

The fact that the model of liberal democracy was developed within a specific cultural context does not imply that it cannot be successfully transferred to regions with a different cultural background. Human history is replete with cultural innovations that have proven their viability in other cultural contexts. Medieval Islamic achievements in mathematics, the natural sciences, medicine and the arts, for instance, have left a deep imprint on the rest of the world. Moreover, many democratic values such as human dignity, tolerance, freedom of speech, equality before the law, etc. are not only elements of Judeo-Christian cultures but also of other cultures and religions.

The most compelling argument in favour of the universality of democratic values and principles, however, can be derived from anthropological assumptions. While a similar line of reasoning can already been found in earlier texts, such as the Federalist Papers or the writings of Ernst Fraenkel (1991), David Beetham (2009) has recently rephrased it in an especially elegant way. Beetham starts out from two fundamental assumptions. The first is that conflicts of interest over scarce resources are inevitable and that only the people themselves have the capacity to determine what is in their own best interest. "There is simply no single 'good' which can be shown to be the supreme end of public policy, unless this is couched in such vague and general terms (such as 'the welfare of the people') as to be either meaningless or open to multiple interpretations. Political decision-making is about hard choices between competing goods, or values or priorities, about which there can in principle be no clearly right and wrong answers." (2009: 283) Nobody can therefore claim to possess *a priori* knowledge about which course of collective action will be the best for achieving the public weal.

Beetham's second assumption relates to what he calls the "limited benevolence or altruism" of political leaders, implying that governments cannot be trusted to decide on behalf of the public interest because the pursuit of particularistic interests usually promises higher returns (2009: 286). Paternalistic ideologies claiming that certain philosophers, religious authorities, charismatic political leaders or experts can serve as 'guardians' (Plato) of the public interest because they are endowed with superior knowledge are therefore unfounded.[1]

---

1 Ernst Fraenkel (1991) used pretty much the same line of argument by refuting the idea that it is possible to identify what is the best in the public interest 'a priori'. Instead, he argued that the public good can only be determined 'a posteriori' and can be best achieved by the free expression and accommodation of conflicting interests.

This implies that all individuals affected by collective decisions should also have the right to participate in them. Beetham concludes: "Now the point to make here … is that this argument against paternalism and in defense of political equality does not stop at borders, or apply only to a section of humanity, but is universal in its reach. If it is valid for my country (wherever 'my' is), then it must be so everywhere" (2009: 286). Even so, democracy presupposes the acceptance of one single albeit centrally important value, which is the belief in the fundamental equality of all human beings, which in turn requires respect for their dignity. It is obvious that ideologies or religions that believe in natural inequalities based on race, sex or other ascribed traits will not easily accept this basic tenet of democracy.

The introduction of democratic institutions requires widespread, although not necessarily unanimous, elite support. Such support does not presuppose that all elite groups have to embrace the philosophical underpinnings of democratic theory. Dankwart Rustow (1970) argued that democratisation may instead result from the insight that it is the only viable solution for ending an inconclusive struggle for political dominance among competing elite factions, because it refers the decision on who should be in charge of the government to the citizens. This is especially likely to happen where it is difficult to predict which of the political camps enjoys more support among the electorate and none can rule out the possibility they might end up in the opposition. Under these conditions, the major elite actors may agree to introduce fair electoral rules and minority rights (Przeworski 1991). Democracy may therefore not result from a widespread belief in its intrinsic value, but primarily because it is considered as a means of conflict resolution. This latter possibility makes even more implausible the claim that it is not universally applicable.

Determinants of liberal democracy: structure vs. culture

In his seminal article on the *social requisites* of *democracy*, Seymour Martin Lipset (1959) used statistical data to determine the relationship between democracy and the socio-economic structure of societies. Lipset concluded that democracy flourishes primarily in economically developed societies with a high degree of urbanisation and a high average level of education. His claim has remained controversial for three reasons. First, the statistical relationship between socio-economic modernisation and democracy is far from perfect. It cannot explain why some highly developed countries such as Germany and Japan became democratic at a relatively late point in time compared to countries at a roughly equal or even lower level of economic development, nor can it tell us why some poor countries such as India have been democratic for a long time. Since social scientific laws are probabilistic rather than deterministic, however, such irregularities may be due to country-specific factors and do not invalidate Lipset's general conclusion.

Lipset's assumption of a causal relationship between socio-economic modernisation and democracy has been subjected to extensive empirical examination, which has generally supported it, even though that relationship is not as linear as Lipset implied and has also varied over time. And although empirical evidence confirms that GDP remains the single most important predictor of democracy, the Human Development Index (HDI), which also takes into account educational level and life expectancy, has even greater explanatory power. Diamond therefore recommended a modest reformulation of Lipset's thesis: "The more well-to-do the people of a country, on average, the more likely they will favor, achieve, and maintain a democratic system for their country" (1992: 468).

A more serious objection relates to the question of causality. Lipset could not convincingly demonstrate the direction of causality between modernisation and democracy. While it is highly plausible that socio-economic development is a precondition of democracy, it cannot be ruled out that causality (also) works in the opposite direction, i.e. that democracy fosters economic development. Although a number of empirical studies have been published that have tried to determine the direction of causality, the results are not conclusive, because the number of cases is simply too small and the number of other relevant causal factors is too large.

Finally, Lipset's structural theory has also been criticised for neglecting the impact of cultural factors, international influences and, last but not least, the behaviour of elites. A major challenge for modernisation theory comes from the theory of value change. Based on the results of the World Values Surveys, Ronald Inglehart and Christian Welzel (2005) have argued that human development leads to rising support for civic liberties both among elites and mass publics, and that this value change has increased the pressure for introducing democratic institutions in ever more countries. However, plausible as this may seem, human development is highly correlated with socio-economic modernisation, which makes it impossible to statistically separate the effects of structural and cultural factors.

Institutional variants of liberal democracy

In many parts of the world the concept of liberal democracy is primarily associated with the institutions and policies of the United States. Conversely, dissatisfaction with US foreign policy, especially US interventions into the domestic affairs of other countries around the globe, influences the reputation of liberal democracy in the Third World. At the same time the knowledge about democratic values and principles among citizens in these mostly poor countries is vague at best, and their authoritarian governments also try to keep it that way. Rather than being aware of the existing institutional variants of liberal democracy, many therefore loathe democracy because they believe that the democratic world is responsible for their own miserable living conditions.

In fact, however, aspiring democrats have an unlimited range of institutional options which allow them to devise a set of constitutional rules that promises the closest fit with their own politico-cultural traditions. Institutional choices have to be made with respect to three fundamental aspects. First, there is the choice between a parliamentary or a presidential system of government. In parliamentary systems such as Great Britain, Canada or Germany, legislative elections determine who will be in charge of the executive, which is in turn politically accountable to the legislature and can be removed from power by a vote of no confidence. In presidential systems which are prevalent in the Americas (United States and most Latin American democracies) the chief executive and the legislature are elected in separate elections for fixed electoral terms.

Both systems have their merits and drawbacks. In parliamentary systems the executive needs the sustained support of a parliamentary majority and can be replaced any time, thus ensuring that the policy initiatives of the government are usually supported by the parliamentary majority. On the other hand, a high degree of political fragmentation may prevent the formation of stable parliamentary majorities and may lead to governmental instability. Presidential systems with their fixed terms avoid this kind of instability. The separate elections for the chief executive and legislature, however, may produce *divided governments* with different parties controlling the presidency and the legislature, and this may in turn produce a stalemate between the two branches of government. This implies that the stability of both systems of government ultimately depends on the willingness of the major political actors to engage in political compromises. Democracy thus presupposes a consensus on basic rules of the game and even the best constitutional rules are not sufficient to ensure its viability where such a consensus is lacking.

The second important institutional choice relates to the electoral system. The basic choice is between plurality/majority systems with single-member constituencies and proportional representation (PR). While a plurality system which is mainly used in Great Britain and former British colonies (USA, Canada, Australia) tends to foster the development of a party system with only two major parties, one of which usually gains a majority of legislative mandates, single-member constituency systems with majority requirement (e.g. France) as well as PR systems (used in most parliamentary democracies) will usually result in multiparty systems that require (informal or formal) coalitions of at least two parties for majority formation.

A third basic decision pertains to the degree of centralisation of governmental power at the national level and the degree of autonomy granted to regions. The strongest vertical separation of powers can be found in federal systems in which regions enjoy considerable autonomy for self-government. In unitary systems such as France, Italy, the Scandinavian countries, Israel and generally in smaller democracies, political power is instead concentrated in the hands of the national government. Federalism is especially suited for large or culturally diverse societies such as the United States, India or Canada, because it allows different ethnic or religious subgroups to govern their internal affairs without much interference by the national government.

It is evident that these three basic institutional choices open up a host of institutional options. Moreover, liberal democracies also differ a great deal with respect to their socio-economic structure and political culture. Cultural traditions may foster a preference for either a majoritarian or a consensual mode of decision-making (cf. Lijphart, 1999). While countries with a majoritarian culture such as Great Britain and the United States tend to prefer a strong executive based on narrow electoral majorities, those with a consensual culture (primarily Switzerland and Finland) tend to accommodate minorities by searching for broad-based compromises and by assigning veto power to independent bodies such as constitutional courts, central banks or regional and local governments.

Liberal democracy and the economy

"Democracy and market-capitalism are like two persons bound in a tempestuous marriage that is driven by conflict and yet endures because neither partner wishes to separate from the other" (Dahl, 1998: 166). While this comment shows that democracy and a market economy tend to coincide, it fails to explicitly acknowledge that this relationship is not one of choice but of necessity. Liberal democracy grants individual liberty rights which also include economic rights. This connection between liberal democracy and a market economy is often not adequately acknowledged, however, especially since even some theorists of democracy have been known to claim that democracy does not predetermine a specific type of economic regime.[2] Many people continue to nourish the illusion that democracy can function without capitalism.

However, while both liberty and equality are fundamental principles enshrined in the democratic creed since the French Revolution, both are also in conflict with each other. The inherent tension between freedom and equality has been analysed by many political philosophers and political scientists. Giovanni Sartori's treatment of this problematique is especially lucid and com-

---

2   In 1992 the *Journal of Democracy* devoted an issue to discussing the relationship between democracy and capitalism.

pelling (1987, Chapters 11 and 12). Sartori starts out by stating that political liberty is foremost *defensive freedom,* which implies the existence of constraints on the power of governments. Because it is an abstract concept and its benefits for the individual are not immediately tangible, its importance for democracy is often not properly appreciated. Most people have instead an intuitive understanding of equality, which they usually associate with economic equality.

Sartori goes on to emphasise that equality implies two different meanings, *sameness* and *justice*, and that both are not equally compatible with liberty. This is only the case for equality in the sense of justice, which implies equality before the law, equal respect and equality of opportunities. Since individuals are different, equality in the sense of equality of conditions would instead require unequal treatment.

These theoretical premises imply that democracy is incompatible with a command economy and that it imposes limits on the right of governments to encroach on the economic freedom of citizens. The upside of this connection between democracy and economic freedom is that democracy protects private property, the freedom to choose one's occupation as well as voluntary contractual relations among citizens. The downside is that free markets tend to produce economic disparities, which frequently violate intuitive norms of distributive justice. Moreover, they also tend to distort political equality, because economic resources can easily be converted into political resources.

Democracy does not mean a completely unrestrained free market, however. It has been frequently – and correctly – argued that below a minimal level of material security, education and personal independence it is not possible for citizens to effectively exercise their democratic rights. Governments therefore need to become economic actors in their own right and have the responsibility to provide for public educational institutions, a public infrastructure and at least basic welfare services.

Robert Dahl mentioned a second, even more important, reason for the necessity of government intervention into the market. A market economy without government regulation is impossible, because "the basic institutions of market-capitalism themselves require extensive government intervention and regulation. Competitive markets, ownership of economic entities, enforcing contracts, preventing monopolies, protecting property rights – these and many other aspects of market capitalism depend wholly on laws, policies, orders, and other actions carry out by governments" (Dahl 1998: 174).

There is considerable disagreement among political theorists as well as political practitioners about the acceptable degree of socio-economic inequality and the degree of government intervention into the market, which is deemed necessary to prevent socio-economic inequalities from becoming unacceptably high. Since the material wellbeing of the populace is of foremost importance for the legitimacy of any polity, conflicts over the economic order and over the appropriate economic policies to achieve the *public weal* are therefore among the most divisive in democratic polities. Democracies have historically developed a variety of institutional solutions to resolve such conflicts and they differ considerably in the ways they regulate the economy. These variations can be reduced to a few main models, which will be briefly discussed in the next section.

An understanding of equality as procedural equality in the sense of meritocratic competition and equality of opportunity implies a preference for minimal government intervention into the market. This is the conception that has always prevailed in the United States. It stands in stark contrast to the mood prevalent in many other developed democracies – and even more so in poor countries – where demands for redistributive egalitarianism are more insistent.

Varieties of liberal democratic capitalism

While many critics of the market economy have insinuated that there is one single model of *capitalism*, this assumption is far removed from reality. As far as government regulation of the economy is concerned, the literature tends to treat it as a continuous variable, ranging from a liberal to a coordinated market economy (Hall and Soskice, 2001). The logical end points of the continuum are a market economy without any political regulation on the one side and total government control of the economy on the other. A totally unregulated market economy is tantamount to market anarchy and implies that market power becomes the only criterion for determining the standard of living. People who have no marketable goods or services to offer will have to rely on their families or on the charities for their survival. On the other side of the continuum total government control of the economy would require the nationalisation of major parts of the economy, i.e. a Soviet-style command economy.[3] It is obvious that both are incompatible with liberal democracy. This means that the democratic end points of the continuum lie somewhere in-between these extremes.

With respect to welfare systems, Gøsta Esping-Andersen (1990) has distinguished three basic approaches that differ considerably in their capacity for *decommodification*.[4] In line with the belief that markets should be left alone as much as possible, the Anglo-Saxon model implies that the responsibility for personal welfare rests primarily with the citizens themselves and that the

---

3   Lipset remarked that when all economic resources are under the control of the government, political power becomes the only source of status and wealth, which will severely curtail freedom and foster nepotism and corruption (1994: 3).

4   Decommodification denotes the degree to which the dependence on market-related income is reduced and income is instead based on legal entitlements.

public welfare system would only cater to the needy. Such *liberal welfare states* therefore rely on "means-tested assistance, modest universal transfers, or modest social insurance plans", as well as subsidies for private health insurance, private retirement plans etc.

Corporatist-subsidiary welfare states, dating back to the late 19th century when Bismarck first introduced social insurance systems in Germany, offer comprehensive coverage to shield citizens from the risks of income loss due to poor health, unemployment, or old age. However, while this model has a partly decommodifying effect, because it ensures that citizens are entitled to benefits that reduce their dependence on market incomes, contributions to and benefits from social insurance plans are primarily tied to (previous) income. This type of welfare system therefore tends to reproduce existing income inequalities. The *social democratic model*, finally, is the most decommodifying in that all citizens are entitled to welfare benefits regardless of their income on the job market.

Among the consolidated democracies the degree of government regulation of the market is relatively low in the Anglo-Saxon countries as well as in Japan and Switzerland. In these countries the share of the GDP spent or regulated by the government is also lower than in the other established democracies (see Table 1). Yet their welfare systems differ in many respects. While for instance, the national health service in Great Britain is paid out of taxes and offers health care for all citizens free of charge, the US health system is largely left to the private sector. Until the health care reform of 2010 a relatively large percentage of the US population did not have any health insurance. Only a small part of the population profits from the two public health care programmes, Medicaid and Medicare.[5] While the 2010 health care reform introduced compulsory health insurance for all citizens, the majority of citizens below the age of 65 have to subscribe to rather expensive private health insurance plans.

At the other end of the spectrum we find the Scandinavian countries and the Netherlands with extensive government regulation of the economy and a well-developed welfare state. But over the last thirty years these countries have experimented with rather different new models for solving the financial problems of their welfare states, so their economic and welfare systems also differ from each other. This shows once more that the model of liberal democracy offers a wide variety of political choices with respect to both political institutions and the economic system.

---

5   Medicaid offers needs-tested health care free of charge for the poor and Medicare is a subsidised health insurance plan for the elderly.

Economic crises and the stability of democracy

In his seminal textbook *Political Man* (1960), Seymour Martin Lipset emphasised the importance of government effectiveness for the legitimacy of political systems. He defined effectiveness as the ability of the political system to "satisfy the basic functions of government as most of the population and such powerful groups within it as big business or the armed forces see them" (1960: 77). Later in the book, however, Lipset used a much narrower concept of effectiveness, as the following quote shows: "In the modern world, such effectiveness means primarily constant economic development. Those nations which have adapted most successfully to the requirements of an industrial system have the fewest internal political strains, and have either preserved their traditional legitimacy or developed strong new symbols" (1960: 82). He thus redefined effectiveness as primarily involving successful economic policy, and this is also how the concept of effectiveness has been understood ever since.[6]

Lipset's analysis of the relationship between effectiveness and legitimacy has become conventional wisdom in the social sciences. His famous fourfold table identifies four different types of polities (1960: 81):

Legitimacy	Effectiveness	
	+	-
+	A	B
-	C	D

Consolidated democracies (A) (examples: United States, Sweden, Britain) are high on both effectiveness and legitimacy. Polities lacking in both (D) are inherently unstable and prone to breaking down, unless upheld by force (examples: Communist Hungary, the German Democratic Republic). Austria and Germany during the 1920s are mentioned as examples of relatively effective democracies which lacked legitimacy (C), because their systems of government were not held to be "legitimate by large and powerful segments of its population" (1960: 81). Societies of type C, however, may eventually develop into consolidated democracies, since "prolonged effectiveness over a number of generations may give legitimacy to a political system" (1960: 82). Lipset thus assumed that in the long run effectiveness may engender legitimacy.

Type B is particularly interesting, because Lipset assumed that high legitimacy would function as a safety valve, stabilising consolidated democracies even in times of poor economic performance. Lipset's assumption has been

---

6   However, Lipset's original concept of government effectiveness also included a well-functioning public administration.

corroborated by historical evidence. Although the United States, the United Kingdom, France and a number of smaller European democracies, primarily the Benelux countries, the Scandinavian countries and Switzerland, were no less severely affected by the Great Depression of the early 1930s than Germany and Austria, democracy survived in these countries because their democratic institutions enjoyed widespread legitimacy (see also Dirk Berg-Schlosser's chapter in this volume).

A more recent study by Przeworski *et al.* (1996) disputed Lipset's conclusions regarding the beneficial effects of democratic consolidation. Based on data for the period between 1950 and 1990, the authors concluded that the stability of democracy is primarily a function of socio-economic development. During that period no democracy in a country with a per capita income of more than $6,000 broke down. Poorer countries were instead more likely to experience a breakdown of democracy, regardless of the length of time the country had been democratic. Since this latter study is more comprehensive and based on more systematic evidence than Lipset's, it shows convincingly that political legitimacy is not a sufficient safety valve against democratic breakdown in poorer countries in the instance of a prolonged economic crisis.

Since democracy and the market economy are closely related, and because democracies are more frequently found in socio-economically developed countries, the question arises whether it is democracy or rather the market economy that is conducive to economic growth. It is obvious that democracy will not automatically lead to economic success. There are several reasons why this might not be the case. The first and most important reason is that authoritarian countries are frequently characterised by collusion between political leaders and large private enterprises, whereby high profits accrue to both sides. The revolutions in Tunisia, Egypt and Libya in early 2011 made it once more abundantly clear that authoritarian leaders tend to exploit their political power to amass private fortunes. Neither side is therefore interested in ending their mutually profitable relationship after democratisation. Unless the old leadership is ousted and a completely new leadership takes over, the old networks tend to persist, which in turn undermines the development of a competitive and successful market economy.

In addition, most new democracies do not have a legal framework of market regulation nor a rule of law tradition, both of which are required for a properly functioning market economy. These drawbacks result in an extended period of institutional engineering and they require scarce resources, which are at the same time needed for alleviating poverty and stimulating economic growth. Many poor democracies therefore suffer from corruption, which is not only bad for the functioning of democracy, but also impairs the economic performance of a country. Corruption fosters the inefficient allocation of resources, impairs productivity and makes a country less attractive for foreign investors. It also contributes to inflating public budgets, because investments in large infrastructural projects promise personal profits for corrupt bureaucrats and politicians, while at the same time reducing the allocation of resources for the maintenance of the existing infrastructure (Tanzi and Davoodi, 2001).[7]

Authoritarian governments, in contrast, may promote the liberalisation of their national markets and stimulate economic success without at the same time liberalising, let alone democratising, their political system. Examples are the German Empire after 1871, Pinochet's Chile after the 1973 coup, or China over the last decades. While democrats of course hope that market liberalisation and the improvement of living conditions will eventually lead to increasing demands for democracy, economic success may also contribute to stabilising authoritarian political systems at least in the short run.

The impact of the Great Recession on the prospects for democracy

It is obvious that the politically problematic side-effects of the close association of democracy and a market economy can severely compromise support for democracy in a deep and prolonged economic crisis. The fundamental flaws of a market economy become more obvious in economically hard times. Disparities in income increase, bargaining conflicts over income levels and the distribution of wealth intensify. At the same time tax revenue decreases and in turn limits the ability of politicians to compensate for income losses by initiating new programmes to increase the demand for labour. Under such adverse conditions the disproportionate political influence of the business sector comes under increasing public scrutiny and the hardships incurred by members of the lower classes nourish feelings of frustration as well as doubts regarding the social balance of democratic politics.

Globalisation is also a factor. It props up the disproportionate political clout of private business, because the "increasingly unrestrained movement of capital between nations has the potential to reduce the policy autonomy of governments while strengthening the political bargaining power of capitalists" (Bernhagen, 2009: 116). It is therefore not surprising that both globalisation, and even more so the global financial crisis of 2008-2009, triggered widespread criticism of capitalism. Public opinion surveys show a decline in the belief that a market economy is the best system for achieving fair allocation of economic resources (e.g. Globescan, 2011). Many people believe that the greed and irresponsible behaviour of a small group of managers in global finance were mainly responsibility for the crisis. There is also a widespread perception that this small group has profited disproportionately from the deregulation of the mar-

---

7   Tanzi/Davoodi (2001) also mention that corruption primarily hurts small and medium-sized enterprises that do not have the means to pay high bribes multinational corporations have.

kets, which allowed them to invent complex and seemingly safe financial products and so lure unsuspecting small investors (including local governments) into buying those toxic products. Governments had to intervene with loans to the order of billions of US dollars to save financial institutions that would otherwise have collapsed. Many observers expect that the less well-to-do will have to pay the bill for these excesses, because the public debts incurred to fight the crisis will eventually lead to tax hikes and inflation. The ensuing dissatisfaction is not only directed against financial institutions, but also against the governments of the rich democracies because of their failure to regulate the financial markets, which could have avoided a crisis of this magnitude.

Interestingly enough, and contrary to expectations, this drop in support for free markets has been most pronounced in countries in which support was already very low before the onset of the crisis. The sharpest drop in support in six of the world's leading economies was noted in the US and Britain.[8] While primarily dealing with the effects of globalisation on advanced liberal democracies and not directly with the current crisis, Jude Hays's (2009) analysis provides a plausible explanation for the sharp drop in US and British levels of belief in the beneficial effects of the market economy. The author claims that for a long time democratic governments have quelled public criticism of globalisation by a policy strategy, which he calls 'embedded liberalism'. People working in globally non-competitive business sectors have been shielded from the adverse effects of increasing global competition by a mixture of unemployment benefits and active labour market policies.

However, the policy of embedded liberalism depends primarily on sufficient tax revenue for financing such expensive public programmes. Hays argued that globalisation will affect more deeply majoritarian democracies such as, for example Great Britain or the United States, which have the most open market economies, than democracies such as the Scandinavian countries or Austria, which have corporatist economies. Majoritarian democracies are more likely to suffer from rising levels of unemployment, because their open-market policies make it easier for businesses to move their capital to wherever they expect to realise higher returns; and they also have more lenient regulations for dismissals of redundant work force. At the same time they rely primarily on capital taxes (rather than on income taxes) and cannot increase revenue accordingly, because raising these taxes would drive capital out of the country. In order to balance their budgets, governments of these democracies will therefore have to cut public welfare programmes, which will in

---

8   At the same time, confidence in the market rose in Germany and China. France and Turkey are especially interesting cases because they are 'anti-capitalist outliers' with an exceptionally high level of scepticism about the benefits of a free market economy (Economist, 07 April 2011). Despite the relatively low number of respondents included in that poll and the lack of corroborating evidence, the results are sufficiently robust to prove that the economic recession following the financial crisis has indeed affected support for the model of market economy.

turn result in declining support for their open market policies. This vicious circle is likely to become even more pronounced during recessions.

Corporatist countries with more restrictive regulations for protecting employment and more balanced tax systems based on both income and capital taxes have been less affected by globalisation and therefore are also less vulnerable during a recession.

In a recent analysis of the impact of the global economic crisis, Larry Diamond (2011) found that the crisis has not led to many breakdowns of new democracies. His analysis shows that the reversals back to authoritarian patterns of the last decade mostly happened when these countries were doing economically rather well, citing in particular the oil-rich countries Nigeria, Russia and Venezuela. Conversely, those Third Wave democracies that have been hardest hit by the Great Recession have shown a remarkable resilience. Rather than turning against democracy, voters in these countries have instead tended to punish incumbent governments and to vote new – and frequently even rightist rather than leftist – governments into power. However, Diamond also notes that the danger is far from over and that a prolonged global recession might damage the prospects of democracy in the poor Third Wave democracies.

In a similar vein Marc Plattner argued that the global economic crisis "has posed some difficult challenges for defenders of democracy and of free markets", but that its consequences have been limited so far (2011: 31). The author concedes that the responsibility of the advanced democracies – and especially of the United States – for precipitating the crisis has the potential "to discredit not only capitalism but the democratic political framework with which it is associated". At the same time he concludes that the crisis has been even more devastating for authoritarian systems – with the exception of China – whose poor economic performance has undermined their weak legitimacy even further. The uprisings that have taken place in the Arab world since the publication of Plattner's article confirm the accuracy of his observation.[9]

While it is still too early to draw firm conclusions about the long-term impacts of the Great Recession on economic development and on support for democracy and the market economy around the globe, the key economic indicators for the fourteen consolidated democracies included in the following Table 1 provide some preliminary insights. They confirm that all of these countries suffered a considerable decline in GDP growth in 2009. With the exception of Australia and Poland,[10] all of them had negative growth rates in 2009.

---

9   Plattner critically observes, however, that the emerging market democracies, in particular Brazil, India, Indonesia and South Africa, are primarily intent on boosting their economies by cultivating trade relations with authoritarian systems such as Iran, Russia, China or Venezuela and show little solidarity with democratic nations when it comes to voting in favor of human rights or against abuses of power by authoritarian governments at UN meetings (2011: 26-38).

10 For reasons of this exception see chapter by P. Mohr, pp. 63-64.

Table 1: The impact of the global financial crisis on economic indicators in 14 liberal democracies

Country	GDP growth[1]				Total general government expenditure as % of GDP[2]			Public budget surplus/deficit as % of GDP[3]				Government debt as % of GDP[4]			
	2007	2008	2009	2010	2007	2008	2009	2007	2008	2009	2010	2007	2008	2009	2010
Australia	3.8	3.7	1.3	3.3	33.4	35.3	n/a	1.7	0.4	-4.0	-3.3	14.3	13.6	19.2	23.6
Canada	2.2	0.5	-2.5	3.0	39.4	39.8	44.1	1.4	0.0	-5.5	-4.9	66.5	71.3	83.4	84.4
Finland	5.3	0.9	-8.0	3.2	47.3	49.4	56.0	5.2	4.2	-2.7	-3.3	41.4	40.6	52.6	58.4
France	2.4	0.2	-2.6	1.6	52.3	52.8	56.0	-2.7	-3.3	-7.6	-7.4	70.0	75.9	87.1	92.4
Germany	2.7	1.0	-4.7	3.6	43.6	43.8	47.5	0.3	0.1	-3.0	-4.0	65.3	69.4	76.5	79.9
Japan	2.4	-1.2	-5.2	3.0	35.9	37.1	n/a	-2.4	-2.1	-7.1	-7.7	167.1	173.9	192.8	198.4
Netherlands	3.6	2.0	-4.0	1.7	45.3	46.0	51.4	0.2	0.5	-5.4	-5.8	52.0	66.0	69.4	74.6
Norway	2.7	1.8	-1.6	1.5	41.1	40.6	46.3	17.7	19.3	9.9	9.5	58.6	56.7	49.5	51.8
Poland	6.8	5.0	1.7	3.8	42.2	43.2	44.4	-1.9	-3.7	-6.8	-7.9	51.8	54.5	58.5	63.9
Slovenia	6.8	3.5	-7.8	1.0	42.4	44.1	49.0	0.0	-1.8	-5.8	-5.7	30.0	29.7	44.1	49.9
Sweden	3.3	-0.4	-5.1	4.1	51.0	51.5	54.9	3.5	2.2	-1.2	-1.2	47.4	46.7	51.9	51.3
Switzerland	3.6	1.9	-1.9	2.7	32.3	32.2	33.7	1.7	2.3	1.2	-0.7	46.5	44.3	42.2	42.1
United Kingdom	2.6	0.5	-4.9	1.6	44.0	47.4	51.6	-2.8	-4.8	-11.0	-9.6	47.2	57.0	72.4	81.3
United States	1.9	-0.0	-2.6	2.7	36.8	38.9	42.2	-2.9	-6.2	-11.3	-10.5	62.0	71.1	84.4	92.8

1 **GDP annual growth in %:** Annual percentage growth rate of GDP at market prices based on constant local currency. Aggregates are based on constant 2000 U.S. dollars. Source: *World Bank*: http://data.worldbank.org *for 2007-2009; for 2010 estimates from the CIA Factbook* (https://www.cia.gov/library/publications/the-world-factbook/rankorder/2003rank.html)

2 **Total general government expenditure as % of GDP:** Expenditures by general government on compensation of employees, subsidies, social benefits, social transfers in kind etc. Source: OECD, 2011: *National Accounts at a Glance 2010*. Paris: OECD: 60-61.

3 **Public budget surplus/deficit as % of GDP:** *Net lending/net borrowing, surplus (+), deficit (-). Source: OECD* - http://dx.doi.org/10.1787/gov-dfct-table-2011-1-en

4 **Government debt as % of GDP:** *General government gross financial liabilities. Source: OECD* - http://dx.doi.org/10.1787/gov-deb-table-2011-1-en

Thanks to the swift implementation of major government programmes to save failing financial institutions and to stimulate economic growth, growth rates were back in the positive range in 2010. This can be seen in the second and third sections of the Table. The figures confirm that total government expenditure as a percentage of GDP rose sharply in 2009 and that the public budgets were strongly affected by either declining surplus or increasing deficit rates. The last section of the Table shows the total government debt, ranging from 23.6% in Australia to nearly 200% in Japan.

Overall the Table indicates the existence of considerable differences in the economic policies of consolidated democracies. In order to assess the full impact of the crisis and the effects of different economic policies to cope with it, more detailed empirical studies will be needed. In any case, it has to be assumed that despite the global economic rebound in 2010, the current crisis is far from over, because the bill for increased government spending will only have to be paid in the years to come.

Conclusions

As the above discussion shows, while the model of liberal democracy is based on a number of common premises, it also allows for a broad range of institutional patterns to organise a democratic polity. This means the model can be adopted by countries with different cultural traditions and historical experiences. The model is based on universal principles and values.

It should have become equally obvious that liberal democracy requires some form of market economy, because political liberties also include economic liberties. However, the existing liberal democracies are not the puppets of a bunch of capitalists, as critics have frequently claimed. Table 1 shows that the governments of advanced liberal democracies control between one third and one half of the overall national income. Democratic governments therefore have sufficient clout to reduce the most flagrant disparities produced by free markets, to actively promote economic development, to invest in a functioning public infrastructure and to introduce protective measures for the economically less advantaged. However, the increased mobility of private capital has also made it more independent from decisions of national governments and thereby increased its political influence even further.

While the wealthy consolidated democracies can be considered strong enough to cope even with major political and economic challenges, the poor Third Wave democracies are much more vulnerable because their political institutions and party systems are not as well established, democratic value orientations are not as deeply rooted in their political culture and they have fewer economic resources to cope with income losses in a recession. But the most vulnerable are authoritarian systems. Their political legitimacy is based exclusively on their ability to secure acceptable economic outputs and therefore poor economic performance has a much more adverse effect on their legitimacy.

Sources

Beetham, D. (2009). Democracy: universality and diversity. *Ethics & Global Politics.* 2 (4): 281-296.
Bernhagen, P. (2009). Democracy, business, and the economy. In: Haerpfer, C, Bernhagen,P., Inglehart, R.F., Welzel, C. (eds.). (2009). *Democratization.* Oxford: Oxford University Press: 107-125.
Charron, N. and Lapuente,V. (2010). Does democracy produce quality of government? *European Journal of Political Research.* 49 (4): 443-470.
Dahl, R.A. (1971). *Polyarchy. Participation and opposition.* New Haven: Yale University Press.
Dahl, R. A. (1982). *Dilemmas of pluralist democracy.* New Haven: Yale University Press.
Dahl, R.A. (1998). *On democracy.* New Haven: Yale University Press.
Dahrendorf, R. (1967). *Society and democracy in Germany.* New York: W.W. Norton.
Diamond, L. (1992). Economic development and democracy revisited, *American Behavioral Scientist.* 35: 450-499.
Diamond, L.(2011). Why Democracies Survive. *Journal of Democracy.* 22 (1):17-30.
Esping-Andersen, G. (1990). *The three worlds of welfare capitalism.* New York: Polity Press.
Fraenkel, E. (1991). *Deutschland und die westlichen Demokratien.* Enlarged edition. Frankfurt/Main: Suhrkamp (first published in 1964).
Globescan, 2011: *Sharp Drop in American Enthusiasm for Free Market, Poll Shows.* Accessible on-line at: www.globescan.com/news_archives/radar10w2_free_market/.
Hall, P. A. and Soskice, D. (200). An Introduction to varieties of capitalism. In: Hall P. and Soskice, D. (eds.): *Varieties of capitalism. The institutional foundations of comparative advantage.* Oxford: Oxford University Press: 1-68.
Hays, J. C. (2009). *Globalization & the new politics of embedded liberalism.* Oxford: Oxford University Press.
Huntington, S.P. (1991) Democracy's Third Wave. *Journal of Democracy.* 2 (2): 12-34.
Inglehart, R. and Welzel, C. (2005). *Modernization, cultural change, and democracy. The human developmentsSequence.* Cambridge: Cambridge University Press.
Keefer, P. (2007). The poor performance of poor democracies. In: Boix,C and Stokes, S.C. (eds.): *The Oxford Handbook of Comparative Politics.* Oxford: Oxford University Press: 886-909.
Kielmansegg, P.G. (1988). *Das Experiment der Freiheit.* Stuttgart: Klett/Cotta.
Klingemann, H-D and Welzel, C. (2007). Theories of the development of democracy. In: Hettne, B. (ed). *Human values and global governance.* Vol. 2. Houndmills: Palgrave Macmillan: 34-49.
Lijphart, A. (1999). *Patterns of democracy.* New Haven: Yale University Press.
Lipset, S.M (1959). Some social requisites of democracy: economic development and political legitimacy. *American Political Science Review.* 53: 69-105.

Lipset, S. M. (1960). *Political man - the social bases of politics*. New York: Doubleday.

Lipset, S.M. (1994). The social requisites of democracy revisited. *American Sociological Review.* 59: 1-22.

Merkel, W. (2010). *Systemtransformation*. 2. Auflage. Wiesbaden: VS Verlag für Sozialwissenschaften.

Morlino, L.(2009). Are there hybrid regimes? Or are they just an optical illusion? *European Political Science Review.* 1 (2): 273-296.

O'Donnell, G. (2004). Why the rule of law matters. *Journal of Democracy.* 15 (4), 32-46.

Plattner, M. F. (2011). From the G-8 to the G-20. *Journal of Democracy.* 22(1): 31-38.

PrzeworsKi, A. (1991). *Democracy and the market. Political and economic reforms in Eastern Europe and Latin America*. Cambridge: Cambridge University Press.

Przeworski, A. et.al. (1996). What makes democracies endure? *Journal of Democracy.* 7 (1): 39-55.

Rustow, D.A. (1970). Transitions to democracy: toward a dynamic model. *Comparative Politics.* 2: 337-364.

Sartori, G. (1987). *The theory of democracy revisited. The classical issues*. Vol.2. Chatham: Chatham House Publishers.

Schmitter, P. C. and Karl, T.L. (1991). What democracy is ... and is not. *Journal of Democracy.* 2 (3):75-88.

Sen, A. (1999). Democracy as a universal value. *Journal of Democracy.* 10 (3): 3-17.

Tanzi, V. and Hamid, D. (2001). Corruption, growth, and public finances. In: Arvind K. Jain (Hrsg.): *The political economy of corruption*. London: Routledge: 89-110.

The Economist (2011). Market of ideas: capitalism's waning popularity. 7 April. Accessible on-line at: www.economist.com/node/18527446.

PART III
An authoritarian response

Some authoritarian capitalisms have recently lost stability, at least partly, as a consequence of the Great Recession; the Arab Spring is often quoted as an example in this context. There is, however, an important exception to this general rule that calls for closer inspection. This exception is China. China not only weathered the crisis amazingly well, but in one respect appeared to have benefited from it. It seems that the crisis helped this economic giant to initiate the badly needed reorientation of the economy towards the huge domestic market so as to reduce tensions produced by an over-heated economy.

China is a world-leading authoritarian capitalist country that lifted hundreds of millions of people out of poverty in a relatively short period. The breath-taking speed of development and the country's relatively solid immunity to the Great Recession call for reflection. It is not difficult to imagine that, barring a political breakthrough, the coming decade or two may see China catching up with the most advanced world economies while still remaining an authoritarian state. This assumption is strengthened by the fact that China is already reaching a world-leading position in a number of economic, technological and military fields.

Should the current rate of the Chinese development be further maintained, one could expect that China might serve as a trend-setter for both poor authoritarian capitalisms and malfunctioning democratic capitalisms. But for the time being China is a trend-setter without followers. It will be of crucial importance for world order whether China will in the not too distant future enter a transition to democracy and join the democratic family, or continue its 'authoritarian economic miracle', prompting others in many different corners of the world to follow suit. Should the latter scenario develop, we may witness another type of global rivalry: not in the military field but rather in economic and technological areas, and not between communist command economies and capitalist democracies but between democratic and authoritarian capitalisms.

China and the crisis in historical perspective

Ursula J. van Beek

Introduction

China is the only ancient empire that survived into the 20th century. For a Westerner to fully appreciate the longevity and richness of Chinese civilisation, it is useful to place it on a comparative timeline. The temporal comparison shows that during the rule of the Shang Dynasty (1600-1100 BCE), a period during which Moses led the exodus from Egypt and the Trojan wars were fought, the Chinese were already engraving symbols and pictures onto shells of turtles and bamboo sticks as a means of expression. As these pictorial characters developed during the Han Dynasty (202 BCE-220 CE) into the unique language system that to this day fosters and preserves the distinctive identity of Chinese civilisation, the Romans invaded Britain. During the same period the Confucian philosophical system was adopted in China. All this took place some centuries before the final collapse of Rome in 476 CE.

For much of its recorded history China was a dynastic empire which towered over the rest of Asia under rulers whose sovereignty was said to have been bestowed upon them by the Mandate of Heaven and whose autocratic rule over the populace was akin to the paternal function of a strict father in charge of a household. China, or the Middle Kingdom, was thought to have been situated in the centre of the world and possessed of a civilisation superior to that of the entire 'barbarian' universe both across the seas and outside its far-flung and ever-changing land boundaries, which were deliberately kept ill-defined. Convinced of its cultural greatness, the imperial Chinese state assigned itself the mission to 'civilise' neighbouring peoples but had little interest in the rest of the world, although in the early Ming dynasty (1368-1644) a large navy was built and sailed the China seas and the Indian Ocean, reaching the east coast of Africa. These voyages merely confirmed to the Chinese that they did not have much to learn from the outside world.

From antiquity the Chinese made significant advances in science and innovation including, among other things, the first recorded observations of comets, solar eclipses and supernovae, the invention of the abacus, the compass, gunpowder, the wheelbarrow, papermaking techniques and printing. Mediaeval Europe borrowed extensively from Chinese science and technology until Europe's own scientific revolutions in the 16th and 17th centuries propelled it to a position from which it gradually outstripped Chinese technological advances. Unconcerned by this shifting balance, up until the early 19th century the Chinese emperors treated with disdain the small and squabbling European states, even when the latter were busy building their commercial empires in Asia. China's rulers refused to deal with European governments on equal terms and conceded at most limited trading privileges at the coast or at the border through which trade was conducted to meet Europe's high demand for Chinese tea, porcelain and silk. Repeated British representations made at the turn of the 18th and 19th centuries to improve the severely restricted trading conditions fell on deaf ears as the emperor who saw little point in making concessions to a state he believed had nothing to offer China in return.

This situation changed drastically once foreign traders discovered China's virtually limitless demand for opium. By the1830s opium represented nearly half of all British exports to China and, when importation was banned in Canton, smuggling began. To put an end to the opium trade and its disastrous health consequences for the Chinese population, the emperor in 1839 ordered all opium in the possession of British merchants to be seized and destroyed. The British response to this action was war. What has since become known as the Opium Wars (1840-1842) ended in the Treaty of Nanking, which included the first of the 'unequal treaties' between China and the West. These treaties, which forced the Chinese to grant equal trading rights first to the British and later to the Americans and the French, ended what the West perceived to be a humiliating assumption of Chinese superiority; the Chinese regarded them as an encroachment on their sovereignty.

The Opium Wars marked a crucial turning point in China's long history. The conflict, which was less about opium than about grabbing the last prize in the Far East, forcibly prised open the Chinese empire to the world as it exposed China's markets and resources to subsequent colonial exploitation. The wars also helped to eventually oust the weak and unpopular last Chinese dynasty (Manchu Qing, 1644-1911) from power. The revolution of 1911, which toppled the imperial regime, opened the door to a failed attempt at republicanism, instability, corruption, rule by warlords and opportunistic Japanese exploits aimed to establish political and economic domination over China. In 1915, taking advantage of the internal turmoil and the Western powers' engagement in World War I, Japan presented China with the infamous Twenty-One Demands, which would have turned the country into a virtual Japanese protectorate had the surreptitious terms not been made public and had the subsequent pressure of world opinion not forced Japan to modify some of the more extreme demands. But the national sovereignty of China was further compromised and the day of the acceptance of the Japanese demands became known as National Humiliation Day.

It has been said that whereas the word *freedom* offers the means to understand core American values and the term *rule of law* is the key to unlock the spirit of England, the essence of Chinese values can be found in the word *history*. Both Chinese national identity and the legitimacy of the Chinese Communist Party (CCP) are outgrowths of the past (Callahan, 2004). The Communist Party elite were the product of an extensive but failed search by traditional Chinese elites to save the post-dynastic country from crippling domestic chaos and foreign imperialist encroachment. The successful communist revolution of 1949 delivered on both counts. And since then Chinese leaders have claimed legitimacy not on the basis of democratic electoral victory, but on the grounds of the historical record of having ended China's century of national humiliation and of having returned the country to a place of global prominence. Behind modern China's remarkable development is a regime carefully cultivating the inherent patriotism and pride of the Chinese people as a means to bolster its legitimacy, which is further defined by substance, that it to say, by testing good governance in terms of how it delivers. China's successful weathering of the recent world-wide economic and financial storm could not but highlight this even further, and not only in China itself but well beyond her national boundaries.

The aim of this chapter is to look through the lens of time to try unveil some of the mystery of why China has become so successful economically and to consider the implications of this success for the post-crisis world and for democracy in particular.

Change and tradition

Even prior to the 2008-2009 global financial crisis China had come to be viewed as a major force in the world's economic and security systems. In the wake of the crisis the country's stature increased further to a position from which to effectively challenge the dominance of the United States in global affairs. The stunning rise of authoritarian China as an economic power and China's continued high rate of growth, at a time when the developed world was overtaken by the most severe economic crisis since the Great Depression, confounds Western economists. The conditions China lacks and that they consider necessary for successful economic development include the limited role of the state; a democratic dispensation as the political mechanism that ensures the balance between state power and decentralised co-operation; and democratically empowered citizens who prevent the state overreaching itself. And so they ask why is it that in the absence of these conditions the Chinese state seems able to arrange productive co-operation on an unprecedented scale without running into the seemingly insurmountable knowledge, incentive and administrative problems that economists expect in such circumstances. Part of the answer can be found in the deep history of China and in the way modern China travelled from the semi-periphery to the centre of global affairs.

The enforced interaction with the outside world, which shattered the traditional Chinese worldview of the centrality of the Middle Kingdom in the world order, brought home two basic truths. The first was that China was but one state among many, and a weak one at that; and the second was that a feeble central power was responsible for the century of humiliation that had transformed the empire into a semi-colony. This in turn led to the conviction that the only way to achieve national survival was to build a powerful modern state with a strong central government. State-building thus became closely associated with the concept of national unity and nationalism. Sun-Yat-sen, the founder of the Republic and co-founder of the Chinese Nationalist Party, Kuomintang (KTM), considered nationalism not only the key to survival of the Chinese nation, but also as a fit state doctrine and the means to ensure the equality and freedom of all races in China (Chou Yu-sun, 1996).

Hidden in the shadow of Mao's revolutionary internationalism, the theme of national unity resurfaced under Deng Xiaoping, who took over as China's *de facto* paramount leader in the late 1970s, and who replaced Mao's ideological philosophy of 'politics in command' by the philosophy of 'economics in command'. For Deng the entire project of mapping out a brand new road forward for China's development rested on the fundamental assumption that national unity was not the source of China's power, as was believed earlier, but that this power depended on whether or not China could catch up with developed countries (Zheng, 1999). In Deng's vision economic wealth was to be the foundation of Chinese power and economic development was the way that would lead to China assuming her rightful place in the world of nations. At the same time, national, or even nationalistic, pride and economic success could became mutually reinforcing, thus providing the Communist Party with a form of substitute legitimacy

Given Mao's near godlike status in China, Deng took a considerable political risk by promoting this momentous change. One of the ideas thought to have inspired him was the Yan Fu argument, a line of reflection pursued at the turn of the 20th century by the famed Chinese scholar and translator, who argued that only by freeing the spirit of initiative in every single Chinese citizen could their total energies be amplified to ensure the survival of the state and to maximise the capacity of the nation as a whole (Schram,1984). This spirit of initiative was badly depleted by Mao's policies of the Great Leap Forward and the Cultural Revolution, which left the people physically deprived, psychologically scarred and, not unlike the Germans after World War II, totally uninterested in politics. Their overriding concern was how to survive and Deng's economic reforms offered some hope, thus creating a platform on which to build consensus between reformist leaders and society. And while the leaders recognised the need to depoliticise peoples' daily lives, they also identified decentralisation of economic decision-making as a major strategy for reforming the economic system. In this way they created an institutional setting in China for what came to be known as development-oriented local government (White, 1984).

As the 'reform and opening' strategy initiated by Deng in 1978 devalued Mao's class struggle rhetoric as a device legitimising the party's continued rule, nationalism was revived. The notion of the century of humiliation came into play once more, as did the party's historically based credentials. But there are inherent dangers, both internal and external, in using nationalism as a legitimising strategy. By its very nature nationalism is ethnocentric and thus exclusive. In a multi-ethnic country such as China it could – and frequently has – come across more as the nationalism of the Han majority than of the Chinese people as a whole, increasing the threat of ethnic tensions and internal alienation. Externally, it conjured unhelpful images of a China that should be feared rather than encouraged to integrate into the world's structures. Recognising this downside, the CCP moved from the theme of injured victimhood epitomised by the century of humiliation to the safer ground of China's proud past and the party's leading role in returning the country to its former global greatness. From the theme of modernisation and rejuvenation of China in the Deng Xiaoping era, the Chinese party chiefs from Jiang Zemin to Hu Jintao started to talk about the Great Renaissance of the Chinese nation, indicating a radical turnabout from the earlier disdain for, to the re-embracing of, elements of traditional Chinese culture (Kang, 2006).

The turning point was the 1989 tragedy of Tiananmen Square. Although Chinese intellectuals were unhappy with the vicious way their government had dealt with the protests, they also objected to the harsh criticism of their country by Western governments. A surge of nationalist sentiment followed that, among other things, produced a number of bestselling books calling for resistance to the West's 'interference' in Chinese society and urging the government to adopt a strong stance in foreign policy (Trailokya, 2010). While initially pleased with this reaction and encouraging it, the Chinese leadership came to realise the possible adverse effects the anti-foreign nationalist outburst could have on China's prospects for further progress and they put an end to it by dusting off the moral teachings of the old sage Confucius. This approach both satisfied the intellectuals who were pleased to see China did not concede to the West, and resonated with the common people for whom traditional values matter.

But opinion is divided among China analysts both inside and outside the country as to how seriously the Communist Party takes Confucianism. Views range from those who claim Confucianism is of marginal and purely utilitarian interest to the party, to those who forecast the CCP's imminent transformation from Chinese Communist Party to Chinese Confucian Party (Bell, 2010). On the basis of the historical record of the CCP it seems fairly safe to say that Confucianism is merely another ingredient added to socialism as a device to legitimise the party's continued rule. The Chinese leaders are above all pragmatic and adapt well to constantly changing circumstances. This pragmatic mentality can be traced back to Deng Xiaoping, whose most famous political adage held that it was immaterial whether a cat was black or white as long as it caught mice. At the same time Deng Xiaoping also made it clear that while economic construction and development moved to the centre stage, the party would never abandon the Four Cardinal Principles: socialist road, dictatorship of the proletariat, leadership of the Communist Party and Marxist-Leninist-Mao Zedong thought. In all probability the Four Cardinal Principles were less ideological than they were functional. Their aim was to send a message to the Chinese people, and to the intellectual elites in particular, that they were free to improve their material living conditions but should keep out of politics and human rights issues, and that they should forget Tiananmen. Pragmatism of this kind has made it possible for the Chinese leadership not only to shift to a fundamentally different policy in response to a changing political environment, but also to respond swiftly to single events, especially if these involve populist or nationalist pressures. The sudden shift in labour policy from suppressing wages to actively boosting wages is just one recent example of the pragmatic mentality among Chinese policymakers.[1]

Ideology has been and continues to be used instrumentally. Sometimes it is used as a guide for action, but mostly it is a means to make moral claims associated with leadership and to forestall the possibility of open talk about politics that could lead to chaos, the most nightmarish of prospects for Chinese leaders from time immemorial. The seeming absence of any tension between ideology and pragmatism is, according to Lucian Pye (1985), a peculiarly Chinese phenomenon and can account for the divergence between doctrinal theories and practice. Whereas in Western culture correctness about doctrinal questions is a value in itself, the Chinese are much more relaxed about matters of belief; one can sense the great difference between Western and Chinese attitudes towards ideology by reflecting on the stark contrast between Western and Chinese approaches to religion. The provenance of the prevailing socialist ideology itself is instructive in this context. Chinese historical consciousness was sustained for centuries by the conviction that China was unique and culturally superior to the West. And yet, ironically, the 'foreign' ideology of Marxism-Leninism was adopted and, astonishingly, with the addition of Maoism was transformed into something believed to be essentially Chinese. At the same time traditional Confucianism was rejected and attacked as a vestige of oppressive feudalism.

At present Confucianism is officially in vogue again. It is used to gain soft power through the establishment of worldwide Confucius centres,[2] which

---

1   For details on this policy see chapter by Han and Lu in this volume.
2   In July 2010 there were 316 Confucius Institutes and 337 Confucius Classrooms in 94 countries and regions http://en.wikipedia.org/wiki/Confucius_Institute#cite_note-2#cite_note-2.

promote Chinese language and culture. At the same time the Confucian-derived notion of a Harmonious Socialist Society has come to occupy a prominent place in the politico-speak of the leaders. The concept was first mooted at the Sixteenth Party Congress in 2002 and was later defined more clearly as a term that describes a society in which order and stability prevail, and in which each individual does his or her best and has a proper place. In 2005 Hu Jintao declared the creation of a Harmonious Socialist Society to be "essential for consolidating the party's social foundation and achieving the party's historical governing mission" (Holbig, 2009). On the one hand, harmonious social governance is meant to enrich and re-actualise Marxism; on the other, it aims to revitalise Confucian norms and responsibilities in society. But in keeping with the ambiguous nature of the policies of the Chinese leaders, their drawing on elements of traditional Confucianism once again does not translate into embracing traditional values as a whole. The effort, rather, is to weave the threads of Confucian tradition into the fabric of Marxism by emphasising elements the two are said to have in common, such as strong leadership, social justice and harmony.

Yet Confucianism in China is a lasting force that deserves careful attention, because it offers a key to understanding both the values and the norms that shape social relations among the Chinese people and their attitudes towards their rulers. Traditional Chinese culture places the relationship of an individual to others in the context of a society of which each member has a responsibility to improve. The core values of thrift, diligence and an ethic of hard work encourage dedication and commitment as a way for the individual to contribute to the development of a harmonious society. Governance based on the concept of a Harmonious Socialist Society taps into these very values. It was devised as a strategic move to respond to the serious social contradictions that emerged in the wake of the increasingly diverse material and cultural needs of the Chinese people and could work to threaten social stability. The aim of the policy is to promote a more 'liberal' governance style, which purports to offer more space for individual self-realisation and self-responsibility.

Traditionally, the justification for the political legitimacy of the rulers flowed from four basic concepts: the Mandate of Heaven, rule by virtue, popular consent and legality. The Mandate of Heaven gave the ruler a divine right to rule, but the rule, according to the moral teachings of Confucius, was circumscribed in that the ruler had to be virtuous and the people had to be content. In this relationship, which was to ensure harmony and social order, the rulers demanded submission of the people to their authority. In return they were obliged to constantly seek popular approval through winning the hearts and minds of the people by looking after their wellbeing. In this concept the true test of the will of Heaven was the acceptance of a ruler by the people. This moral contract constituted the foundation of the imperial political system; the accompanying laws and regulations were based mainly on family rules, norms, customs and social traditions, and although during the Qing Dynasty more emphasis was put on rule by law, the use of law was primarily a means by which to strengthen, rather than restrict, the power of the ruler.

It is not too difficult to find parallels in the relationship between the Chinese people and their rulers then and now: power continues to emanate from the top and the rulers, though their virtue might be questioned (as it often had been in the imperial era), continue to seek popular consent, nowadays by readjusting their claim to legitimacy in step with changing circumstances. And as unlikely as this might seem, continuity did not reassert itself with the more recent official return to the essence of Chinese culture and tradition, but was preserved in the wake of the success of Mao's communist revolution in 1949, when the victorious CCP carefully replaced the traditional Confucian Mandate of Heaven with an ideology that seemingly resembled the yearned-for ideal society of harmony and social justice, and thus found an easy resonance with the people. At the same time full use was made of history or, more precisely, of the historic mission the party fulfilled when it restored the territorial map of China to correspond roughly with that of the pre-1919 Qing era. This pride-reaffirming feat that no other Chinese force was able to claim since China's humiliating defeat in the Opium Wars, gained the CCP a popular mandate to rule through the legitimising support of the people.

On these foundations grew the paradox of modern China, a country at once far removed from its imperial past and yet firmly rooted in that past. The most significant expression of that paradox is the curious mix of Confucianism and Marxism. The two ideologies share an emphasis on humane government and the centrality and self-cultivation of the human being. But in socialism with Chinese characteristics, the Marxist notion of class struggle has been replaced by the notion of social harmony, combined with scientific development. At the same time hierarchy and the supremacy of the collectivity over the individual as a means of societal organisation have been retained, placing a powerful instrument of power in the hands of the Communist Party.

The linking ideological theme is the continuing belief that each individual is a part of a whole and that harmonious relations with others are the key to the wellbeing of the whole. In a concept of society construed in this way the rulers frame the broad goals for the society by taking cognisance of bottom-up ideas, demands and reactions. In contrast to a democratic society, which is thought of as a horizontal structure, a top-down and bottom-up dynamic is thus established and is adjusted as conditions change, though the ultimate aim remains reaching goals set by the leadership. Under Deng Xiaoping this system took on the appearance of democratic centralism, whereby policies originating at the centre were tested and evaluated on the ground and then reports on results and on problems encountered were channelled back to the system's centre for debate. According to Naisbit (2010), this vertical structure encompasses a democratic model that fits Chinese history and thinking, and allows a steady flow of ideas up and down the hierarchy.

Implications

This is in theory. In practice the flow has been interrupted by political patronage and ineffective monitoring of agents of the state, which results in endemic cadre corruption. This problem, like much else in China, is not new. It can be traced back to the middle of the 14th century when the founder of the Ming dynasty, Hung Wu, issued an official imperial edict in which he bemoaned the great misfortune befalling China in the form of the 'idle riffraff' concerned only with establishing connections with local officials who, utilising the prestige of the government, help them oppress the masses below. Hung Wu, who came from a humble background himself, was familiar with the suffering of the poor under the combined oppression of the scholar-bureaucrats and the wealthy. He lamented that if he were to punish them, he would be considered a tyrant; and if he were lenient, the law would become ineffective, order would deteriorate and the people would deem him an incapable ruler. The emperor reached the conclusion that "To be a ruler is indeed difficult" (Pye, 1985).

Today, as then, the culture of bribery and corruption is both rife and well recognised by Chinese leaders, who consider venal local officials a grave problem not only because they damage the credibility of the CCP at the local level, but also because they tarnish the party's image as a whole; government corruption was one of the major issues behind the Tiananmen demonstrations of 1989. According to the former Prime Minister, Li Peng, who tried to decentralise and downsize the Chinese bureaucracy, with varying degrees of success, "The fight against corruption is a matter of life and death" (Tuck, 1995). But like the Hung Wu emperor of old, the Chinese leaders of today are damned if they tackle the problem head-on and they are damned if they do not. Hence efforts to eradicate corruption are nothing more than isolated instances that hardly touch the surface of the inherent patron-client relationships between state officials and business elites. A real effort would require a fundamental institutional overhaul, which the party-state with its fear of the chaos that this would be likely to produce, has yet to initiate (Pei, 2006). In the absence of such a consolidated effort, the national leaders aim to diffuse pent-up resentments by trying out semi-democratic substitutes for elections in the form of public hearings and releases of information through the media. Several authors (e.g. Lu, 2000; Pei, 2006; Ngo, 2008) point to the existence of many other problems plaguing China. Along with weak accountability, seen as the main reason for corruption, there is also the glaring absence of the rule of law, of political opposition and of civil liberties. These factors are not likely to create the developmental state to which China professes to aspire, but a predatory one.

Is China such a state? It is in the nature of a predatory state apparatus for the rulers to plunder state coffers without regard for the welfare of the people; available surpluses are used for self-enrichment rather than for reinvestment in the economy to maintain its growth and, in the process, provide collective goods to the populace. China's continued economic success alone suggests that the Chinese rulers are unlikely to be primarily driven by predatory instincts, but that concerns about the livelihood of the people also come into play. One example is that the government identified poverty eradication as the most fundamental human right (Zhan and Su, 2009), achieving remarkable results.[3] The handling by the government of the economic crisis in general, and in the rural areas in particular, also made this clear. According to reports, some 20 million rural migrant workers were laid off in coastal towns towards the end of 2008 as the world's economy slowed down, which led to a sharp reduction in demand for Chinese exports (Hsu *et al.*, 2010). As the laid-off workers began to return to their inland home provinces, social instability grew in step with mounting economic hardships and anxieties about the future. But by mid-2009 the government's swift proactive economic package policy response halted and even reversed this trend, thus calming much of the economic uncertainty. Significantly, experiences on the ground alerted the Chinese leaders to the need for a more balanced relationship between nationally and internationally driven economic interests. Hsu *et al.* (2010) suggest this is likely to lead to a policy shift away from an export-led model of development located primarily in the coastal regions to a more inward-oriented model of development. Such a shift would have a positive impact on the tens of millions of Chinese who, even though they have been involved in the most dramatic economic transformation in recent history, have been also partly excluded from it. The crisis, in short, has been used as an opportunity to assume a more equitable approach to the professed project to build a Harmonious Socialist Society.

The intriguing question is: why should the Chinese rulers care about the people in the absence of any institutional mechanisms to check their power? And here again one might usefully turn for guidance to history, and more specifically to the Mandate of Heaven that bestowed the right to govern on the ruler, but *only* if he ruled well and justly, made the people happy and led through moral example not by force. Of course, it would be ludicrous to suggest that the divinely inspired Mandate of Heaven has any significance to the

---

3   Between 1981 and 2004 the fraction of the population consuming less than a US dollar a
     day fell from 65% to 10%, and more than half a billion people were lifted out of poverty.
     Facts about poverty in China challenge conventional wisdom. The Wall Street Journal, 13
     April 2009.

Chinese Communist Party. At play rather is that part of the qualifying provision of the Mandate that allows for incompetent or despotic rulers to be removed by force in a rebellion, which in terms of Confucian philosophy bestows instant legitimacy on the successful rebel leaders. China's history is replete with examples of popular revolts and upheavals that frequently fractured the continuity of dynastic rule from the third century BCE onwards (Perry, 2001). The most recent victory was that of the communists themselves who, under Mao Zedong, claimed power along with legitimacy. With well over a billion potential rebels, the CCP, like every emperor before it, has little choice but try to keep the people happy, albeit strictly under the party's control. Viewed with a more jaundiced eye, the communist regime's efforts are not so much driven by the needs of the people as by the need to stimulate economic growth to ensure the regime's legitimacy. And, as noted by Philip Mohr elsewhere in this volume, the pursuit of economic growth is not only the goal of the central government but also of the local ruling structures, who act as if they were private corporations instead of involving themselves in the task of redistribution and social development.

China's growth-oriented development path seems more in tune with the traditional Chinese power structure than with the Great Leap Forward and the Cultural Revolution, when arbitrary top-down autocracy ruled supreme and people's needs were disregarded. The present one-party leadership with strong bottom-up participation aims to be more inclusive and more transparent for, as President Hu noted, "Power must be exercised in the sunshine to ensure that it is exercised correctly" (Naisbit, 2010: 42). No one can tell with any degree of certainty where this development path might lead, but it seems increasingly unlikely that it will lead to a political system that is recognisably democratic in the Western sense, as many commentators predict. What might emerge instead is a more internationally legitimate and internally less repressive China.

Internationally there is already certain currency attached to the term Beijing Consensus, which implies an alternative economic development model to the increasingly more controversial, if not discredited, Washington Consensus model.[4] According to Joshua Ramo, who coined the term, the Beijing Consensus is guided by three main characteristics, all of which set it apart from the Washington Consensus. First, there is commitment to innovation and experimentation on an ongoing basis, and a dynamic developmental path that gets adjusted when circumstances change, because of the belief that no single plan can work in every situation. Secondly, GDP is not the only measure of progress; the other two important indicators are the sustainability of the economic system and an even distribution of wealth. The third guideline refers to a policy of self-determination to allow less-developed nations use

---

4   For a more thorough comparative discussion on the Beijing Consensus and Washington Consensus models see the chapter by Philip Mohr in this volume.

leverage to keep the superpowers in check and assure their own financial sovereignty. In contrast to the Washington Consensus, which largely ignores questions of geopolitics, in the Chinese context geopolitics and geoeconomics are fundamentally linked. What has linked the two since the Sixteenth Party Congress in 2002 is the rhetoric of harmony, which is supposed to underpin both China's internal socio-political structure and her foreign relations. The idea of a harmonious and peaceful world is seen as the key enabling mutual development. The concept of harmony is also meant to indicate that China's rise to a global power is peaceful and non-militaristic.

The notion of a harmonious world also has an ancient origin and was rooted in the concept of All under Heaven, which placed China in the cultural and political global centre as the Middle Kingdom. Foreign relations with peripheral states were conducted through what was known as the tribute system, which was based on symbolic obedience to the authority of the Chinese emperor, or the Son of Heaven, but was mutually beneficial. Rule under the All under Heaven principle was open to any qualified candidate who best knew the Way (Tao) to improve the happiness of all peoples universally. Around 500 BCE the founder of Taoism, Laozi, wrote: "A king could rule a state by his orders, win a war by strategies, but enjoy All-under-Heaven only by doing nothing to decrease the freedom and to deny the interests of people" (Tingyang, 2006). If the prescription of the heavenly mandate was followed correctly, a harmonious society and a harmonious world would emerge; if it was violated disharmony would ensue.

The Chinese emperor's self-assigned identity as the Son of Heaven was motivated by the need for legitimacy and security. These two requirements remain as important for Chinese leaders today as they were during the dynastic period, if not more so, given the pressing need for China's development-oriented modernisation strategy within far more complex internal and external social and political environments. The rhetoric of a harmonious world today calls for multilateral structures as mainstays of security interests and peace; an international trade system characterised by fairness, equality and absence of discrimination; and the rejection of Huntington's clash of civilisations thesis in favour of inter-cultural dialogue and exchange in which competitors look for common ground but preserve their cultural differences.

A concept of a harmonious world construed in this way was presented by President Hu Jintao in his 2009 foreign policy programme, which took into account "the profound changes" in the world situation and went on to propose constructing a "harmonious world" by means of "joint development, shared responsibilities and enthusiastic participation" in global affairs. According to Zhang Xiaotong, one of the Party's leading ideologues, the President's programme amounted to a "major theoretical innovation" based on the "scientific judgment of the development and changes of the times" (Lam, 2009). It also represented a fundamental departure from Deng Xiaoping's famous diplomatic credo of "adopting a low profile and never taking the lead" in international affairs (Xinhua News Agency, 2009). Of all the components of the Hu leadership's foreign policy outlook, "shared responsibility and enthusiastic participation" were the two most novel and significant, as they indicated for the first time that Beijing was willing to co-jointly shoulder responsibilities for global obligations.

Conclusions

This chapter aimed to address two questions: What makes authoritarian China such an economic success story in the absence of democratic conditions that are typically associated with thriving economic development? And, second, does China's success translate into post-crisis global reconfiguration, and if so, with what possible implications for democracy?

The simplest answer to the first question would be to say that authoritarian regimes have been known to be economically successful because capitalism does not necessarily need democracy to prosper, and there are many examples – besides China – to prove this. But such an answer would fail to register the relevant aspects of traditional Chinese philosophy and the historical path communist China took to get where it is today. Therefore the more useful question is to ask why *communist* China succeeded where other communist countries failed so dismally. The fundamental difference is in the method. For Lenin and Stalin and their successors both in the Soviet Union and across the Soviet bloc the revolution meant putting immovable laws of history into practice. This teleological approach allowed the vanguard parties in the respective countries of the bloc to assert they were in possession of the ultimate 'truth' and to claim that they alone knew what was best for the people and could therefore decide which policies should be implemented. All grassroots initiatives and experimentation were frowned upon and quashed.

The method of leadership in China, on the other hand, followed practice-based epistemology. And interestingly it was not Deng Xiaoping but Mao Zedong who first understood that learning from experimentation was crucial to innovation and that therefore policy implementation, not policy debate, was the key. Many academics believe that Mao, along with a whole generation of political thinkers and party activists, was strongly influenced by John Dewey.[5] In a series of lectures at Chinese universities during 1919 and 1920 the American scholar presented the experimental method as the core feature of modern science and the most important tool for obtaining scientific know-

---

5   Mao is said to have attended one of Dewey's lectures in the spring of 1920 and to have read and recommended the Chinese edition of Dewey's Five Major Lectures. He stocked this book in the bookstore he opened that year (Di, 1992).

ledge. Dewey's modern approach stressed that theory should be tested through practical application as this was the only way in which to revise one's outlook, assess methodically all learnt facts and discover new facts. Subsequently Dewey's Chinese students placed experimentation at the centre of social reform initiatives. In practice this translated into the so-called 'point-to-surface' controlled experimentation whereby model villages were established and expanded between the 1930s and mid-1950s[6] for the purpose of conducting experiments, the results of which were then disseminated to the centre with a view to progressively refining policies (Heilmann, 2008).

Deng Xiaoping and his group were disciples of Mao and therefore his legitimate heirs, but they still needed a justification for shifting China's development away from Mao's subsequent hugely devastating revolutionary path. Deng found it in Mao's early conviction of making practice the sole criterion for testing truth. Ironically, as Elizabeth Perry put it, in this way "elements of China's revolutionary inheritance have actually furthered the stunningly successful implementation of market reforms" (2007). The link between central policymakers and local enterprise re-established under Deng proved essential both as a mechanism for mediating conflicts over strategy and as an outlet for freeing the individual spirit of initiative propagated by Yan Fu.

China's economic success, strongly underscored by the recent crisis, begs the question not so much of whether the country will become a leading global player, but what kind of a player it will be. The official rhetoric of a harmonious world coupled with membership in the World Trade Organisation and a greater involvement in world issues as well as in UN peacekeeping activities might suggest that, contrary to a long-established historical tendency, China has developed a more universal vision of the international community into which it is becoming integrated and in which it wants to play an active role. But such perceptions are soon belied by China's standing commitment to the principles of national sovereignty and non-intervention, and by the frequent cultural references to 'Chinese characteristics' indicating a continuation of a traditional inward-oriented cultural exceptionalism. As reported by Lam (2009), the Chinese leader, Hu Jintao, has been urging party and government officials to make a contribution towards "fostering humankind's peace and development" by synthesizing "independence and sovereignty" with globalisation. The Chinese leader has also made it repeatedly clear that China's more active participation in global affairs would not affect its unique model of development, and that countries should respect and learn from each other so as to "safeguard the world's pluralism and the multiplicity of development models".

These utterances point towards a Chinese vision of a regional, rather than global, order within which international societies sharing region-specific val-

---

6   The practice was abandoned during the frenetic activities of the Great Leap Forward and the Cultural Revolution, when Soviet-style top-down policy implementation was instituted.

ues operate under the pluralist management. East Asian countries, for example, already form the nucleus of an emerging market group bound by common values. In January 2010 China signed a free-trade agreement linking it to the Association of South-East Asian Nations (ASEAN), and in March the ASEAN countries (China, Japan and South Korea) set up a pool of foreign exchange reserves to give them some element of monetary policy coordination (*The Economist*, 2010). According to one commentator, the economic crisis provided a considerable opportunity to move in the direction of regionally focused global solutions, because the undoing of the Washington Consensus provides "more room, and more need, for experiments in alternative modes of international political economy." Going that route will let China retain the combination of nationalist politics and liberal economics and will allow it to rise on the back of the global market while remaining non-democratic (Buzan, 2010).

For many countries not satisfied with Western liberal economic and political systems China symbolises a new and tempting alternative to democracy and the perception has grown in the post-crisis period. The Chinese 'model' has no internationally infectious doctrine to offer. It attracts because the unrestricted use of power makes for more efficient decision-making, as China's crisis management has demonstrated; because it shows faster economic growth than that noted in market-led democracies; and because it seems to hold the potential for greater regime longevity, something of much interest to autocrats and would-be autocrats the world over. What is forgotten, though, is that in contrast to the tried and well-tested democratic mechanisms that diffuse tensions, the Chinese authoritarian system has no such built-in safety valves, which makes China susceptible to implosion in response to any number of issues related to social and/or nationalist demands. Any country wishing to emulate China, but coming from a different development path, would be even more vulnerable in this respect.

There are some aspects of the Chinese experience from which countries could learn. South Africa, for example, might do well to note that innovative policy implementation, not endless policy debates, is the secret to successful service delivery. But the benefits of learning selectively from China should be clearly distinguished from the folly of trying a wholesale imitation of a culturally distinctive form of authoritarian governance. The countries with the most to lose, but among the ones most likely to try it, would be imperfect democracies that show poor economic performance.[7] At present they are obliged to at least uphold the pretence of a democratic rule in order to access global markets and money; under China's patronage things would be different since the Chinese principle of non-interference attaches no conditions for governments to reform, be transparent or respect human rights. Given the cul-

---

7   For the most likely candidates see E. Wnuk-Lipinski in this volume

turally idiosyncratic type of autocratic rule in China, trying it outside the Chinese context would be most unlikely to produce the desired economic outcomes, but would be sure to eradicate the meagre vestiges of democracy that the citizens of these countries still have as their last means to keep some degree of check on their governments.

Sources

Bell, D. (2010). The Chinese Confucian Party. *Globe and Mail.* 19 February.
Buzan , B (2010) .China in international society: Is 'peaceful rise' possible? *Chinese Journal of International Politics.* 3(1): 5-36.
Callahan, W.A. (2004). Historical legacies and non/traditional security: commemorating National Humiliation Day. Paper presented at Renmin University, Beijing. April.
Chou Yu-sun (1996). Nationalism and patriotism in China. *Issues and Studies.* 32 (11): 67-86.
Di Xu. (1992). *A Comparison of the educational ideas and practices of John Dewey and MaoZedong in China.* San Francisco: Mellen Research University Press.
Helimann, S .(2008). From local experiments to national policy: The origins of China's distinctive policy process. *The China Journal.* January. 59: 1-30.
Holbig, H. (2000). Remaking the CCP's ideology: Determinants, progress and limits under Hu Jintao. *Journal of Current Chinese Affairs.* 38 (3): 35-61.
Hsu, S., Shiyin, J. and Heyward, H. (2010). The global crisis' impact upon China's rural migrants. *Journal of Current Chinese Affairs.* 39 (2):167-185.
Kang, Xiaoguang (2006). Confucianisation: a future in the tradition. *Social Research.* 7(1): 77–120.
Lam, W. (2009). Jintao unveils major foreign policy initiative. *China Brief* (December). 9 (24): 2-4.
Lu, Xiaobo (2000). Booty socialism, bureau-preneurs, and the state in transition. *Comparative Politics.* (32(3): 273-295.
Naisbitt, J. and Naisbitt, D. (2010). *China's megatrends. The 8 pillars of a new society.* New York: HarperCollins Publishers.
Ngo Tak-Wing (2008). Rent-seeking and economic governance in the structural nexus of corruption in China. *Crime, Law and Social Change.* 49(1): 27-42.
Pei, M. (2006). *China's trapped transition: The limits of developmental autocracy.* Harvard University Press.
Perry, E. J. (2001). Challenging the Mandate of Heaven: Social protest and state power in China. Watertown (MA): East Gate Books.
Perry, E.J. (2007). Studying Chinese politics: Farewell to revolution?. *The China Journal.* January. No. 57
Pye, L. and Pye, M. (1985). *Asian power and politics. The cultural dimensions of authority.* Cambridge (Ma): Harvard University and London: The Belknap Press.
Ramo, J. (2004). *The Beijing Consensus.* London: Foreign Policy Centre.
Schram, S.R. (1984). Economics in command? Ideology and policy since the Third Plenum, 1978-84. *The China Quarterly* (September). 99: 417-461.

The Economist (2010). Brazil, Russia, India and China matter individually. But does it make sense to treat the BRICs – or any other combination of emerging powers – as a block? 15 April.

Trailokya Raj Aryal (2010). Confucianism and communism in China. *Republica Opinion,* 22 June.

Tuck, C. (1995). Is the party over? Political instability in post-Deng China. *Contermoarary Review* (May). Accessible on-line at:
http://findarticles.com/p/articles/mi_m2242/is_n1552_v266/ai_17041146/

Tingyang Zhao (2006). Rethinking empire from a Chinese concept 'All-under-Heaven' (Tian-xia). *Social Identities.* January. 12 (1): 29- 41.

White, G (1984). Developmental states and socialist industrialisation in the Third World. *Journal of Development Studies.* 21 (1): 97: 120.

Xinhua News Agency, 24 November, 2009. In: Lam, W. (2009). Jintao unveils major foreign-policy initiative. *China Brief.* December. 9 (24). Accessible on-line at: http://www.jamestown.org/programs/chinabrief

Zhan Zhongle & Su Yu (2009). Poverty eradication and human rights safeguards: China's progress and reflections. The second Beijing forum on human rights: harmonious development and human rights. Beijing, November.

Zheng, Yongnian (1999). *Discovering Chinese nationalism in China. Modernisation, identity and international relations.* Hong Kong: Colocraft

A new bi-polarisation?

Edmund Wnuk-Lipinski

Introduction

Reading the global press or surfing the net one gets the distinct impression that the 21st century belongs inevitably to China. China is currently second (after Germany) in investment into renewable energy and, according to estimates, may soon be a global leader in the production and supply of this kind of energy. Its continued high economic growth rate is an extraordinary achievement, considering that other major economies struggle with the consequences of the global financial crisis and at the time of writing have merely succeeded in returning to the path of earlier growth after a significant drop in their GDPs. Over the last decade China has become a giant in global exports and it will probably soon be No. 1 in the global economy. John Toon from Georgia Institute of Technology wrote in 2008: "A new study of worldwide technological competitiveness suggests China may soon rival the United States as the principal driver of the world's economy – a position the U.S. has held since the end of World War II. If that happens, it will mark the first time in nearly a century that two nations have competed for leadership as equals. The study's indicators predict that China will soon surpass the United States in the critical ability to develop basic science and technology, turn those developments into products and services – and then market them to the world. Though China is often seen as just a low-cost producer of manufactured goods, the new "High Tech Indicators study done by researchers at the Georgia Institute of Technology clearly shows that the Asian powerhouse has much bigger aspirations."

At the same time China's military power is not only growing, but is also being fundamentally modernised. The fire power of the Chinese army recently surpassed the similar strength of the Russian army and, according to Global FirePower, may be positioned in the second place, just after the US Army fire strength. The already accomplished programmes to modernise the army are impressive and further modernisation to be implemented in the coming decade will fundamentally change Chinese military capabilities. First of all, China will move from the position of a regional military power to the status of a global player. Secondly, in the area of cyber attacks and cyber warfare technology it will probably be the best developed nation-state in the world. Such conclusions at least can be drawn from the Annual Report to the US Congress prepared by the Office of the Secretary of Defence in 2007. In the same year the *Christian Science Monitor* (September 14) published a more open assessment by James Mulvenon, expert on China's military and director of the Center for Intelligence and Research in Washington. Mulvenon said the Chinese "are the first to use cyber attacks for political and military goals. Whether it is battlefield preparation or hacking networks connected to the German chancellor, they are the first state actor to jump feet first into 21st-century cyber warfare technology. This is clearly becoming a more serious and open problem."

Even if the above assessments are somewhat cursory, it is still fair to say that the Chinese giant is waking up. The wounds of the Cultural Revolution have been healed, the memory of the Tiananmen massacre is receding and the ideological fervour of the earlier decades of communist China has been replaced by a pragmatic task-oriented attitude among both the elites and the masses. Paradoxically, the global financial crisis reinforced the already strong position of the Chinese economy on the global market. For this economy proved to be relatively resistant to the financial turbulence; the huge Western currency reserves discouraged attacks by global 'casino-capitalism' investors in local Chinese currency, and exports surplus as well as steady demand on the domestic market kept the economy on a path of growth. 'State-led capitalism', to use David Lane's (2010) phrase, combined with the huge size of the country produced an outcome that can be summarised in a simple statement: China's is the fastest growing emerging market in the world. And yes, China is an economic success story that cannot be without consequences on a global scale.

China is being watched with increasing concern by the core countries of globalisation and particularly by the US. This is not surprising, given some convincing predictions that China will soon become a new and probably demanding partner in the current club of global players. But one can assume that China is also being watched, and possibly with growing hope, by a number of either formally democratic or authoritarian peripheral countries who cannot claim their development to have been a success story either in economic or in political terms. For the periphery the Chinese example may be a more and more attractive alternative to the patterns offered by democratic countries, still affluent but evidently more vulnerable to the global financial crisis. This, of course, would be a fundamental shift from the previous 'no-other-alternative' route – a route that became quite popular in the wake of the somewhat premature belief in the final victory of liberal democracy and free market economy proclaimed by Francis Fukuyama after the collapse of the world communist system. The recent financial crisis has shaken the global market and revealed the vulnerability of the global economy to regional turbulence. It also undermined a belief in the stability of market rules, and in the capitalist economy itself.

The general question pondered in this chapter is: If peripheral democracies suffer as a result of the global financial crisis while authoritarian China manages to reinforce its global economic standing despite the trying circumstances, can we expect a gradual shift from the current pattern of development that combines liberal democracy with a free market economy to a pattern in which authoritarian rule is combined with a free market as a shortcut to a more secure and in consequence better position on the global market?

Democratic and authoritarian capitalisms

The collapse of the Communist bloc in 1989 gave a new impetus to Huntington's Third Wave of democratisation thesis. The impetus was so powerful that it prompted some students of democracy to announce triumphantly that it was only a matter of time before liberal democracy would prevail all over the world. Soon afterwards, though, it became clear that this kind of optimism was groundless. According Freedom House estimates, around the year 2000 the number of electoral democracies stood at 120 or 63 percent of all independent nation-states. According to the same source, more recently there has been not only stagnation but even a decline in the number of electoral democracies from 124 in 2005 to 116 in 2009. It is too early to conclude that the Third Wave of democratisation is over, but there is little doubt that it has lost momentum. A decline is also evident in the area of civil liberties; Freedom House estimates that in 2009 alone a decline occurred in 14 countries and only in four did the civil liberties index rise. In short, the global wave of democratisation, so vigorous in the last decade of 20th century, seems to have come to a turning, which is either just a temporary slowdown or, what seems to be more likely, the beginning of the reverse wave.

The one truly global consequence of the collapse of the communist system was that it put an end to the dismal failure of the experimentation with a command economy of the Soviet type and that since then countries in transition have been encouraged to adopt some kind of market economy. Only North Korea and Cuba deviate from this general pattern. As a result the really global market economy is capitalist and consists of a whole range of solutions to the problems of various local economies, from liberal in the US through to welfare state capitalism in the EU to a mixture of state and private capitalism in China. Thus, what had in fact been victorious globally as an outcome of the momentous year 1989 was not so much liberal democracy as capitalism.

It goes without saying that democracy, and especially citizenship, can hardly be functional without a market economy and private property rights. The opposite, though, is not true: the market economy, or more broadly capitalism, may well function both under a democratic or a non-democratic regime. What is needed for capitalism to work are predictable rules of the game, an army of consumers and a non-rebellious society willing to trade human rights for economic wellbeing and social peace. Krzysztof Gawlikowski, a Polish sinologist, commenting on the specificity of the 'Asian value systems' claims that the

Asian cultural context, and notably Confucian values, that shape the worldview of the Chinese people are substantially different from – and incompatible with – Western values. Gawlikowski (2005) refers to empirical studies conducted by David I. Hitchcock (1994) on East and Southeast Asian elites that show striking differences when compared with American elites. For example, the elites of East and Southeast Asia value much less than the Americans do personal freedom (32 and 82% respectively), individual rights (29 and 78%), free expression (47 and 85%) and open debates on the solution of social problems (29 and 74%). Asians, on the other hand, appreciate much more an orderly society (71 and 11%), harmony (58 and 7%), consensus (39 and 4%), respect for authority (42 and 11%) and the rights of society (27 and 7%). Hitchcock adds that a significant number of Asians considered decisions taken behind closed doors as the proper way of solving social and political problems (29% compared to 0% of Americans). As far as respect for learning was concerned, the figures were 69% for Asians and merely 15% for Americans. Asians also valued self-discipline more highly than Americans did (48 and 22%). These findings explain why civic and political rights that are taken for granted in Western liberal democracies could be perceived in the Asian, and especially in the Chinese cultural context, as an imposition of norms from an alien culture and as such produce cultural resistance understood by local populations as a defence of their traditional identity.

Citizens with civic and political rights are not a necessary condition for the wellbeing of capitalism. Moreover, too many social rights for the citizenry may slow down capitalist effectiveness and increase the cost of the various elements of production as well as making the economic system more vulnerable to global crises. The global division that seems to have emerged currently is one between democratic and authoritarian capitalisms. According to Freedom House, of the 192 independent nation states only 113 (58,8 %) enjoy the status of electoral democracies. And the category 'electoral democracies' covers all nation-states that practise minimal procedural democracy, i.e. they hold competitive elections in a multiparty system. Liberal values that are attached to a democratic regime and are taken for granted in the Western world are not necessarily perceived as an integral part of democracy in other world regions and civilizations. And China's economic achievements could undermine the near-axiomatic conviction in political science that democracy goes hand in hand with economic success, while an autocratic regime is likely to be associated with poor economic performance. More on this later. For now it will suffice to say that it is increasingly less clear whether democracy increases the probability of economic success or rather – and this is more likely – whether it produces improvements in the living standards of wide segments of a society but only when good economic performance is already in place The legitimate question to raise in this context is whether the Chinese model of authoritarian capitalism might become an attractive alternative to liberal democracy of the Western type, which is combined not only with a market economy but also with the whole package of civic values such as human rights, the role of the individual in society etc. And, if so, to whom might the Chinese model appeal most? Before offering tentative answers to these questions, it will be useful to briefly survey the volatile world order that emerged after the collapse of the communist system.

Two world divisions: poverty and democracy

The self-liberation of Central and East European countries from communist rule and especially the end of the Soviet Union led to a rearrangement of the global chessboard; the bipolar division of the world came to an end and all of a sudden most of the global strategies (political and military) based on the premise accepted for decades that this bipolar construction of the world order was solid and stable was proved to be without foundation. There was no Cold War any longer and the threat of a global military conflict disappeared, along with that of an expanding communist sphere. The so-called 'free world' lost a basic point of reference. To put it differently, the communist threat that sustained the unity of liberal democracies and forced them into economic, technological and, above all, military alliances so as not to be outdone by the Soviet bloc was no more. NATO underwent an identity crisis and the question of a new world order jumped to the top of the agenda. Indeed, the last decade of the 20th century saw a fundamental reshuffling of the global scene.

The question is which factors of the former world order remained important when the bipolar division of the Cold war era passed into history? There were at least two. One was the level of economic development and the other was the level of freedom offered by the various political systems around the world. These two dimensions partly overlap (see Table 1).

Table 1: World according to wealth and democracy (2009)

Nation states	Total	Affluent	Neither affluent, nor poor	Poor
Total	192 (100,0)	51 (100,0)	94 (100,0)	47 (100,0)
Electoral democracies	113　(58,8)	42　(82,4)	54　(57,4)	17　(36,2)
Others	79　(41,2)	9　(17,6)	40　(42,6)	30　(63,8)

Source: own calculations on the basis of Freedom House (2010). Freedom in the world 2010: erosion of freedom intensifies (*http://www.freedomhouse.org/uploads/fiw10/FIW_2010_Tables_ and_Graphs.pdf* (without Tuvalu and Nauru) and data from: World Development Report 2010, The World Bank, Washington D.C. p. 377 ("Affluent" – annual income per capita for 2008 equal to 11,906 US $ or more; "neither affluent, nor poor" – income per capita for 2008 between 978 US $ and 11,905 US $; "poor" – income per capita for 2008 equal to 975 US$ or less).

In statistical terms there is a clear correlation between the democratic order and the wealth of nations measured by per capita income. This is nothing new as a number of empirical studies confirm this association. Most of the affluent societies are electoral democracies, and most of the poor countries are not democratic; they do not even fit the minimal procedural criterion of democracy that is applied here. But the problem lies in the question of whether a given society is affluent because it is democratic, or whether it is democratic because it is affluent. Empirical findings are not clear; in the literature one finds some arguments supporting both of the opposite theses, but because they are expressed in causal terms they cannot both be true. This theoretical controversy deserves an in-depth analysis that would, however, go beyond the scope of this chapter. For the sake of further reflection it will be enough to say that so far electoral democracies have been positively associated with good economic performance, creating the widely shared conviction that a democratic system offers the best entry ticket to the club of economically successful nation-states. This conviction was strengthened by the fact that the club consisted exclusively of liberal democracies. However, the global financial crisis and the following deep recession hit leading democratic capitalisms the hardest exposing the fragility of economic growth and the vulnerability of democratic capitalisms to financial mismanagement. This in turn undermined the widely shared belief that the best recipe for a prosperous future is electoral democracy combined with a free market economy. This was especially evident in the fact that an economic giant such as China didn't suffer much from the crisis and even used it to show off its striking competitive edge on the global market.

As Table 1 illustrates, there are also electoral democracies among the poor nation-states. In fact over one third of poor countries are formally electoral democracies. Looking at the same issue from a different perspective one can see that of all electoral democracies only 37,2% belong to the club of affluent nations-states; nearly half are neither affluent nor poor (47,8%), and 15% of electoral democracies fall into the category of poor nations. Among all non-democratic nation-states 11,4% belong to the category of affluent societies; half of the non-democratic countries (50,6 %) are neither poor nor rich, and 38,0% fall into the category of poor nation states.

As already mentioned, the criterion applied by Freedom House to form the category of electoral democracies is a purely procedural element. It includes all nation-states that organise competitive elections at regular intervals, but it ignores a set of values (a package of civil and political rights of an individual) which in the Western hemisphere is attached to democratic procedures as an integral part of democracy. As already said, what is generally taken for granted in the Western cultural zone can be (and indeed is) questioned elsewhere, and particularly in China. Table 2 provides data on the association of wealth and freedom in the set of independent nation-states.

Table 2: Freedom and wealth among the nation-states (2009)

Nation-states	World total	Affluent	Neither affluent, nor poor	Poor
World total	192 (100,0)	51 (100,0)	94 (100,0)	47 (100,0)
Free	87 (45,3)	42 (82,4)	38 (40,4)	7 (14,9)
Partly free	58 (30,2)	2 (3,9)	33 (35,1)	23 (48,9)
Not free	47 (24,5)	7 (13,7)	23 (24,5)	17 (36,2)

Source: own calculations on the basis of Freedom House (2010). Freedom in the world 2010: erosion of freedom intensifies (*http://www.freedomhouse.org/uploads/fiw10/FIW_2010_Tables_and_Graphs.pdf* (without Tuvalu and Nauru) and data from: World Development Report 2010, The World Bank, Washington D.C. p. 377 ("Affluent" –annual income per capita for 2008 equal to 11,906 US $ or more; "neither affluent, nor poor" – income per capita for 2008 between 978 US $ and 11,905 US $; "poor" – income per capita for 2008 equal to 975 US$ or less).

Today fewer than half of the independent nation-states fully observe civil and political rights. But most affluent societies (82,4 %) protect the civil and political rights of citizens, whereas poor countries show the opposite trend: they are – in the vast majority of cases – either "partly free" or not free at all. So the panoramic view of today's world reveals a picture where wealth and freedom are concentrated at one end of the pole, and poverty and neo-enslavement at the other. As a result of the global circulation of information, both ordinary people and political elites in poor countries are well aware of their position and know that the distance to the other pole is not getting shorter; but may indeed be getting longer. In the period between the collapse of the world communist system and the onset of the 2008-2009 global crisis the remedy to help those countries escape from the poverty zone seemed clear. International institutions, such as the IMF or the World Bank, and some democratic nation-states led by the US were willing to provide aid under the condition of thorough local reforms that would restructure the economic and political system of a given country along the lines of Western liberal democratic capitalism. This was the model before the onset of the global financial crisis that highlighted China's good economic performance despite the unfavourable global economic climate. China's economic success and its crisis-proof growth not only reinforced authoritarian rule in China itself by proving that its policy works, but it also shifted China from the status of a poor and backward country to the position of a global player, at least on the world market. The communist ideology that plays its ritualised role to legitimise an authoritarian hold of power is undergoing modifications, as discussed by Ursula van Beek in this volume. But generally ideology no longer moves the Chinese people. They are rather mobilised on a massive scale by the high consumption standards to which they aspire. One need not be a dedicated communist any longer to participate in the success of the Chinese system; it is enough to be pragmatic in the market and at the same time avoid suspicion

that one has political aspirations that might challenge the ritualised communist power structures.

John and Doris Naisbitt (2010) argue that the Chinese 'economic miracle' rests on a specifically Chinese model of social relations that has roughly the following attributes:

1. Top-down strategic decisions supported by bottom-up participation;
2. Ideological indoctrination replaced by encouragement for innovative
   thinking in business;
3. Political legitimacy of power provided by economic performance and not
   by democratic procedure;
4. Top-down and bottom-up forces in a delicate balance that forms a new
   model of power relations called by the Naisbitts "vertical democracy",
   however strange this might sound to Western ears;
5. Placing social order and harmony, fundamental to the teaching of Confucius, at the top of the Chinese value system;
6. Central power defines border conditions that cannot be trespassed by individuals or groups, but within a framework of conditions that allow relative economic freedom, expressed in a poetic Chinese way as 'Framing
   the forest and letting the trees grow';
7. Rigid directives from the centre replaced by a trial-and-error strategy,
   elimination of fear of risk, and encouragement of experimenting in the
   economy and in intellectual life; and finally,
8. Opening to the world, and above all to the world market, combined with
   the evolution from imitation to innovation, that is "from manufacturing
   brands to creating brands".

Such a model of pragmatic market communism, no matter how odd it might
sound, seems to have worked well during the global financial crisis and is unlikely to be overlooked by the world, and especially by poor countries that
show perennially poor economic performance.

These countries are located on the peripheries of the global network of
political and economic relations and are either authoritarian or electoral democracies. The peripheral electoral democracies are sometimes called 'defective democracies', because of their many institutional malfunctions and subs-
tandard adherence to the rights of citizens. In fact, nearly one quarter (24,8%)
of electoral democracies are evaluated by Freedom House as "partly free". In
other words, a substantial number of procedural democracies show some
shortcomings, predominantly in the area of civil and political rights of individuals. This is even stronger in the category of poor countries, where of the
17 electoral democracies that fall into that category only 4 are estimated by
Freedom House as "free" (Benin, Ghana, Serbia and Ukraine), and 13 as
"partly free" (Bangladesh, Burundi, Comoros, Guinea-Bissau, Haiti, Liberia,
Malawi, Mali, Mongolia, Senegal, Sierra Leone, Vanuatu and Zambia). 'De-

fective democracies' are the weakest element of the Third Wave of democratisation.

The question of world leadership – politics and economy

Not many people today would doubt US world leadership in technology, the economy and military affairs. However, the world order is shaped by dynamic economic, technological and political forces, which may in the relatively short time of a decade or two change the established situation.

When we speak about leadership we may think about one of its two dimensions. First, leadership means that some nation-state achieves the best score in a given area. And this kind of leadership can be easily verified by empirical proof (statistics, observable performance etc.). Secondly, leadership may mean that a given-nation state is simply followed by other nation-states either in policies implemented or paths of development (leadership in a stronger sense); or the position of this nation-state is so powerful in a given area that other nation- states will be discouraged from doing anything explicitly against the will of this privileged nation-state.

If leadership is understood as achieving the highest score in a specific area, then one can say the US is the world leader in military strength and in technological progress. In this leadership position the state of the American economy shapes many economies around the world. The 2008-2009 global financial crisis was born in the US and produced recession not only in that country but also in many different regions of the world, including Europe. As long as the American economy is in a good shape the world economic order is more or less stable, but if the American financial system or the economy catches a cold, the world economic order may well fear that it will be getting the flu. This correlation, which the last crisis so brutally revealed, might be too close for comfort to some and might in consequence be redefined as a constant threat by an increasing number of national economies – a threat that is beyond their political control structures. One of the outcomes of the crisis has been an urgent search for an answer to the question "How can we make the global economic order more immune to financial turmoil or even to financial fraud, which can always occur in one of the global economic players, but especially in the US?"

American leadership in the second sense is less obvious. First of all, the leadership is challenged by various authoritarian nation-states, and especially by the countries of militant Islam. It is also increasingly being challenged by China. In a sense, the relation of China to the US serves as a factor that is used for the formation of a new and more nationalistic identity of China after the collapse of the Maoist totalitarian ideology. But even among American allies there are clear signs of ambivalent attitudes towards US political and military leadership. A good indication of this phenomenon is the winding road of transatlantic US relations with the EU, where friendship is mixed with competition. In these relations US leadership is accepted as long as it does not become too powerful.

The end of the Cold War redefined the criteria that determine the position of a global leader. Military strength, though still important, is gradually losing its formerly overriding power as the threat of a global military conflict recedes. What matters more now is economic expansion and technological progress as well as economic cooperation within structures that transcend the borders even of giant nation-states with huge domestic markets.

There is an additional trend that may soon change the global balance of power and put the question of leadership into a new context. Bilateral relations are gradually being replaced by multilateral cooperation, while the traditional direct power relation on the global scene of hegemony vs. submissiveness gives way to the 'soft power' of norms and regulations. In this context the question of leadership moves from the issue of who matters most in a cluster of bilateral relations to the issue of who is powerful enough to impose norms and regulations that shape multilateral cooperation above the nation-state level. The Chinese strategy of world expansion seems to take this evolution in the nature of international relations into account seriously. Southeastern and central Asia are its natural areas of expansion, but one should note that China is becoming increasingly active also in Africa and the Arab world. Two organizations, the Forum on China-Africa Cooperation (FOCAC) and the Sino-Arab Cooperation Forum (SACOF), serve as an experimental field to implement Chinese strategy of world expansion through soft power, which regulates China's cooperation with two large regions of the world. Nicola Contessi (2009) writes that "As rules (or norms) are often epiphenomena of underlying interests, multilateralism has come to represent an effective way for China to increase her power projection in the two regions, while sidelining direct confrontation with the superpower." The increasing presence of China in various multilateral initiatives, combined with its economic strength, gradually changes the status of that country from 'norm taker' to 'norm broker', even if the norms are always filtered through indigenous Chinese culture.

From the perspective of authoritarian capitalisms, US leadership is not only challenged but also denied. This is so not only because of natural economic competition on the global market, but also because one of the significant elements of American international policy is to promote world democracy. Part and parcel of this package is the American lifestyle and a set of values regulating public life known as American 'political correctness'. Needless to say, this element of American foreign policy produces a direct threat to authoritarian rule and is thus rejected by political rulers of non-democratic states. It also undermines any indigenous cultural identity.

Towards a new world order

The present world order is unstable because of many and sometimes conflicting global processes, such as climate change; 'casino capitalism', which moves huge financial resources around the world in search of the best returns on investments; local economic breakdowns that disturb the global financial system; and – last but not least – global terrorism. The remedies applied by international organisations and by the most powerful nation-states are limited and defensive. Responsibility for the global order is dispersed, which in practice means that nobody feels responsible for world affairs as long as particular national interests are not threatened. Peripheral nation-states (authoritarian and democratic alike) with a low level of economic development are left on their own and can hardly cope with the regional and local consequences of the global turmoil. Therefore the future is increasingly less predictable. One could expect that such a situation will not last long.

According to many indicators, some of which were mentioned earlier, China is not only challenging the military supremacy of the US, but is also trying hard to fill the technological gap and take up the position of a global economic leader. Chinese world exports have had an impressive record over the past decade. According to PRC National Bureau of Statistics, China's total volume of exports was equal to 249,2 billion US$ in 2000 and in 2009 climbed to 1,201,7 billion US$ (an increase of 482%!). According to the US International Trade Commission, China's trade with the USA alone reached 366 billion US$, but the surplus of Chinese exports over imports grew to 226,8 billion US$ (in 2000 the Chinese surplus was 83,7 billion US$). According to *The Economist* (31 March 2010), China, which is still seen by various rating agencies as an emerging market, is now a leading global exporter, with a 9,6% share in world exports, and has surpassed not only the US (8,5 %) but also Germany (9,0 %).

Such rapid growth has already changed the economic map of the world. China is becoming one of the leading global centres for investments and trade, and is an advertisement for the effectiveness of economic development in the context of authoritarian capitalism. As such it might be an appealing pattern for other authoritarian capitalisms to follow. Similarly, for defective peripheral democracies with poor economic performance such a pattern might also become more attractive as a potential exit route from their disadvantaged position. Should this be the case, the Third Wave of democratisation may not only remain stagnant but might even be reversed. All it would need for this to happen would be for defective democracies to abandon democratic procedures and turn to authoritarian solutions in politics in order to imitate the Chinese example in economics.

Conclusions

It is far from clear whether the continuing evolution of China will leave its internal political structure intact. There is some solid scholarship in social theory suggesting that the probability of social emancipation from authoritarian rule increases in step with economic development and growth of welfare. But it is equally well known that culture matters and hence that the Chinese culture might turn out to be a fertile ground for the emergence of a new model. In this model the harmonious development of the economy combines with vertical social relations that stabilise the political system, which is authoritarian – according to Western standards. The other scenario for China is an acceptance of Western norms of liberal democratic order, which would mean submission to Western soft power and in consequence the Westernisation of Chinese culture and a transition of social identities from indigenous to imported models. And this seems rather unlikely. What is more probable is that China, rather than following the trends set by others, will within a decade or two become a trendsetter that might find followers not only among poor authoritarian capitalisms but also among defective democracies. Should this be the case, the emergence of a new bipolar division of the world will be only a matter of time.

Sources

Awdry, C. (2010). *China cements status as world growth leader.* Available on-line at: http://www.ftchinaconfidential.com/MacroEconomy/CapitalMarkets/Features/Gu estColumn/article/20100114/98d2ff8c-fe6f-11de-a148-00144f2af8e8/China-cements-status-as-world-growth-leader.

Contessi, N. P. (2009). Experiments in soft balancing: China-led multilateralism in Africa and the Arab world, *Caucasian Review of International Affairs.* 3 (4):404-434.

Department of Defense (2007). *Annual Report to Congress. Military power of the People's Republic of China 2007.* Washington D.C.

Freedom House (2010). *Freedom in the world 2010: erosion of freedom intensifies. Available on-line at*: www.freedomhouse.org/uploads/fiw10/FIW_2010_Tables_and_Graphs.pdf.

Gawlikowski, K. (2005). From false 'Western universalism' towards true 'universal universalism'. *Dialog and Universalism*, No. 5.

Global FirePower.com . Available on-line at: http://www.globalfirepower.com/.

Hitchcock, D.I. (1994). Asian values and the United States: How much conflict? Washington, D. C. Centre for Strategic and International Studies.

Lane, D. (2010). Post-socialist states and the world economy: The Impact of global economic crisis, *Historical Social Research.* 35 (2): 218-241.

Marquand, R. and Arnoldy, B. (2007). China emerges as leader in cyberwarfare. *Christian Science Monitor* (14 September). Accessible on-line: http://www. dtic.mil/cgi-bin/GetTRDoc?Location=U2&doc=GetTRDoc.pdf&AD=ADA508213

Naisbitt, J. & D. 2010. *China's megatrends. The 8 pillars of a new society.* New York: Harper.

Toon, J. (2008), *China as global technology leader?* (http://www. ventureoutsource.com/contract-manufacturing/trends-observations/2008/china-as-global-technology-leader)

World Development Report (2010). The World Bank. Washington D.C. Accessible in-line at: wwwr.worldbank.org/wdr2010

Worldwatch Institute (2008). *China on Pace to Become Global Leader in Renewable Energy* (http://www.worldwatch.org/node/5497)

Chinese crisis management: consolidated authoritarian capitalism as a new brand of political regime?

Han Sang-Jin and Lü Peng

Introduction

"Welcome to the People's Republic of China," declares a Chinese officer as he crisply salutes a flood of refugees from all over the world who have fled to Tibet as their homes were destroyed by an apocalyptic deluge. It is a line that thrilled thousands of Chinese filmgoers, who voted writer-director Roland Emmerich's latest blockbuster *2012* the most popular Hollywood film in China. The plot panders to Chinese audiences: the giant arks that will save humanity are both made and landed in China. When the apocalypse comes, China will save the world. At least that's how Chinese audiences interpret this movie. For the first time that anyone can remember a Hollywood disaster movie has cast the Chinese as a significant beneficial force.

The aim of this chapter is to explore some salient characteristics in the Chinese pattern of crisis management to see why China has been so successful in economic development that even a Hollywood movie alludes to the notion that it might save the world from its economic woes in the wake of the global financial crisis; the Chinese themselves seem to be more confident after the global economic downturn. Of course, it is an exaggeration to say that China will save the world economy, but it seems quite certain that it is making a significant contribution to that end. In order to discover why that is, we will focus on the specific rules selected for crisis management by the party-state of China and the successful consequences of the institutionalised selectivity. However, the ultimate goal of the analysis is not to simply present this success as a positive development but also to consider it as a possible threat to the future of China. In this connection we want ponder the problem of democracy[1] and citizens' participation as important issues that need to be addressed. For this purpose we shall examine the attitudes of Chinese elites towards democracy before the global financial meltdown and in the course of the Great Recession.

---

[1] We refer here to democracy as a system where top political leaders are selected via free and fair elections. If one accepts this thin definition, China is definitely not a democratic regime.

Where does China stand today?

The 2008-2009 economic crisis, which originated in the meltdown of the financial and housing markets of the United States, spread all over the world but had only a limited direct impact on China. It is true that Chinese companies with heavy investments in the West felt a massive blow, but thanks to the relatively slow-paced development of China's financial system and the fact that foreign investment by China's banking industry is subject to foreign exchange controls and regulatory approval, the banking industry's overall open foreign exchange exposure has been relatively low. More importantly, because of its insulated banking sector that relies primarily on deposits, the domestic financial market in China has not experienced a cash-flow crisis. Furthermore, there has been almost no direct impact on small and medium-sized banks.

China was also spared the effects of the other 'culprit' of the global crisis, the housing market, which despite a huge bubble did not collapse in China as it did in many Western countries. In fact, the Chinese housing market has skyrocketed by almost 60% since 2008, when the financial crisis broke out. The price of land in and around Beijing has gone up by a factor of 9 in the last 6 years. Many observers believe the question is no longer whether there is a Chinese housing bubble, but when it will burst.

As far as China's real economy is concerned, the international crisis left its mark in several respects. To begin with, international trade was badly affected. In November 2009 exports fell (for the first time since 2001) by 2.2%, while in December imports declined by 17.9%. Secondly, the manufacturing sector taking orders from the US and the EU began to feel the pinch; in early October 2008 the China Manufacturers Purchasing Index, based on monthly questionnaires sent to 400 Chinese manufacturers, indicated the steepest fall in the volume of foreign orders since the survey began in 2004. In addition, orders from the West for Christmas products made by Chinese manufacturers fell off the cliff in that year. It was reported that as a result 23 million migrant workers were laid off in major manufacturing cities and had to go back to their home towns in the inland provinces (Cai and Chan, 2009; Wang, 2010b).

Such factors as decreasing exports and increasing unemployment as well as the loss of Chinese banks' foreign assets can be considered exogenous. And while they did affect China, they have caused a *slowdown* rather than a *meltdown* of the Chinese economy in terms of export growth, which in some respects remained booming. In the first three quarters of 2008 the country's domestic consumption, another engine of the economy, still grew by 22%, which was 6.1% higher year-on-year. This does not mean that China's endogenous economic sectors are perfectly healthy. As we will point out below, China has its own serious problems. Therefore the question of how to expand domestic demand has become of crucial importance to prevent the exogenous crisis from jeopardising China's real economy.

Figure 1: Breakdown of the 4Tn stimulus package

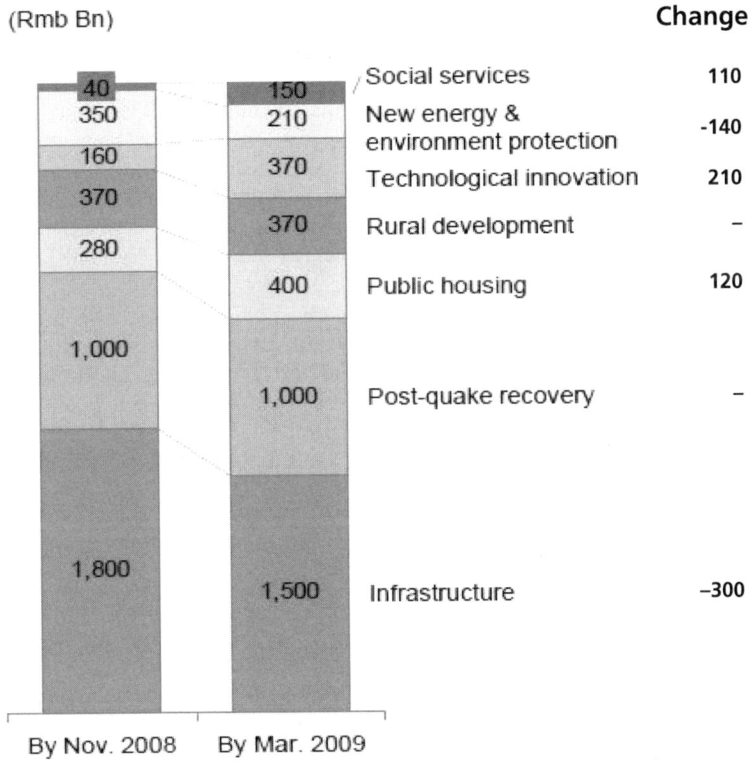

(Rmb Bn)			Change
40	150	Social services	110
350	210	New energy & environment protection	-140
160	370	Technological innovation	210
370	370	Rural development	–
280	400	Public housing	120
1,000	1,000	Post-quake recovery	–
1,800	1,500	Infrastructure	–300
By Nov. 2008	By Mar. 2009		

The Chinese response may be seen as a policy of extreme Keynesianism. In November 2008 the Chinese government launched a swift rollout of 4 trillion RMB (about US$ 586 billion) as a stimulus package to be spent in the following 2 years. This package was the largest (as a share of GDP) in the world and was equivalent to 13% of GDP in 2008. Its principal aim was to spur domestic demand, reduce domestic savings and increase consumption to make up for the fall in exports. Figure 1 above shows the overall composition of this massive scheme. With 1 500 billion RMB (37.5%) assigned to infrastructure, the real injection earmarked for projects related to infrastructure and construction amounted to about 2 900 billion RMB (74.5%). Both public housing and post-quake recovery were of use to land developers, while a total of 550 billion RMB was allocated to enhance China's social welfare net to help increase individuals' purchasing power in social services and rural development. The object of the monetary element of the stimulus plan has been to expand the banks' credit supply and increase existing loans. In January of 2009 new loans reached a record of 1.62 trillion Yuan. This figure increased to 4.59 trillion in March (see Zhang *et al.*, 2009). Seven months later the composition of the stimulus package changed significantly. This was in response to wide criticism levelled at spending too much on infrastructure and construction, which led the government to increase investment on social welfare. For example, 110 billion and 120 billion RMB went for social services and public housing, respectively. But heavy investment in infrastructure and construction is still the dominant feature of the package.

Figure 2: How is it financed?

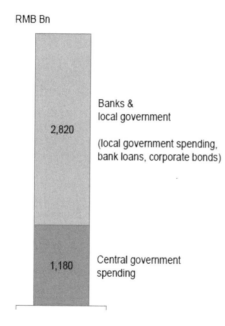

RMB Bn

2,820 — Banks & local government (local government spending, bank loans, corporate bonds)

1,180 — Central government spending

To be more specific, 1 000 billion RMB of the 4 trillion package, or roughly US$ 146.5 billion, was earmarked for recovery after the devastating earthquake that occurred on 12 May 2008 and killed 68 000 people. Some of the investment had already been announced before November 2008. The extra funds might amount to less than a third of the announced stimulus package, but the gross amount of the stimulus package is still huge and promotes market confidence domestically and internationally.

The stimulus spending was not only high, but it was also rapid. As Figure 2 above indicates, the package was not fully financed by the central government. About 30% of the total amount came from Beijing, while the rest was supposed to come from local governments and from lending by state-owned banks. The efficiency of the party-state was impressive. Within weeks local governments were meeting to compile lists of shovel-ready projects along guidelines set by the central government. Each provincial government announced its own parallel 'stimulus package' for two years, making the total budgets amount to 10 trillion RMB. By the end of April 2009, that is six months after the stimulus package was announced, about 57% of the total 4 trillion RMB budget (2.28 trillion RMB) was already allocated. Subsequently the central government asked its branches to spend 100 million RMB (about US$ 14.72 million) on large projects within 110 days. Such giant projects would be impossible under the conditions of a liberal-democratic political system, where state power is always under heavy periodic pressure to gain legitimacy and support from the electorate. The Chinese government, on the other hand, can mobilise resources across the nation and invest colossal amounts of money efficiently to carry out specific projects (e.g. the post-earthquake recovery) or support specific events (e.g. the sport programmes for the Olympics). Some commentators see this as evidence of the "strong state capacity" of the Chinese government.

Selectivity of crisis management

How, with what purpose and to whom was the heavy stimulus package distributed? We cannot offer a definite answer to this question because of the confidential nature of information of this kind, but we can formulate a few reasonable hypotheses. First, the greater part of the package was channelled into infrastructure projects as they can absorb the largest number of workers in a short period of time. Second, state-owned enterprises (SOEs) rather than private enterprises benefited most from the stimulus package; the party-state explicitly attempted to protect the interests of SOEs since functionally they represent the most important sector in China. Channelling money in this way is meant to prevent workers from becoming a socio-political factor in an aggressive challenge to the regime. In this sense the party-state is not significantly different from a typical capitalist state in the West. The very logic of state activity in China is to steer the economy and to manage the society in such a way that enterprises make profits and workers become submissive.

The heavy investment in infrastructure and construction is not specific to China. However, the need to absorb as many workers as possible is particularly strong in China, where people have become accustomed to a fast-growing economy. In order to insulate Chinese industry from the effects of the global downturn, the government's most urgent priorities were to safeguard living standards and to contain unemployment by means of state-led investment and the facilitation of credit. In this process even the textile industry, a labour-intensive but overgrown industry in China, became substantially subsidised.

The selective preferential treatment of SOEs needs more explanation. First, big infrastructure projects have been dominated by SOEs and preference for SOEs and infrastructure are just two sides of the same coin. Secondly, as far as other domains are concerned (for example, energy, high technology, ecology industry and manufacturing), Chinese state enterprises are no longer the small companies they used to be in the past. Instead, they now send shockwaves to the business world. In the *Global 500* list of the world's largest companies released by *Fortune* in July 2009, 37 Chinese firms made the list and they were all state-owned. In the list of 2010, three Chinese state-owned companies were listed among the top ten, while 6 American and 1 Australian company made up the remainder.

The reason for this can be found in China's reform of state-owned enterprises during the late 1990s called *zhuadafangxiao* (hold on to the big and let the small go). On the one hand, the 'let the small go' part soon turned into a chaotic wave of straightforward privatisation, often involving local governments and corrupt officials. On the other hand, after a series of restructuring efforts, the 'hold on to the big' part of the guideline generated several behemoths. This was somewhat similar to what had happened in Poland during the 1990s, when large SOEs were reorganised and upgraded under the scrutiny of a specific government department. But the difference was that the 'strategic and mainstay' Chinese enterprises were ultimately not privatised, but remained under the control of the government through the offices of the state-owned Assets Supervision and Administration Commission (SASAC), which represents the state in order to 'fulfil the duty as the investor' of the SOEs. By means of robust taxation and other profits from these aircraft-carrier-like state firms, the state gained more economic might to invest in its social welfare system. In other words, a stimulus package that selects state firms as a priority can be profitable in some cases, not to mention that those state enterprises have much stronger networks to lobby or bargain for higher budgets for themselves than private or foreign companies are able to do.

The stimulus package favours state enterprises not only for economic reasons but also for political ones. Chinese leaders believe it is much easier to control labour in state-enterprises than in private or foreign companies, because managers and workers do not care much about profits as long as the state invests enough money to keep their payroll and welfare going. It is therefore not surprising that in the past 60 years employees working in state entities have never launched a successful national protest in China. One factor is that up until the mid-1990s, and even during the Tiananmen Event workers in the SOEs were the 'privileged'. The other factors still in operation today that make a national strike impossible today is the lack of an independent union, such as Solidarity in Poland, and the promise of sustained welfare by the state. For both the Chinese economy and politics a national labour strike could be a disastrous event, incomparably more serious than the heated debates on the exchange-rate regime. This is why the party-state is more keenly interested in subsidising state enterprises as 'strategic economic domains' than in subsidising private enterprises.

The consequences of crisis management

As pointed out above, the beneficiaries of the stimulus package of both the central government and local governments are found overwhelmingly among state-owned and state-controlled enterprises. Be that as it may, the result was that expanded investments from the state began to have a discernible impact on the economy from the first quarter of 2009. At least in the short term this 'primacy of internal investment' strategy has achieved some positive effects. Three major economic indicators illustrate the strategy.

First, economic growth in terms of GDP remained robust in the past two years as China's economy expanded by 9.6% in 2008 and by 9.1% in 2009, by far the best performance in the G20 economies. Several prestigious investment banks estimated that the 4 trillion package contributed 2 to 3 GDP points to the growth, with Morgan Stanley and Citigroup estimating 2 points and Merrill Lynch estimating 3 points (Michael, 2009).

Second, China's exports have shown a strong recovery and as a result factories are reopening and employment is up. In the first four months of 2010 the total value of China's imports and exports rose by 42.7% year on year to US$ 855.99 billion, where the export value rose by 29.2% to US$ 436.05 billion. Actually, as a result of the export recovery Chinese factories in a few coastal cities have been struggling to find workers to help fill export orders despite exhaustive recruiting drives.

Third, the ratio of household consumption to GDP, the weak link of the Chinese economy, is not as high as expected, but it is rising rapidly. In 2009 it accounted for 52.5% of GDP growth, up from 46% in 2008. Household consumption showed a corresponding rate of increase over the same period, accounting for about 39% of GDP growth in 2009, compared with 33% in 2008 (Lo, 2010).

In sum, as the international financial crisis spread from developed countries to emerging economies, and as it spilled over from the financial sector to the real economy, China has not remained immune to the recession in the West, but neither has the exogenous financial crisis caused an endogenous economic meltdown and/or social turmoil in the country. In some respects, as Bobo Lo (2010) argued, the crisis has actually turned out to be a blessing in that it relieved the Chinese leaders' previous concern of an over-heating economy and encouraged a reorientation of production towards the domestic market.

Conditions for success

To get a full picture it is not enough to describe the set of selective rules employed by the state in its intervention into the economic crisis in China. What is also important is to examine the conditions which allowed the party-state to perform such a role with considerable success. Given the overwhelming importance of the role the party-state plays in the overall policy direction to be pursued, it is a pity that no serious debate has emerged in China to conceptualise the Chinese state in a manner acceptable to the international community of social science.

To begin with, the party-state of China differs significantly from both a 'totalitarian' state conventionally used in reference to Nazism, Fascism and Stalinism, and from a 'liberal-democratic' or a 'social-democratic' state in the Western sense. The Chinese party-state lies in between these two opposite poles and has some general characteristics, outlined below.

First, it has an extensively developed bureaucratic apparatus with heavy networks of consultation and influence over the society as a whole. This condition is possible only when a country reaches a considerable degree of economic and social modernisation.

Second, ambitious young people with recognised educational credentials both at home and abroad are recruited into the state bureaucracy. In other words, they are protected by state power to act fairly autonomously according to the rules of the state's activities. Insulated from external pressures, they are in a better position to pursue developmental goals than they would be if they were subject to external pressures.

Third, the system of governance by this kind of bureaucracy entails a considerable degree of organisational discipline, which regulates interactions. Although elements of corruption, factionalism and clientalism exist, the party-state still maintains a discipline of meritocracy, an effective ability to formulate and evaluate national policies of development, rules of objective testing and competition as well as an emphasis on public good over private interests, public deliberation and norms of general social welfare. Furthermore, the party-state is able to discipline private entrepreneurs as well as the workers.

Fourth, a considerable degree of cohesion has emerged among the power elites, particularly between those who steer the economy and public security, that is, between socio-economic technocrats and the military. These two power groups are united in the belief that national wealth and military power ought to be increased through a state-led process of modernisation. The internal cohesion makes it possible for the state apparatus to pursue economic policies consistently. Consequently, political dissidents are effectively shut out of decision-making processes.

A salient aspect of the Chinese party-state is that rather than striving to reach a compromise between government and enterprise, the state attempts, often forcefully, to induce enterprises to comply with its already established goals. The state uses various means to this end, among them financial inducement schemes as well as fiscal and tax benefits. The secret lies in the state's control of capital supply to the private sector. The state also uses such devices as loans, industrial subsidies and other legally stipulated means by which it reduces or exempts from duties, alleviates customs taxes and defers debt redemption.

In the prevailing order of things the state positions itself above the private sector. This position is deeply anchored in the Confucian norm of public service and has had an enormous influence on state policy over economic enterprises. While the state plays a large role in developing state-owned enterprises, it also wants to play an important role in the private sector, which it tries to discipline, albeit not in the traditional way but in a capitalist way. It is therefore not accurate to describe the relations between the government and economic enterprises as symbiotic, as is often done in the case of Japanese capitalism. Rather, the concept of a 'disciplinary' regime (Amsden, 1989) is more applicable. The state disciplines not only the workers but also the entrepreneurs. We may call this type of regime a bureaucratic authoritarian state with a built-in emphasis on economic growth.

However, this description involves idealisation. The fact is that although the Chinese state turns out to be highly successful in accelerating economic growth, it is undeniable that it also suffers from serious limitations and contradictions. This leads us to ask whether the Chinese ruling elite are aware of the possibility that the Chinese pattern of crisis management described above could store up problems over the long term, such as large amounts of bad loans. We would like to tease out how such a scenario would be likely to impact on the future of China, particularly with regards to democratisation.

Political elite: consensus on stability

In China as in other countries the paramount concern of the government is regime longevity. Though political factions exist and matter, a consensus among most Chinese leaders since the reform-and-opening-up policy of 1978 has been to promote stable and rapid economic growth at all cost as the key to maintaining regime legitimacy. Any project believed to jeopardise economic growth is to be postponed, suspended or even abandoned.

Chinese leaders believe that the recipe for successful economic transformation is the absence of political reform. Social and political unrest in Central and Southern Europe since 2008, along with the troubles experienced by America's economy and the Congress stalemate, have only re-confirmed the belief in the superiority of the resilience of Chinese authoritarianism over Western liberal capitalism. In fact, both because of China's success relative to other leading economies and because of the country's pivotal importance in any global recovery, the diplomatic pressure from core democracies, especially the US, to democratise China has been largely neutralised.

The Chinese leaders are gaining even *more* confidence in the authoritarian model when they look at their domestic 'achievements'. Perhaps not ideologically, but in practice they have so far been relatively successful in boosting the economy and maintaining stability. No other political crises anywhere approaching the scale of the Tiananmen protests in 1989 have taken place since then, while the mass upheavals of the Falungong Movement in 1998, the turmoil in Tibet in 2008 and the Xinjiang unrest in 2009 were eventually all managed and did not deteriorate into national political disasters.

The conclusions the Chinese leaders drew from these experiences made them chose to consolidate rather than to relax the Party's authority. Indeed, since the global downturn in 2008 Chinese leaders have been much more engaged in maintaining social stability than in delivering democracy. The so-called 'Leading group to maintain social stability', a powerful Party organ that supervises the police, the judiciary and other related branches, has been heavily funded in recent years. A research team at the prestigious Tsinghua University in Beijing (Sun *et al.*, 2010) reported that for the first time ever at the annual session of the National People's Congress (NPC) in March 2009 the state revealed its budget to maintain public security (and social stability). The expected expenditure totallled 514 billion RMB (US$ 72 billion) in 2010, up by 8.9% from 2009. This is almost equal to the central government's 518.6 billion RMB budget for defence. And the 8.9% growth in spending on public security is higher than the 7.5% increase in the defence budget.

Although tough on political dissent and separatist movements, the Chinese party-state has taken a surprisingly lax policy line towards the masses. Higher living standards, access to consumer goods and the huge expansion in public access to the media (as long as it does not cross certain political lines) proved to be effective. Jeffrey Wasserstrom, a veteran of China studies at the University of California, Irvine, argues that it is more helpful to think of China in terms of Aldous Huxley's Brave New World than George Orwell's 1984. "Orwell emphasizes the role of fear in keeping people in line, while Huxley pays more attention to how needs and desires are created, manipulated and satisfied" (Wasserstrom, 2010). This also falls squarely within the Chinese tradition of benevolent autocracy, and since the economic crisis left China relatively unscathed, the state has ample money to continue its paternalism.

Economic elite: Seeking interests inside the system

Despite pessimism about the Chinese political elite, the global business community and a large number of political scientists share the optimistic view that encouraging the private sector will eventually bring about a democratic transition in China. The prospect, however, seems dim. Based on national surveys and in-depth interviews, numerous empirical studies have demonstrated that members of China's business elites show few signs of becoming the bearers of democracy or civil society (Pearson, 1997; Dickson, 2003). Rather, they prefer to use adaptive informal networks such as personal ties to influential officials.

Will their honeymoon end during the economic downturn? As mentioned above, the 4 trillion RMB stimulus package favours state-owned enterprises. While this favouritism is certainly not a new phenomenon, it still raises a lot of concerns. For example, over 70% of middle- and upper-level managers surveyed by the *China Economic Magazine* in April 2009 expressed the view that the stimulus plan was repressing the private sector. Their anxieties are not unfounded because the state-led companies that received massive stimulus-related loans now have the means to buy private enterprises. For example, in September 2009 a consortium led by the state-owned China National Oils, Foodstuffs and Cereals Group, the country's largest importer and exporter of food, grabbed 20 per cent of Mengniu Dairy, China's largest milk producer, making the state the single largest shareholder. The state's expansion is even more robust in energy industries. Given these cases, it is widely believed that the economic crisis exacerbated a phenomenon known as *guojinmintui* – the state advances as the private sector recedes. Some media even use a stronger tone about this process.

Political leaders repeatedly deny that the government is implementing a policy of re-nationalising parts of the economy and most analysts agree there is no formal policy to support *guojinmintui*. But still, private entrepreneurs and their representatives express their anxiety and anger via business groups, parliament and other adversarial political bodies such as the Chinese People's Political Consultative Conference (CPPCC). They do not, of course, dare to criticise the party-state; instead their complaints are directed against the colossal Central Enterprises, that is, the 136 large-scale SOEs controlled directly by the central government. Since government officials and the SOE tycoons usually compare giant state corporations to 'the eldest son of the People's Republic', private entrepreneurs call themselves the 'step-children' or 'servant girls' of the state. This can be viewed as increasing the strength of the lobbying forces among private owners (Kennedy, 2005).

On the one hand, a realistic businessman must be aware that complaining is one thing, but acting smart is another. One way to gain access to bigger deals and finance has been for private firms to hook up with the state-owned firms' patronage system, because state-owned firms not only have the upper hand in bidding for stimulus-related projects, but they also hold the power to decide which businesses to select for supplies and sub-contracting jobs, particularly in the massive infrastructure construction projects. It was reported that this strategy was acknowledged and even encouraged by the Chinese political leadership. For instance, the Chinese Vice-Premier Zhang Dejiang suggested during the meeting of the National People's Congress on 5 March 2010 that private businesses should lean on their state-owned 'brothers' for support in time of crisis. At the same occasion he advised private businesses that "if you want to grow big, you first need to attract the attention of state-owned firms who are stronger and better funded... Once you have clinched on to the big brothers, lean on them, co-operate with them and gain opportunities to upgrade your own business, technology and management" (Liu *et al.*, 2009).

On the other hand, the state also responds. For example, in May 2010 the Chinese central government released a document called 'Several opinions on encouraging and guiding the healthy development of private investment'. This document contains 36 clauses, a follow-up to the government's policy released five years earlier, known as '36 clauses for the non-state-owned economy'. Some policy watchers believe that these so-called 'new 36 clauses' are meant to address the complaints of private entrepreneurs by encouraging further liberalisation of transportation, telecommunications, energy and enabling access to large areas of a specific industry. In addition, local governments have a strong motivation to maintain a 'local growth coalition'; they allow private capital access to the financial pipeline of the state, because they need investment from private owners.

In sum, the global economic crisis has to a large extent made private entrepreneurs seek more patronage from state officials. The entrepreneurs are pragmatic and creative, but they are not budding democrats. As long as most entrepreneurs still think the system generally works for them (via personal or institutional conduits), there seems little chance they will support democratisation.

Cultural elite: whether democracy is good is debatable

At the same time the global economic crisis damaged the appeal of democracy itself among the Chinese cultural elite. This is evident from the increased influence of 'new leftists' and from the conservative attitudes shown by Chinese intellectuals. In the 1980s almost all independent intellectuals identified themselves as 'liberals', while intellectual dissidents were considered to be the 'seeds of democracy' (Goldman, 1995). The intellectual climate changed dramatically when the new left came onto the scene. This group of scholars emerged in the 1990s in response to the fall of the Soviet Union, the harsh neoliberal shock therapy imposed upon Eastern Europe, the massive marketisation of SOEs as well as the dismantling of social welfare in China initiated in 1993. The new leftists and their opponents who identify themselves as liberals engage in debate on almost all issues, including democracy, and have divided the Chinese intelligentsia into two basic camps.

But in China the labels 'new left' and 'liberal' produce somewhat different associations in the popular mind to those in the West. The new left is striving mainly for a 'Chinese alternative' consisting of a state-interventionist economy and nationalism based on Chinese tradition, while the liberals are keen to promote private property and individual freedom. Both camps generally embrace 'economic and political democracy', but they are in sharp disagreement over how and when to democratise China. Liberals argue that it is only through democracy and direct and open elections that China could overcome its problems with corruption and distributive inefficiency. The Chinese leftists by contrast criticise (liberal) democracy for having deteriorated into a 'money game' in developed countries and a 'smoke grenade' in the developing economies, where it has often given rise to domestic unrest and/or populism, or activated regional conflict or civil war. They also argue that political reform in China should not come through a new political system in which people choose their leaders in free elections. They consider it more important to push party leaders to stay in touch with the people and provide a popular check on corruption by means of 'mass democracy' or 'participatory democracy'. "The people express their will and the government becomes responsive to it. That is what democracy is", said Wang Shaoguang, a political scientist at Hong Kong Chinese University and a leading scholar of the new left Chinese intellectuals (Wang, 2008).

It is widely believed that the new left's ideas resonate primarily with young people and nationalists, and are sometimes supported by the party-state, especially under the current slogan of the Chinese administration to build 'a harmonious society' and also since the launch of a movement to resist 'universal values', a euphemism for human rights, legal systems and democracy in China. The liberals' discursive power has been steadily declining. At the same time the new leftists enjoy greater global influence than do liberals in international intellectual circles. This is partly because almost all members of the Chinese new left have been either educated at prestigious Western universities or were invited there as visiting scholars. They are therefore usually theoretically inspired by – and are better connected with – their 'mentors' in Western new leftist circles. In addition, they often publish in international journals and some even serve on the editorial boards of top English language journals. Most Chinese liberals, on the other hand, have been educated in China and publish mainly in Chinese. To make things even odder, the new leftists are not party intellectuals. Most work at prestigious universities in mainland China, Hong Kong or even Western institutions, while several leading 'liberals' used to be or still are members of government/party organs or think-tanks. This contributes to the rather bizarre situation in which Western-educated intellectuals are more likely to oppose Western-style democracy – although 'oppose' might be too strong a term since new leftists usually prefer to identify their stance with the expression 'not to oppose, but to rethink' (Mierzejewski, 2009).

The Great Recession has apparently allowed the Chinese new left to enjoy more discursive power. Several leading new leftists, echoed by their even more influential Western mentors, vowed to construct a new authoritarian 'political civilisation', one superior to (liberal) democracy as the global financial crisis has discredited laissez-faire Anglo-Saxon capitalism and strengthened the case for greater state control. These arguments find resonance with the economic package and the ideological assertions of the Chinese party-state.

Neither the liberals nor the new left constitutes a clearly defined intellectual circle, and a large number of intellectuals actually do not identify themselves with either of these two camps. But the majority of those with clear labels choose a pro-meritocracy rather than pro-democracy stance for economic and political – and not for intellectual – reasons. Since the 1990s talented intellectuals, scientists and technocrats have been lured increasingly into the existing system as 'interest shareholders' with offers of abundant government funding, affluent living conditions and prestigious political/academic titles. To some extent this is what happened in Hungary during the reformist communist era, when the Party recruited technocrats to key positions and when intellectuals became a class on the road to power (Szelényi and Konrad, 1979). These are the same cultural elite who were sympathisers or even radical activists in the democratic movements of the 1980s, but who are now no longer involved in any radical effort to democratise China, even if they have still not completely lost their faith in democracy.

The 'crisis of crisis management' as a new beginning?

The political consequences of the socio-economic intervention by the state in response to the crisis need to be examined more carefully. If crisis management works, the crisis might be diminished or suspended; if it fails a 'crisis of crisis management' is likely to occur and the original crisis might then be aggravated. If the crisis is blamed on the regime itself, a legitimacy crisis may emerge. The economic crisis might then be transformed into a political issue and various reform-minded elites and social groups might start to mobilise for action.

We argued above that the crisis management adopted by the Chinese government has worked well so far. Yet another interpretation is possible. One may be inclined to view China's stimulus package as one that does not solve anything in the long term, but somehow exacerbates the already existing economic, social and political problems. In this context two questions deserve attention. First, what kind of political consequences can be anticipated if the current crisis management fails? Second, and conversely, what new possibilities could emerge if the crisis management continues to be successful and as a consequence the urban middle class along with the working class increase not only in numbers, but also as potential voices of opposition? The latter option requires us to take a bottom-up perspective rather than the mainstream view of the ruling elite.

Many experts on China closely monitor the frequent eruptions of public protest throughout the country over various issues, which involve complaints related to working conditions, local government corruption, land seizures and so on. For instance, since late May 2010 a multitude of serious strikes have taken place at several Honda assembly plants in the Pearl River Delta cities of Foshan and Zhongshan. "Chinese workers challenge Beijing's authority," cried *The Wall Street Journal* headline on 13 June 2010. The headline reflects the common perception of the international community in which millions of Chinese migrant workers could become a powerful social and political power if they joined forces to protest against working conditions, low wages and possibly other sources of grievance.

Not only the working class but other social classes have been expected by social scientists to become the potential actors building a civil society in China. Sympathetic attention has been drawn to the rising number of new homeowners in cities, who have formed self-managed committees to organise and pursue their interests and to resist the unfair treatment by local governments and government-linked property developers. These middle-class citizens engaged in collective assemblies and movements are seen to represent a real, if tentative, manifestation of civil society.

However, it is an open question how to interpret the meaning of these rapidly increasing collective manifestations. It may be too hasty to see this political reawakening as a demand for a liberal democratic change in the Western sense. Instead, participants in these activities seem to focus more on issues related directly to their economic interests, property rights and social justice. In this sense the conflicts may be more conflicts of interests than class or identity conflicts.

Therefore, the foremost question is what is new in those recent occurrences of collective movements? At a glance two things are new. First, the striking workers belong to the younger so-called '80s and 90s generation'. Second, in the Honda plant in Zhongshan workers formed a factory council, which a *New York Times* article characterised as a "sophisticated, democratic organization", demanding the right to form a trade union separate from the government-endorsed one. These two characteristics can be viewed as a political awakening of young Chinese migrant workers (Pei, 2010).

But a new puzzle emerges. A series of suicide attempts by migrant workers shocked China: 16 young workers tried to kill themselves (resulting in 12 deaths) in just the first five months of 2010 (three in the last ten days of May) in a single giant factory complex of Foxconn in Shenzhen, the world's largest contract electronics manufacturer for major brand names such as Apple, Dell and Toshiba.

Both the suicides and the strike events led to a rise in workers' salaries. At Foxconn the company hastened to introduce damage-control measures by offering raises of about 25 percent to workers. In Honda the strikes ended after three weeks with the workers winning 10 to 30 percent raises. In addition, the Chinese government put the motion of 'collective bargaining over payment' on its urgent agenda and started to modify its 'minimum downpayment requirements' by asking companies to raise salaries in direct proportion to the increase of their profits. Raising salaries, if truly implemented, can be an achievement of huge significance both economically and politically. Economically speaking, it has been widely accepted that the secret of the 'Chinese magic' relies on cheap labour, while economists extol this model as 'comparative advantage' (Lin and Chang, 2009). A critical view is that the increase of the 'lowest wage standard' is less than 40% of local average pay (*South China Moring Post*, 2010). Yet Steven N.S. Cheung, a provocative right-wing economist in Hong Kong, warns that "collective bargaining" will cause more strikes and is a bad idea for the Chinese economy (Cheung, 2010).

As in many other countries, competing views on democracy and its future prospects also emerged in China, as the debate between the new left and the liberals indicated. While there is no one dominant official view on the subject, mainstream opinion tends to see the future of China from the perspective of the ruling elites in politics, business and culture. Seen from that angle, there is no apparent reason to launch a reform toward democracy from the top, since the party-state is capable of managing crises and regulating and controlling social unrest effectively, while ordinary people want to keep social stability and economic growth and can conceive of no reasonable alternative to the current regime. The confidence generated by the so far successful crisis management reinforced this dominant mentality, leading to the idea of a consolidated bureaucratic-authoritarian state with an organic commitment to economic growth as a new brand of political regime.

The feasibility and viability of this view hinges to a very great extent on whether the Chinese economy will continue to grow. Ruchir Sharma, head of the Emerging Markets Branch at Morgan Stanley, likened China's possible fall below the 8 percent official growth target to the storyline of the Hollywood thriller *Speed* in which a bomb on a bus was set to detonate if the vehicle slowed to below 50 miles an hour. "In China, the bomb would be triggered by the slump in job creation and explode in the form of labor unrest" (Sharma, 2010).

Many observers worry that despite China's dealing well with the crisis so far, an economic recession has merely been delayed. From the point of view of structural reform, inherent problems such as weak domestic demand for consumer goods have not been resolved but have grown worse. As a recipe the Beijing government wants to gradually downsize its huge stimulus package, but that is not as easy as its launch was on 5 July 2010. On that occasion Premier Wen Jiabao said Chinese economic policies were set to "face increasing dilemmas", since China cannot hold back steps to "solve current significant and urgent problems", while at the same time "laying foundations for a stable and relatively fast economic growth in and beyond 2011" (Liu *et.al.*, 2010). There is no easy way out of this dilemma.

Conclusions

Many observers believe that if the booming Chinese economy stopped flourishing, someday radical movements would emerge and challenge the authority of the party-state. A revolutionary change would then take place in response to public demands for social justice and equality. In our opinion, however, it not certain that under such circumstances the possible rupture and antagonism would lead to the institutionalising of democracy. Historical experience shows that when threatened by radical movements from below, the middle class tends to support authoritarian counter-movements, thus contributing to political polarisation.

On the other hand, it is an open question whether or not the basic assumption of modernisation theory could be applied to China – and, if it can, to what extent. To be sure, the expectation that rapid economic progress may help liberalise the political system still remains to be tested in China. Though the record of political progress lags behind expectations, it is important to remember that the party-state of China is not a fixed system closed to changing environments, but has evolved in a specific way, gradually enlarging the avenues of political consultation and participation rights. If we adopt a broader understanding of democracy rather than the narrow conception based only on electoral competition, we can perhaps better understand the political developments that have taken place over the past several decades in China.

What is suggested here is that it will not be piecemeal change from the top but increasing demands for change from the bottom that might result in further political evolution. There is ample evidence to demonstrate that, contrary to the mainstream view of the ruling elites, the 'grassroots segment' of the Chinese middle class lacks trust in public authorities and is far more disillusioned than the mainstream segment with the performance of the party-state of China as far as social justice and fairness are concerned (Han, 2009, 2010). Likewise, the grassroots segment is far more actively engaged in civil initiatives of various kinds and is supportive of democratic change in China. This amounts to saying that the potential for democratic change is developing from the bottom up, although it is not clear when and how such a change might eventually come about.

As O'Donnell and Schmitter (1986) argued, the landscape of democratic transition is shaped significantly by the relationships among political elites, particularly the hard-liners and the soft-liners within the ruling bloc as well as the radicals and moderates within the opposition camp. The best available option is democratic transition in terms of negotiation between the reform-oriented soft-liners of the ruling bloc and the reform-oriented moderates of the opposition camp. This scenario may become a more realistic proposition when increasing numbers of the middle class and the working class start favouring a negotiated transition to democracy rather than war-like violent confrontation. One may expect that China will eventually follow its own path of evolution along this way.

Coinciding with the title of the movie mentioned at the beginning of this chapter, the year 2012 will be important for China as the Party's 18th National Congress will be held then and a new generation of Chinese leaders will come to power. But the drift of mainstream thinking can perhaps already be gleaned from the proclamations made by Xi Jinping, the country's current Vice-President, who is expected to become the next General Secretary of CCP in 2012, and in 2013 possibly also the next President of China. During his visit to Mexico on 16 February 2009 Xi proudly stated that China had already made a significant contribution towards overcoming the financial crisis of the world by retaining its role as an engine of the global economy. He is reported to have added: "… there are a few foreigners, with full bellies, who have nothing better to do than try point fingers at our country… China does not export revolution, hunger, poverty, nor does China cause you any headaches. So, just what else do you want?"

The phrase "having a full stomach and nothing better to do" is meant to insult cynical troublemakers. Though Xi's speech was quickly deleted from websites and news reports by censors inside China, some observers still feel anxious about this inflammatory 'extemporaneous address'. As an alternative, one might be tempted to think that a low-level performance or even a collapse of the Chinese economy might provide a better chance for democratic change. Here we disagree. Although such a scenario might trigger a collective effort towards democratisation, it might also instigate a civil war. The question thus is not *whether* China will become democratic but *under what conditions*, and this requires further sober analysis and reflection.

Sources

Amsden, A. (1989). *Asia's next giant: South Korea and late industrialization*. Oxford: Oxford University Press.

Cai, F. and Chan, K. (2009). The global economic crisis and unemployment in China. *Eurasian Geography and Economics*. 50(5):513–531.

Chan, E. (2009). China's stimulus package and its effect on China's SOEs: bad for the economy and bad for the prospect of democracy. Avalaible on-line at: http://www. chinaelectionsblog.net

Dickson, B. (2003). *Red capitalists in China: The party, private entrepreneurs, and prospects for political change*. Cambridge: Cambridge University Press.

Gilley, B. (2004). *China's democratic future: how it will happen and where it will it will lead?* New York: Columbia University Press.

Habermas, J. (1973). *Legitimation crisis.* Boston: Beacon Press.

Han, S-Jin (2009). The dynamics of the middle class politics in Korea: why and how do the middling grassroots differ from the propertied mainstream? *Korean Journal of Sociology.* 43(3): 1-19.

Han, S-J. (2010a). The grassroots identity of the middle class and participation in citizen initiatives, China and South Korea. In Cheng Li (ed.) *China's emerging middle class: beyond economic transformation.* Washington DC: Brookings Institution Press (forthcoming).

Han, S-J. (2010b). Redefining second modernity for East Asia: a critical assessment. *British Journal of Sociology.* 61(3): 465-489.

Kennedy, S. (2005). *The business of lobbying in China.* Cambridge: Harvard University Press.

Lee, J. (2009). Global financial crisis makes it more difficult for China to pursue political reform. *Executive Highlights.* 29 June. 859.

Lin, J. and Chang, H. (2009). Should industrial policy in developing countries conform to comparative advantage or defy it? A debate between Justin Lin and Ha-Joon Chang. *Development Policy Review.* 27(5): 483-502

Liu Li, Ruan, V. and Batson, A. (2010). China's economic policies face dilemmas, says Premier Wen. *The Wall Street Journal.* 5 July.

Liu, Z. et al. (2009). Private business sidelined by China's stimulus. *Economic Observer* (Jingji Guancha Bao). 16 March. 409.

Lo, B. (2010). China and the global financial crisis. Available on-line at: www.cer.org.uk/pdf/essay_974.pdf

Lubman, S. (2010). Are strikes the beginning of a new challenge? Available on-line at: http://blogs.wsj.com/chinarealtime/2010/06/25/stanley-lubman-are-strikes-the-beginning-of-a-new-challenge/

Michael, D. (2009). China's stimulus package: opportunities and roadblocks. A report of Boston Consulting Group.

O'Donnell, G. and Schmitter, P. (1986). *Transitions from Authoritarian Rules: Tentative Conclusions about Uncertain Democracies.* Baltimore: Johns Hopkins University Press.

Offe, C. (1984). *Contradictions of the welfare state,* Cambridge: MIT Press.

Offe, C. (2006). *Strukturprobleme des kapitalistischen Staates,* Frankfurt: Campus Verlag.

Pearson, M. (1997). *China's new business elite: the political consequences of economic reform.* Berkeley: University of California Press.

Pei, M. (2006). *China's trapped transition: limits of developmental autocracy.* Cambridge: Harvard University Press.

Pei, M. (2010). China's political awakening? The diplomat. Available on-line at: http://the-diplomat.com/ 2010/07/14/china

Read, B. (2003). Democratising the neighbourhood? New private housing and homeowner self-organisation in urban China. The China Journal. 49(1): 39-59.

Sharma, R. (2010). The post-China world, *Newsweek,* June 20.

Shih, V. (2009). *Factions and finance in China: elite conflict and inflation.* Cambridge: Cambridge University Press.

South China Morning Post. (2010). Don't be so panicked about raising wage. 9 June.

Sun, L. (2009). The logic of financial crisis and its social consequences. *The Chinese Journal of Sociology.* 2: 1-15.

Sun, L. et al. (2010). New thinking on stability maintenance: long-term social stability via institutionalized expression of interests. *South Weekly.* 14 April.

Tsai. K. (2007). *Capitalism without democracy: the private sector in contemporary China.* N.Y.: Cornell University Press.

Tsou, T. (1995). Chinese politics at the top: factionalism or informal politics? Balance-of- power politics or a game to win all? *The China Journal.* (34): 95-156.

Wang, K. (2010a). A China paradox: migrant labour shortages amidst rural labour supply abundance. Available on-line at: Faculty.washington.edu/kwchan/Chan_paradox_shortages_paper.pdf

Wang, M. (2010b). Impact of the global economic crisis on China's migrant workers: a survey of 2,700 in 2009. *Eurasian Geography and Economics.* 51 (2):18-235.

Wasserstrom, J. (2010). *China in the 21st century: what everyone needs to know.* Oxford: Oxford University Press.

Wong, C. (2000). Central-local relations revisited: the 1994 tax-sharing reform and public expenditure management in China. *China Perspectives.* 31: 20-41.

Zhang, Z. et al. (2009). Handling the global financial crisis: Chinese strategy and policy response. Available on-line at: www. unpan1.un.org/intradoc/groups/public/documents/.../unpan038696.pdf

PART IV
Towards a new global configuration

The Great Recession revealed the uncomfortable truth that both our individual and collective lives depend increasingly on factors beyond our control. This might be a trivial truth in academic circles, but for the wider public it has been a rather unpleasant revelation. This painful lesson did not spare policy makers either. Both at the global and regional (EU) level they have come to realise that the best they can do is to respond to the damage that has already been done. These defensive and reactive policies, which were implemented to limit the disastrous effects of the crisis, placed on the agenda the question of the accountability of the global players both at the nation-state level and within transnational financial and industrial corporations. The other and perhaps more important question that emerged has been how to maintain the stability of the global financial and economic markets, which cannot be achieved without commonly agreed upon and globally binding rules of the game.

But such globally binding rules – rules that would temper the micro-rationalities of the individual profit-seekers, which in turn affect the stability of the whole global market – place on the agenda the problem of power. Who is to set up the rules? Who would execute them? Who could bring to book the violators of the rules, and how? In short, if we are to learn from the Great Recession, then the problem of the elevation of legitimate power from the level of nation-state to the global level must be addressed seriously; what we have already learnt is that the 'invisible hand' of the market at the global level can and has led our world into trouble.

The idea that we are back to 'business as usual' is dangerously short-sighted: if we do not wish to be driven by the blind forces of globalisation, the world needs democratic control. And this is probably the biggest challenge we face in 21st century.

The Great Recession and its potential impact on popular culture in liberal democracies

Pierre du Toit

Introduction

The global political, economic and military dominance of the well-established democracies of Western Europe, North America and the Pacific Rim emerged from the aftermath of World War II, and became even more deeply entrenched after the end of the Cold War, symbolised by the fall of the Berlin Wall. States located in these regions have democratic regimes and high-technology capitalist economies. They boast affluent societies and they are inclined to support social values that are expressly liberal. They also engage in high levels of trade with one another and are inclined to be peaceful. This peace is both domestic, in the sense that these states tend to have fewer civil wars and, most strikingly, they rarely engage in hostilities with one another. And although they have been known to go to war against non-democratic countries, they have done so with apparent reluctance. These countries therefore form a notable 'liberal democratic zone of peace' and coalesce into a distinctly recognisable cluster of affluence and stability in the global landscape. Their distinctiveness is underscored by a dense diplomatic engagement with one another, bilateral and multilateral economic co-operation, military co-ordination in alliances such as NATO, and regional integration, the epitome of which is said to be found in the European Union. This zone of peace is continually shifting, as new countries are drawn formally or informally into the fold, and others drop out.

Is this admirable and enviable enclave of peaceful and prosperous democracies and the popular culture in which they are embedded under threat from the recent global financial crisis?

The basic correlation

The existence of what is termed the liberal democratic peace has been confirmed by many studies. B.M. Russett (1993), for example, showed there were no wars between democracies between 1946 and 1986; and R.J Rummel (1997), drawing on a data set from 1900 to 1987, found a correlation between democracy and domestic peace. Other studies, covering different time periods, have reached the same general conclusion.

But the democratic peace proposition is not without its critics. In most studies, according to Azar Gat (2006), the correlation between democracy and peace becomes more blurred the further back in time the measurement is applied. This is in part because not many states complied with contemporary benchmark definitions of democracy. What was considered democratic one hundred years ago hardly qualifies as such in this century. Troublesome cases include pre-Civil War USA, for example: was the USA liberal, given its extensive slave economy? And what about the many cases that had less than universal franchise, such as Britain at the start of the twentieth century? Not to mention Germany just before the First World War, with its universal male franchise, rule of law, a constitutional monarchy but with an executive responsible to the monarch instead of to parliament? Should those features have qualified Germany as a democracy *at that time*, the First World War would have to be seen as a glaring, even fatal, exception to the democratic peace proposition. If one goes back even further, the ancient Greek democracies fail entirely with their limited citizenship criteria.

The second criticism against the democratic peace proposition is that it is spurious. A neo-realist interpretation claims military and economic interests discourage war between democracies, meaning it is not so much the democratic nature of the countries involved that matters but rather the fact that they work together in military alliances, such as NATO, and in regional economic organisations, such as the EU. Yet another critical interpretation holds that affluent peaceful democracies are grouped into a cluster in which the USA acts as a dominant force that more or less settles the terms of engagement for other democracies both among their own ranks and in their engagements with non-democracies.

The explanation

Given these contradictory views, the proponents of the democratic peace thesis are compelled to find persuasive reasons to show what it is about democracy that inhibits war and facilitates peace. So far three distinct answers have emerged.

The first argument is structural and points to the constraining impact that democratic institutions have on the exercise of public violence. Reaching formal decisions about going to war in democracies is more often than not a complicated time-consuming and protracted affair. Institutional constraints such as special legislative majorities, separation of powers, human rights charters and concerns with public finance can all slow down the process of deciding to go to war, or even prevent such decisions from being taken at all.

More fundamentally, democracies may be constrained by domestic public opinion. Popular support for war has to be obtained and the cost-benefit calculation in favour of war may not be forthcoming. Citizens have to weigh up the obvious costs of war in the form of destruction of infrastructure, casualties and deaths, against the less obvious benefits of material gains or intangible betterment. These calculations have varied hugely through various eras. In times when the traditional benefits in the form of loot, plunder, booty and land were attainable, popular support for war was indeed to be found in democracies. Modern ideologies of nationalism and imperialism have added an element of intangible reward to victory in war, and even as recently as a century ago public outbursts of jingoism accompanied the declaration of war (Gat, 2006). During the course of the twentieth century, however, the ever more effective technologies of war, culminating in nuclear weapons, raised the prospective costs of war to new levels. The structural inhibitions on war present in democratic regimes are therefore supported by an interest-based calculation in which the benefits of peace are likely to outweigh those of war. With nuclear war that delivers mutually assured destruction, even the most basic attraction that war could hold, the prospect of winning, becomes untenable.

The second explanation of the liberal democratic zone of peace centres on civic and political culture. The explanatory argument does not rule out confrontational policies on the part of democracies; it merely maintains that such policies are unlikely. If enfranchised majorities do find reasons to engage in international conflict, they are free and able to do so. Similarly, as Rummel (1997) noted, if resentful majorities want to act violently against despised minorities, they have democratic structures available to them to vote into power leaders with the appropriate mandate. The point is that durable peace requires that the citizens of democracies themselves be disposed to amicable relations with fellow citizens and neighbouring states.

The values, attitudes and beliefs broadly defined as a *liberal political culture* are what is widely considered to be required for such a peaceful disposition. Beliefs about the essential dignity of humans and the concomitant rights to life, liberty and equality are taken to be the bedrock from which the attitudes of trust and tolerance emerge. The additional belief in the inherent reasonableness of humans, and the belief in their capacity for and preference for rational calculation over emotional and impulsive decision-making serves as the anchor for the liberal conviction about the superiority of bargaining, negotiation and compromise in the resolution of conflicts. These structural and cultural factors can serve as mutually reinforcing forces of moderation. Institutions can shape cultural dispositions, and cultural values can also impact on the choice of structures and can shape how they function.

The third explanation for the correlation between democracy and peace is based on the impact of modernity in general and affluence in particular. Azar Gat (2006) asks what it is *about* modern liberal societies that makes them so loath to engage in war. He finds the pacifying effect of modernity to lie in affluence, and in the particular way in which affluence has been acquired in modern high-technology urban capitalist societies. Capitalist modernity, according to Gat, deeply affected the cost-benefit calculation in favour of peace and away from war. Modern industrial technology, as applied to the weapons of war, greatly increased the destructive effects of such confrontations, whether to maim or to kill, as both World Wars have shown. Modern communications have further amplified the horrors of war by bringing them into many civilian homes, thus shaping popular culture.

At the other end of the cost-benefit calculation, capitalist modernity has greatly increased the rewards of peace. Ever expanding trade and commerce within and between societies increased mutual prosperity between trading partners. Modern technology has been able to convert such wealth into a positive-sum exchange for entire regions, such as Europe after the Second World War, tangibly experienced by entire societies and reflected in higher life expectancy and improved living and working conditions. Trading with an opponent, rather than trying to conquer him, has become a far more attractive and potentially more lucrative enterprise.

Capitalist modernity also impacted on popular culture and values. Modernity has eroded many traditional values and few have been affected more than those associated with the ethos of the warrior elite (Gat, 2006). As Martin van Creveld (1991, 2008) explained, in the culture of war achievement in battle is taken as an expression of some of the very finest of human qualities: bravery, unconditional altruism, loyalty to comrades, the capacity to endure hardship, as well as a display of discipline and valour. In this glorified view war represents a test of both metal and mettle, where warriors have to measure up to the most acute conditions of danger, risk and uncertainty. Those who excel in this field are deserving of respect, honour and medals. In the extreme expression of this culture war is seen as an end in itself, rather than as a means to an end, and the end is to achieve and express these very qualities regardless of the actual outcome, be that victory or defeat.

The steady rise of liberal values in the form of the human rights doctrine where life, liberty, equality and human dignity are seen as supreme and incontestable claims that individuals can bring against state and society has, according to Gat, contributed significantly to the decline in the social standing of those who excel in the kind of public violence sanctioned by war. Most crucial has been the impact of the right to life, which represents the idea that a person is entitled to devote himself/herself to the pursuit of liberty, prosperity and the pursuit of happiness. This has made societies more risk averse and less willing to submit to military discipline with its drudgery, discomfort, danger and the ever present risk of having to make the ultimate sacrifice of one's own life.

What made these rights so compellingly attractive is that in the late stage of capitalist modernity the prospect of a life that could be enjoyed, rather than just be endured, became a realistic prospect for entire societies. The wealth-generating capacities of capitalist market economies driven by high technology and global economies have created mass societies in which a high-consumption materialistic consumer culture has thrived. People could now become prosperous without having to do so at the expense of others.

The social and physical context in which this modern consumer-oriented lifestyle was achieved and has been maintained also contributed to undermining the values that legitimise the exercise of public violence. This context is one of urban and suburban populations working in high-technology occupations within the industrial production sector or increasingly in the service sector of the economy, with fewer and fewer found in agriculture or in primary production such as mining. Everywhere, even in the last two sectors, workers have been enduring less hardship, have found protection in highly mechanised production, and have been subject to protective rules governing employment conditions; they have also benefited from a state-sponsored social safety net. Furthermore, these more prosperous and more protected workers have found pleasure in consumer lifestyles and in entertainment made available by modern high-technology communications media. According to Gat (2006), these citizens are ill prepared for the discomfort, deprivation, hardship and exposure to danger that confronts the average soldier during war, and they are highly unlikely to be attracted to military work as a career option.

These liberal, democratic, affluent and peaceful societies have also achieved demographic stability, with low or even negative population growth rates. Smaller cohorts of young people, especially young men, are found in these societies. The latter group, especially when they were marginalised and weakly integrated into society, have historically served as the primary basis of recruitment into the armed forces. Within these more affluent populations the relationship between men and women has also changed fundamentally. In the ancient hierarchy war was almost exclusively the domain of men, while women were either innocent non-combatants, bystanders, or worse, highly valued objects of war. The old hierarchy has been superseded by social relations based on the norms of gender equality.

In these societies, then, the values endorsing public violence have been profoundly weakened. Where the right to life and dignity prevails, war by the agents of the state against any cohort of its own citizens (civil war) has become de-legitimised, and states have even found it hard to justify the use of the death penalty as a form of punishment against their own citizens. In the liberal imagination the notion of war as a means to an end, even against patently undemocratic countries where few if any human rights are respected, has come to be seen as increasingly meaningless, absurd and even unthinkable, while a militaristic culture has become almost an object of ridicule and disgust. The pacifist values ensconced in contemporary popular culture are vividly expressed in the slogan of the counter-culture of the 1960s, with its call to 'Make love, not war'.

The question of whether the longstanding peace between these rich democracies is ultimately driven by considerations of military and economic interests as defined by the democratic rulers of these countries, along with the domineering presence of the USA, or is instead driven by the popular culture and sentiment of the citizens within these democracies, or by some combination of both sets of factors, is not the focus of this chapter. This question will be allowed to simmer. The rest of the chapter will elaborate on factors that have already affected the growth and contraction of this zone of peace, as well as those that may do so in the future. One such prospective factor is the Great Recession.

Expanding the zone of peace

The post-World War II liberal democratic zone of peace was largely framed by the contours of the bipolar structure of the Cold War. Liberal democracies coalesced around the pivotal powers of the USA and Canada in North America; Britain, France, the Low Countries and Scandinavia in Europe; and countries on the Pacific Rim. Up to the early 1970s general academic opinion held that further democratisation would be a slow incremental process, requiring the fulfilment of many necessary pre-conditions (see Dahl, 1971). The subsequent rapid democratisation of Portugal, Greece and Spain in 1974 and 1975 that initiated the so-called Third Wave of democratisation in many places in the world was therefore highly unexpected. With the fall of the Berlin Wall in 1989 and the collapse of communism as a viable ideology and regime type, this wave received an additional forward thrust. The most notable endorsement came from Francis Fukuyama (1989), who published his celebrated paper announcing the end of ideological conflict and the global victory of liberal values and democratic institutions.

But were these new democracies all respectable entrants into the zone of peace? Hardly so. Democratisation brought new constitutional rules and liberal bills of rights, but these written rules had yet to convert into an established liberal civic culture. And many of these societies were still very poor, with domestic economies hardly able to generate the affluence needed to pacify domestic citizens. Finally, many of these economies were yet to be drawn into favourable trade relations with the countries at the centre of the global economy.

On the basis of the annual ratings provided by Freedom House, Larry Diamond (1996) argued that many of the celebrated new democracies such as Turkey, Brazil, Pakistan and Nigeria were becoming ever more 'shallow' in the sense that they were losing their liberal attributes while holding onto obvious democratic procedures such as elections. Illiberal democracies were emerging (Zakaria, 1997). In some cases democratisation brought into power more radical parties, such as Hamas in the Gaza strip, which ran counter to the political, military and economic interests of the USA and other established democracies. And in other cases new types of hybrid regimes containing a mix of authoritarian and democratic features were forming. These included Armenia, Kyrgyzstan, Jordan, Algeria, as well as Tanzania and Kenya.

In yet other cases elections remained as ostensible expressions of the democratic process. But the democratic substance of these events has been often 'hollowed out' by a dominant party merging state bureaucracy with that of the party, in effect rigging elections to perpetuate the dominant party's rule. A critical example of such a new kind of authoritarian rule, and one which was crucial to the expansion of the democratic zone of peace, was the hollowing out of the democratic regime in Russia. After a deeply flawed election held in Russia in 2007, the Freedom House agency downgraded the country from the category of "Free" to "Not Free" (Puddington, 2007).

It is not surprising, therefore, that by 1996 questions were being asked about whether the Third Wave had run its course and a backwash was imminent. The turn of events in Russia in 2007 is considered to effectively mark the end of the Third Wave of democratisation, and with this any likelihood of expanding the liberal democratic zone of peace in the immediate future (Diamond, 2008). By 2009 the number of democratic and less than fully democratic countries had seemingly stabilised. In the Freedom House ratings for 2009, 89 countries representing 46 percent of the world's independent states and 46 percent of the world's population, were rated as Free, that is, both as liberal and democratic. This represents the outer limits of the possible zone of peace, should all these countries become wealthy, liberal and peaceful. At the edges of this core there is continuous movement across categories. For example, in 2009 Montenegro moved up from Partly Free to Free and Kosovo rose from Not Free to Partly Free. Declines were registered in Lesotho, which was downgraded from Free in 2008 to Partly Free in 2009, while Bahrain, Gabon, Jordan, Kyrgyzstan and Yemen slipped down from Partly Free to Not Free (Puddington, 2010). Overall the Survey identified Central Asia, Sub-Saharan Africa and the Arab Middle East as the most difficult regions in which to establish and consolidate democracies. Seen against this background, it is uncertain whether the 2011 uprisings against authoritarian rule in Egypt, Tunisia, Lybia, Yemen and Syria could produce liberal-democratic outcomes. The outcomes may be some form of renewed authoritarian rule, or dominant party systems that can be described as competitive authoritarian regimes, or, lastly, illiberal democracies.

Threats

The expansion of the liberal democratic zone of peace can be taken as problematic, given that many of the preconditions for establishing and securing democratic regimes are not adequately met on the periphery of semi-democratic regimes. There are a number of states along the periphery with the ability to modernise without having to become more liberal or democratic. Russia and China are the pre-eminent cases, along with India, which is still generally considered to be democratic, but has dubious liberal attributes given the persistent status inequalities that follow from the caste system.

What is not always brought into the discussion is that the threat to democracy exists not just at the edges but also at the very core of the liberal democratic zone of peace. Maintenance of this core could be endangered by a variety of forces (Gat, 2006).

First, the most direct and immediate threat is the use of weapons of mass destruction. The conventional logic of defence is that based on deterrence, at any level of technology. But when biological or nuclear weapons are deployed by terrorists, deterrence fails since the terrorists are likely to be supremely motivated to do damage at any expense, even the loss of their own lives. The use of weapons of mass destruction by states cannot be ruled out either. And an effective defence against nuclear and biological weapons, once they have been deployed, has yet to be devised.

Second, ethnic nationalism remains a volatile ingredient in the politics of multicultural societies, and with larger migrations of people as a result of globalised capitalism, the multicultural character of many urban concentrations both in the centre and on the periphery is set to increase. A number of states have suffered disintegration or partition since the end of the Cold War with adverse consequences for liberalism and for democracy in many cases.

Third, there is the phenomenon of state collapse with regional ramifications, especially in the Horn of Africa. Somalia, for example, returned to a 'state of nature' that is closer to the one envisioned by Hobbes than the one imagined by Rousseau, and it would be more accurate to describe it as a *realm* rather than as a state. The actions of stakeholders in this realm have thus far been entirely hostile to the democratic zone of peace, and Somalia has emerged as the centre of international marine piracy.

Fourth, the prospect of the re-emergence of a bipolar global structure has a bearing on the above set of factors. It remains to be seen whether the three major modernising giants of Russia, India and China are going to democratise, let alone become more liberal. Conceivably they could consolidate into authoritarian capitalist regimes, as Russia has already started to do. The Great Recession, with its shift of economic power to the developing world, could accelerate such a trend. Hassner predicts that Russia will join China in countering Western efforts to export liberal democracy:

Russia and China jointly are able to use their indifference to human rights to block Western attempts to sanction rogue states, from Uzbekistan and Burma to Sudan and Zimbabwe, and instead to deal with these countries in purely economic and strategic terms. In this Russia and China are at one with almost all the countries of the global South, including India, for whom national sovereignty and non-interference in internal affairs trump democracy promotion and the defence of human rights (Hassner 2008: 14).

Fifth, the role of scarce resources and demography deserves consideration in the wider context. With the notable exception of the USA, many if not most of the established democracies in the core have very low population growth rates, with some showing negative growth rates. This is especially noticeable in the post-communist democracies, some of which (Poland, for example) have become staunch members of the liberal democratic core. Long-term demographic decline in the form of aging populations and labour forces, with the concomitant demand for labour that can only be met by in-migration from other regions, can impact negatively on these democracies. Likewise, explosive growth on the periphery, especially sub-Saharan Africa, is likely to increase pressure on elected governments to deliver public goods, and to expand social and physical infrastructure (Goldstone, 2010). Relative and absolute resource scarcities are likely to increase social tensions and competition both in the democratic centre and on the periphery. Rapid global climate change is likely to further induce increased migration, as well as local and regional resource scarcities (Schwartz and Randall, 2003).

The Great Recession and liberal popular culture

The sixth and last significant destabilising factor is the Great Recession, in evidence since the global financial crisis of 2008-2009. In the interpretation of the impact of capitalist modernity and prosperity on liberal values and the appeasement of such societies, a central focus is placed on the role of popular culture. This refers to the culture that was formed predominantly after World War II and was most thoroughly shaped by the 'baby boom' generation of the post-war period. The values of this generation were deeply influenced by, and found expression in, the counter-culture movement of the 1960s. This counter-culture entailed the deliberate rejection of established cultural norms and was a rebellion against most, if not all, norms of restraint and forms that prescribed actions relating to sexual conduct, the use of intoxicating substances, and in the case of the USA, loyalty to the so-called military-industrial complex (Mills, 1965). The general preference was for 'sex, drugs and rock & roll', embodying a hedonistic, materialistic lifestyle of instant gratification and a rejection of establishment authority. A particular focus of dissent was the Vietnam War and the involvement of the USA in this war. A rejection of war in any form came to be the cornerstone of this youthful generation and this value has been carried over to subsequent generations in the established liberal democracies. And, as has been argued, all of this has been buoyed by the wave of prosperity that swept through these very societies in the last 50 years.

The 1960s generation reshaped some core liberal values. Equality was extended from a criterion applicable largely to political rights to such areas as sexual orientation and gender relations. Third-generation rights, bearing on environmental quality, gained acceptance. And progress came to be interpreted in post-materialist and post-industrialist terms as a matter of increased 'quality of life'. Again, these values found expression in societies that experienced ever higher standards of living.

How is the Great Recession that produced a sustained decline in this trajectory of affluence likely to affect these more recently re-shaped as well as the older liberal values such as trust and tolerance? The latter are values crucial to the maintenance of civility in domestic politics. Under conditions of economic (and other forms) of hardship, out-groups are prone to be singled out as the cause of calamities. Such scapegoats are often identified in ideologies of exclusive ethnic nationalism and in attitudes of prejudice, racism and xenophobia. Should acute economic decline undermine liberal values, democratic regimes may persist but most likely as highly illiberal democracies, as envisioned by Fareed Zakaria (1997). And these would be present in the centre of the democratic zone, not at the edges. At worst, democracy itself may give way to more extremist regimes and ideologies. The demise of the Weimar Republic comes to mind as an instructive example.

In Europe, at the very centre of this zone, an emerging issue likely to test the resilience of liberal values in popular culture is that relating to immigration. At the time of writing, data from surveys on public attitudes in Europe about migration issues mostly pre-date the Great Recession. Yet much of the data reveal sentiments that express unease, if not enmity, towards migrants from outside the EU region. At the start of this century about 5 percent, just on 56 million, of the population of the EU were listed as non-European immigrants. To this must be added millions of second- and third-generation migrants who continue to be considered as 'guest workers' of a temporary nature. These communities are not all welcomed.

One survey, undertaken in 2008, for example, found that 50 percent of respondents in Germany, Italy, Holland and France endorsed the view that Western and Muslim ways of life are irreconcilable (Petrou, 2010). Already in 1997 the Eurobarometer Survey registered that 45 percent of Europeans thought there were too many foreigners living in their respective countries. A general overview of survey research on this topic concludes that "the rejection of ethnic and social groups is approaching dangerously high levels in both Western and Eastern Europe" (Zick, Pettigrew & Wagner, 2008: 244).

The perceived sense of threat presented by Muslim culture, in particular, appears to exaggerate the presence of migrants and their culture. In Switzerland the building of minarets on mosques was banned in response to the presence of only four such minarets in the entire country. Fifty-seven percent of participating voters approved of the banning of what they perceived as a threatening piece of architecture, and majorities in 22 of the 26 cantons supported a constitutional amendment to this effect (Petrou, 2010).

One conceivable trend in public opinion is that such expressions of public intolerance could escalate in the medium and longer term within an environment of persistent economic and financial instability, and the liberal character of the established European democracies could decline accordingly. It is still too early to identify persistent trends that relate the effects of the Great Recession to anti-immigrant hostility, and at the time of writing systematic research on such trends has yet to appear.

Conclusions

Liberal democracies emerged in tandem with the benefits of capitalist modernity. The affluence generated by the economic system, along with many of the other features of modern life, tilted the cost-benefit calculation away from domestic and foreign belligerence towards tolerance, civility and pacific relations. This rising affluence converted the structure of conflict over prosperity into one where entire societies could raise their standards of living without dispossessing others. These conditions favoured a popular culture in which liberal values could flourish. But what happens when these conditions change? The proposition one can offer is that a deep and sustained decline in material prosperity, which effects a return to zero-sum politics, can contribute to the unravelling of such a pacific popular culture.

This proposition also raises the question about the prospects for popular culture in undemocratic or semi-democratic regimes. They have also become infused with the materialistic high-consumption culture that typifies late modernity, and these countries have also engaged less in war. The obvious reason is that the cost-benefit analysis favouring peace over war applies to them as much as it does to affluent democracies. What is crucial, and subject to empirical investigation, is the extent to which liberal values conducive to peaceful dispositions have been also established in the rise to modernity in such authoritarian regimes among both the general public and among the ruling elites. The cases of Russia and China are again of decisive importance.

If both elites and the general public in such authoritarian regimes subscribe to values conducive to aggression, such as a fundamentalist version (either secular or religious) of the ideology of nationalism, rather than liberal values, a sustained period of decline in affluence, coupled to an existing or emerging conflict over resources, may also facilitate the growth of aggressive popular dispositions towards perceived opponents. Should authoritarian leaders/elites choose to enter into forceful aggression, then the absence of the constraining forces of liberal constitutionalism on those regimes will be telling.

Sources

Dahl, R.A. (1971). *Polyarchy. Participation and opposition.* New Haven: Yale University Press.
Diamond, L. (1996). Is the Third Wave over? *Journal of Democracy.* 7(3): 20-37.
Diamond, L. (2008). The democratic rollback". *Foreign Affairs.* March/April: 36-48.
Fukuyama, F. (1989). The End of History? *The National Interest* 16: 3-18.
Gat, A. (2006). *War and civilization.* Oxford University Press: Oxford.
Goldstone, J. A. (2010). The new population bomb. *Foreign Affairs.* January/February: 31-43.
Mills, C. W. (1956). *The power elite.* New York :Oxford University Press.
Petrou, M. (2010). Europe's war against Islam". *Maclean's,* 123(1): not paginated.
Puddington, A. (2008). The 2007 Freedom House Survey: is the tide turning? *Journal of Democracy.* 19(2): 61-73.
Puddington, A. (2010). The Freedom House Survey for 2009: the erosion accelerates. *Journal of Democracy.* 21(2): 136-150.
Rummel, R.J. (1997). *Power kills. Democracy as a method of non-violence.* Brunswick (NJ) : Transaction Publishers,.
Russett, B. M. (1993). *Grasping the democratic peace. Principles for a post-Cold War world.* Princeton (NJ): Princeton University Press.
Schwartz, P. and Randall, D. (2003). *An abrupt climate change scenario and its implications for United States national security,* mimeo.
Van Creveld, M. (1991). *The transformation of war.* New York: Free Press.
Van Creveld, M. (2008). *The culture of war.* New York: Ballantine Books.
Zakaria, F. (1997). The rise of illiberal democracy. *Foreign Affairs.* November/December: 22-43.
Zick, A., Pettigrew, T.F and Wagner, U. (2008). Ethnic prejudice and discrimination in Europe. *Journal of Social Issues.* 64(2): 233-251.

Global solutions? Searching for democratic approaches to a new world order

Christer Jönsson

Introduction

Four times in modern history statesmen and diplomats have convened to create a new world order: at the signing of the Peace of Westphalia in 1648, after the Thirty Years War; at the Congress of Vienna in 1815, following the Napoleonic Wars; in Paris in 1919, in the wake of World War I; and in San Francisco in 1945, at the end of World War II (John Keegan in Schlesinger, 2003: xv). The Peace of Westphalia established a European system of secular authority that laid the foundations for the modern state, while the Congress of Vienna produced the Concert of Europe, a club of great powers dedicated to preventing the emergence of revolutionary states. The legacy of Westphalia left us with a system of states that spread beyond Europe to the rest of the world; the legacy of Vienna has been the club model, whose current global applications are the G8 or G20.

Only at the Paris and San Francisco conferences did the word 'democracy' enter into the discussions of a future world order. The League of Nations, in the words of Inis Claude (1964: 47),

rested upon two assumptions: that the age of democracy had arrived, providing a sufficient number of soundly democratic states to unite in an organization for maintaining world peace; and that the democratic method of arriving at agreement by civilized discussion rather than coercive dictation could be applied to the relations of democratic states as well as to those of individuals. [US President Woodrow] Wilson had fought his war to make the world safe *for* democracy; he created his League to make the world safe *by* democracy.

For Wilson national self-determination was an essential corollary of democracy. "Just as the people had the right to govern themselves within the national system, so the nations had a right to govern themselves within the global system" (Claude, 1964: 47).

Despite the failure of the League of Nations, similar ideas guided the creation of the United Nations at San Francisco, with two noteworthy additions. First, the UN Charter set forth special responsibilities and privileges for the Big Five, in line with the club model. Second, the Charter starts by referring to "we the peoples" and Article 71 empowers the Economic and Social Council (ECOSOC) to grant consultative status to non-governmental organisations (NGOs) on issues in which they have competence. Thus, somewhat paradoxically, the reversion to great power politics was combined with the potential for broadened participation beyond states.

The recent global financial and economic crisis did not give rise to a new assembly of statesmen and diplomats to deliberate on a new world order. One reason is that the previous reordering attempts all came in the wake of major wars. The financial crisis, by contrast, did not threaten world peace, even if it has had grave worldwide effects. But the contemporary situation differs from the previous four in at least two other, more profound, ways. First, today government representatives would not be able to chart a new global order even if they had the political will do so, because states are no longer the sole sovereign arbiters of world affairs. Second, the present disorder concerns global flows rather than the redrawing of territorial boundaries that preoccupied the previous reordering attempts.

The fact that new actors have entered the international arena along with states means that traditional multilateralism in terms of interstate collaboration is insufficient to offer viable solutions to pressing global problems. Different labels have been suggested to capture the new reality: "multiple multilateralisms", "new multilateralism", "complex multilateralism", "polylateralism" and "plurilateralism" (cf. Weiss *et al.*, 2009: 204; Tallberg and Jönsson, 2010). In the end the concept of global governance has become the favoured umbrella term of both social scientists and policymakers for denoting the new and complex patterns of authority in world politics that involve a variety of actors and networks along with states and international institutions.

Today various actors from the economic sphere and civil society claim, and are increasingly granted, the right of access to various national and international forums. This means that any assessment of viable democratic features in future global governance arrangements must take into account the broader set of *transnational* actors. These are individuals and groups who act beyond national borders yet are not controlled by governments. In fact, several transnational actors already lay claim to enhancing democracy at the global level, which means that it is no longer possible to limit the perspective to states and citizens by arguing that only assemblies of democratic states with electoral support from their respective *demoi* constitute democracy at the global level. While controversial, the claims of the transnational actors are widely acknowledged.

Furthermore, the financial crisis demonstrates another crucial feature of contemporary international affairs: the growing importance of *flows* across national borders beyond the control of individual governments. It has been suggested that the historically rooted spatial organisation, the 'space of places', is being superseded by the *space of flows*: it is the flows and transactions, rather than physical territory and places, that shape the significant spatial patterns in a globalising world (Castells, 1996). We have become increasingly dependent on flows across geographical boundaries, and our security is today more dependent on defending these flows than on defending territory. Our welfare has become increasingly dependent on undisturbed air, sea and land transport of goods and people as well as uninterrupted flows of communication via the internet.

Global finance is a case in point. Capital market liberalisation in the 1990s opened up markets to the free flow of short-term, hot, speculative money. In a few decades the financial market grew out of proportion. As we entered a new millennium, the *daily* turnover in the international currency trade exceeded the reserves of the largest central banks, outstripped all World Bank loans throughout its existence, and amounted to around forty times the value of the daily production of merchandise in the world. These flows of money of an almost unimaginable magnitude were, by and large, beyond the effective control of governments or intergovernmental organisations.

This chapter will first review the existing formal and informal mechanisms of 'complex multilateralism' in the contemporary world by assessing their democratic qualities and probing their applicability to the realm of finance. It will then discuss two popular theories of global democracy which address the 'deterritorialization' of contemporary politics – 'the all-affected principle' and 'discursive representation' – with a view to establishing their practical feasibility. Whereas the first section offers a normative appraisal of real-world arrangements, the second section evaluates the realism of prevalent normative ideas.

Managing complex multilateralism

One may distinguish three principal types of regulatory arrangements in to-day's world: *markets, hierarchies* and *networks* (cf. Thompson *et al.*, 1991). Within each category there is a considerable variety of institutions and instruments.

Markets presuppose a large number of autonomous actors with little interdependence. Their independent decisions, based on self-interest, lead to mutually advantageous exchanges and efficient allocations of resources. Control is decentralised and regulation is the result of 'the invisible hand'. Economic actors – buyers and sellers, firms and consumers – populate markets.

Hierarchies consist of vertical chains of authority and delegation between superordinate principals and subordinate agents. The exercise of control is overt and centralised. This provides the foundation of states and interstate forums. Hierarchies imply bureaucratic actors within a framework of formal rules.

Networks, finally, rest on the coexistence of autonomy and interdependence. They involve informal relationships between essentially equal actors. Networks tend to be inclusive, providing meeting places for government, market and civil society actors. In contrast to markets, networks presuppose interaction between autonomous actors; in contrast to hierarchies, networks are relatively flat with no formal ranks of authority.

The typical output of global markets is equilibrium between supply and demand; global hierarchies produce international law and conventions; and global networks usually initiate 'soft law', standards and codes of conduct. The questions here are : What is the nature of each of the three types of regulatory arrangements in general, and how do they relate to finance in particular? And more specifically: What are the democratic qualities of the various regulatory arrangements in terms of three basic dimensions of democratic governance: *transparency, accountability* and *inclusion*?

Transparency is a democratic prerequisite. In order to have a say on global policy issues, affected individuals need to be informed of the decision-making process. At the national level accountability is a straightforward concept: it is the touchstone of representative democracy as it holds the government accountable for its actions before the people in elections at regular intervals. In global governance, however, the question of who is accountable to whom? is far less clear-cut. Inclusion means that affected communities – either directly or indirectly, through representatives – can meaningfully participate in negotiations and deliberations.

A self-regulating financial market?

In theory markets have certain democratic qualities as they generate outcomes that are the results of autonomous individual choices. All actors are assumed to be free to pursue their self-interest. In practice, however, market failures – situations in which the outcomes of market-mediated interactions prove to be suboptimal – frequently occur. The financial market is a case in point, as demonstrated in the chapter by Stan du Plessis in this volume.

Economists tell us that market self-regulation does not work in markets where a small group is well informed and the vast majority are ill informed or ignorant. Such information asymmetries are glaring in the financial market. It is hard to imagine any other field where the market requirement of information symmetry is so far removed from reality. Alan Greenspan, for instance, after he stepped down as Chairman of the Federal Reserve, admitted that the complexity of some of the new instruments in the financial market were hard to comprehend, even for him: "And I figured if I didn't understand it and I had access to a couple hundred PhDs, how the rest of the world is going to understand it sort of bewildered me" (quoted in Sorkin, 2009: 90). Without appropriate government regulation and intervention, such a market does not lead to economic efficiency (Stiglitz ,2006: xiv).

As du Plessis in this volume points out, the financial market illustrates the dangers of 'moral hazard', situations in which one party makes the decision about how much risk to take, whereas another party bears the cost if things go wrong. If those who take risks believe they will not carry the full burden of losses, their propensity to take greater risks to gain potentially higher returns increases. Thus, lending institutions extend risky loans because they believe they will be bailed out by governments, central banks or other institutions should they become unable to meet their liabilities. And the financial market in recent decades created increasingly complex products many levels removed from the underlying assets, entailing extraordinary degrees of risk.

As the problems of information asymmetry and moral hazard demonstrate, the global financial market does not fulfil any of the three democratic criteria. There is minimal transparency as transactions of enormous sums of money, which have significant repercussions for individuals around the world, take place without broader insight into the processes and actors involved. There is no mechanism through which ordinary citizens can find out who is responsible and who should be held accountable. And important market transactions take place within exclusive cabals bereft of any popular representation.

Hierarchy through international organisations?

International or intergovernmental governance structures rest on the sanctity of state sovereignty. States are the principals delegating functions and conditional authority to international organisations as agents. To the extent that the principals – member states – are democratic, international organisations can be said to have democratic qualities indirectly. For instance, a democratic constitution is a prerequisite for membership in the Council of Europe. But for the most part intergovernmental organisations (IGOs) are characterised by a 'democratic deficit': universal or near-universal membership shows a mix of authoritarian and democratic states, and powerful states tend to predominate in international organisations, whether membership is restricted or universal.

The international financial architecture created after the end of World War II was US-centred. The International Monetary Fund (IMF) and the World Bank (originally known as the International Bank for Reconstruction and Development, IBRD) have been premised on leadership by the United States and other advanced industrial countries, as reflected in their 'club' rules. The head of the IMF is a European, with a US representative in the number two position; the US President appoints the head of the World Bank. The voting power of member states in the policymaking bodies of both organisations is weighted according to their financial contributions. The United States, with around 17 percent of the votes in both, dwarfs all other member states, while developing countries have marginal, if any, influence.

But since the turn of the millennium a series of reforms have made this architecture gradually more inclusive. The IMF established a new Interna-

Christer Jönsson

tional Monetary and Financial Committee (IMFC), which enabled all IMF members to debate and influence the role of the organisation beyond what was previously possible. A new regulatory initiative – the Financial Stability Forum (FSF) – was founded in 1999 to promote financial stability by bringing together key regulators from about a dozen states and several international economic organisations (Germain, 2002).

The FSF was the result of discussions among finance ministers and central bank officials of the G7 countries. This group of seven industrialised states, formed in 1976, assumed an increasingly important but largely informal position in global finance. In response to the contagion effects of the Asian financial crisis in 1997-98 a larger grouping of countries, known as the G20, was established in September 1999. It provides a mechanism for bringing the emerging market economies into the decision-making structure of the global financial system. Originally a forum of ministers of finance, the G20 was upgraded to a venue for heads of state as a result of the global financial crisis. The G20 summit in November 2008 agreed to expand the membership of the FSF to include China and other emerging economies; and the 2009 summit decided to establish a successor to the FSF, the Financial Stability Board (FSB), including all G20 members.

Discussions in the G20 also resulted in certain adjustments of the voting power in the World Bank and the IMF. The World Bank decided to grant another seat on its board to Africa south of the Sahara and to increase the voting share of developing and transition countries by three percent to 47.19 percent. The reform gave China a larger voting share than Germany, the UK or France. A reshuffle of the IMF's 24-member Executive Board, initiated in March 2011, increases the representation of emerging markets and developing countries, while Europe loses two seats.

Thus, the financial crisis has entailed important efforts to redress the imbalances in favour of the US and Europe in relevant international organisations. Representing two-thirds of the population and accounting for 87 percent of the total GNP of the world, the G20 emerged as the most inclusive international body to date. Yet the G20 remains a club of the economically most powerful states, while poor countries in the developing world continue to be excluded. And even if their voting share has increased marginally in the World Bank and the IMF, the United States and Europe remain in control.

The G20 has established itself as the foundation of the new international financial architecture. Yet it is noteworthy that this is an organisation without a permanent secretariat, a necessary component if the G20 is to develop into an 'economic security council', as many hope. It has been suggested that the OECD (Organisation for Economic Co-operation and Development) might formally assume that role, as it has been trying to do informally thus far. However, that would once again underscore the leading role of the rich developed countries in the North.

The 'transnational turn' in global governance opened up several IGOs to participation by transnational actors such as NGOs, advocacy networks, party associations and multinational corporations (cf. Jönsson and Tallberg, 2010). However, this general trend does not apply fully to international finance bodies. Whereas the IMF has been reluctant to let transnational actors in, the World Bank draws on the expertise of NGOs in the formulation of country reports, engages in operational collaboration with civil society actors in the field, and conducts policy dialogue through the NGO-World Bank Committee. The G20 allows in only government representatives, with other groups typically organising protests in the streets.

Intergovernmental organisations in the financial sector are not only less than inclusive, but they also score low on transparency, even if some recent improvements have been made. The IMF, for instance, by helping develop Special Data Dissemination Standards (SDDS), enabled market participants to make sounder investment decisions based on the best available information. In addition, both the IMF and the World Bank initiated an information disclosure policy, while the well-publicised agendas, meetings and working groups of the G20 are now open to public scrutiny. Yet the inner workings of these organisations remain inaccessible to the general public.

Accountability is equally problematic. This is partly related to poor transparency. Lacking knowledge of the policy process makes it difficult to hold the organisations accountable. Whereas both the IMF and the World Bank are formally accountable to all member states, effective accountability is limited to the great powers led by the United States. The G20 has broadened accountability to twenty states but, unlike the IMF and the World Bank, does not grant even formal accountability to the governments of developing countries.

The financial crisis has indeed led to a notable expansion of international initiatives, and the G20 initially managed to agree on measures to avoid a full-scale depression. Yet national responses to the crisis have been varied and largely insufficient, and no global consensus around regulatory countermeasures has emerged. The revelation that not only banks and traders but also states are guilty of irresponsible financial behaviour has spawned conflicts rather than occasioning concerted action. The first prominent example, Greece, was soon joined by Ireland, Portugal, Spain and Italy – together they represent the so-called PIIGS group.

What kind of global regulation, then, can IGOs produce? Two types, in particular, have been discussed at recent G20 meetings and elsewhere: transaction fees in the financial market and fiscal consolidation plans among states. Taxing financial transactions has been suggested as one way of achieving financial stability. A so-called Tobin tax, suggested originally by Nobel laureate James Tobin, is an internationally agreed uniform tax on currency transactions. Variants of this have long been on the global agenda, but no consensus seems in sight. Fiscal consolidation plans setting a cap on budget deficits as initiated in the European Union and suggested globally by the G20 have proven to be ineffectual. The gap between states with large deficits (such as the United States) and those with large surpluses (such as China) is too wide to expect any global consensus. What G20 and other IGOs can realistically accomplish is not so much to eliminate existing imbalances, but to contain them at a sustainable level and to reduce the volatility of exchange rates.

Flexible transnational networks?

Transnational networks may take many different shapes. They may be exclusive, promoting the specific interests of a specialised group, or inclusive, encompassing various types of actors in a specific issue area. They may be more or less institutionalised and may range from temporary loose coalitions formed around a specific issue to long-standing tightly knit groupings within a given field. Their common denominator is that they include groups that are not governmental actors, which is not to say that they necessarily exclude governmental actors.

In global finance exclusive networks predominate. A central node in the fairly institutionalised network is the Basel Committee on Banking Supervision (BCBS) established in 1974 at the Bank for International Settlements (BIS), itself a forum for central bankers created after World War I. Up until 2009 the Committee consisted of representatives of central banks as well as the authorities responsible for domestic banking supervision in twelve countries. Since then the Committee has expanded its membership to include all G20 countries. Another key player is the Institute of International Finance (IIF), a consultative group of major US and European banks, which has long enjoyed a close relationship with the BCBS based on its personal contacts in national regulatory agencies. Other important actors include the International Swaps and Derivative Association (ISDA) representing over 860 institutions in the privately negotiated derivatives industry, and the Group of Thirty, a Washington-based association of senior bankers.

The regulatory authority of the BCBS was vested in the so-called Basel process. Its aim has been to set prudential standards for the international banking system *via* the rule of capital adequacy requirements that are to provide a buffer against unexpected losses and allow banks to continue to operate during periods of stress. In 1988 the Basel I Accord set minimum capital requirements for internationally active banks, but by the late 1990s the Accord came to be viewed as inadequate and in June 1999 the BCBS proposed a new framework. After five years of negotiations the Basel Committee agreed on Basel II, a new capital adequacy framework, which in addition to specifying minimum capital requirements also provided guidelines for regulatory intervention and information disclosure standards for banks. However, the final accord fell short of the initial aims expressed by the BCBS and by mid-2007 only the European Union had adopted the Accord. Basel II came to be viewed as a failure, with some analysts going as far as to see it as one of the underlying causes of the recent financial crisis. In their view the disproportionate influence of large international banks over the Basel process resulted in an Accord allowing the institutions that pose the greatest threat to the stability of the financial system to hold the least capital.

Since 2008 there has been a strong demand for regulatory change at the same time as the G20 emerged as a regulatory authority to rival the BCBS. In September 2009 the G20 requested the BCBS to formulate a new set of rules and set a deadline for the end of 2010. In December 2009 the Basel Committee issued a set of preliminary proposals to guide subsequent negotiations, and at its Seoul summit in November 2010 the G20 endorsed the Basel III rules proposed by the BCBS in September. The speed is unprecedented. By comparison, it took a decade to negotiate Basel II.

Basel III more than triples the amount of capital that banks will have to hold in reserve. Moreover, the capital has to be of better quality than before. It also introduces capital buffers above the minimum requirements that can be drawn upon in bad times. The toughest set of global banking regulations ever formulated, Basel III is to be gradually implemented starting on 1 January, 2013, and to be fully phased in by 1 January, 2019.

While welcomed by many, Basel III also has its critics. Some in the banking sector argue that the banking system is too broken and the world economy too fragile to support more onerous regulation. Sceptics suspect that Basel III might fall short of expectations for exactly the same reasons that Basel II had failed, namely for being equally prone to 'regulatory capture', that is, *de facto* control of regulatory agencies by the regulated interests (Lall, 2010). The slow pace of implementation reinforces such suspicions. Continuous lobbying by banks or an eventual economic recovery could blunt the will to enforce Basel III. Finally, capital requirements are not sufficient to solve the problems of global finance. Other necessary measures include more effective supervision, more transparent derivatives markets and improved global accounting rules (cf. Reuter, 2010).

In short, the most important networks in international finance lack basic democratic qualities, especially transparency. The Bank for International Settlements in fact has one of the lowest scores on the index of transparency published in the Global Accountability Report by One World Trust. Accountability is equally low. Ruling standards are the result of protracted discussions between unelected regulators with a high degree of operational independence, on the one hand, and representatives of influential financial institutions with privileged access to information, on the other. And networks remain exclusive rather than inclusive.

One particular form of formalised inclusive networks that is becoming increasingly common in global governance in several issue areas is the so-called public-private partnerships (PPP). Such partnerships are voluntary co-operative arrangements between actors from two or more societal spheres (state, market, civil society) with non-hierarchical decision-making procedures (cf. Bexell and Mörth, 2010). The idea is to include relevant stakeholders in a specific issue area in what is often termed 'stakeholder democracy'.

The exclusive and opaque settings in which global finance is discussed are a far cry from this form of partnership. Nor do any reform proposals include any significant civil society involvement. Global networks typically produce 'soft law', which are rules of conduct that in principle have no legally binding force, but which nevertheless have regulatory effects and may elicit significant degrees of compliance. In contrast to hard law, which can have virtually immediate effects, soft law is more closely related to long-term socialisation (cf. Mörth, 2004). The Basel Accords are examples of soft law. The first two have proven to be too soft, encouraging circumvention rather than compliance. Whether Basel III will deviate from that pattern remains to be seen.

Global democracy: from practice to theory

Having concluded that existing global governance practice falls short of basic democratic criteria, we need to raise the hypothetical question of what global democracy might look like in general, and how this might relate to global finance in particular. Global democracy has recently become a prominent theme among political theorists. While agreeing that traditional models originally developed for the national context are not directly transferable to the global arena – for instance, representative democracy as we know it domestically is hardly realisable on a global scale – they have advanced varying blueprints for reforming global governance to meet standards of democratic decision-making.

Two recent attempts to envisage the democratisation of global governance in the absence of a well-defined global *demos* have received considerable attention among political theorists: the all-affected principle and discursive representation (Näsström, 2010). The all-affected principle asserts that the 'people' cannot be defined in advance, but are those who are affected by the decisions of a certain agency. According to the concept of discursive representation, discourses rather than peoples are what should be represented.

The all-affected principle

Most theories of democracy presuppose a given people (*demos*). Only after defining the *demos* is it possible to discuss the proper domain of democratic rule as compared to more private concerns. The all-affected principle turns the argument around by determining the delimitation of the people on the basis of the scope of political decision-making. In each individual instance the people are those affected by the decision in question. Thus, the all-affected principle suggests a way to democratise global governance without having to fall back upon a pre-constituted people (see Shapiro, 1999).

In democratic elections all votes count as equal. All citizens have an equal say regardless of inequalities in wealth, power and skills. By contrast, the all-affected principle implies that the democratic principle of counting each equally is replaced by one which says that we need to count each differently. Those whose basic interests are at stake in a particular decision are seen to have a stronger claim to inclusion in the *demos* than others. Thus the franchise is defined activity by activity, decision by decision. Votes, then, are proportional rather than equal: everyone should have an influence proportional to the stakes that one has in a question. Thus parents of young children should have a proportionally greater say on questions of schooling; HIV-infected individuals should have a greater say on AIDS policy; investors and borrowers should have a greater say in global finance.

The all-affected principle calls attention to how the ideal of 'one person, one vote' has become perverted under present political conditions where national borders do not coincide with existing power structures. We are all affected by decisions taken elsewhere. For example, decisions taken in Washington and Beijing, or by the World Bank and the G20, may affect individuals in remote corners of the world without them having any possibility to influence them. If the all-affected principle is to remedy this contemporary predicament, it needs to address two crucial questions: Who is affected and to what degree by a particular decision? And who is to determine which claims about being affected should be accepted? As it is unable to provide satisfactory answers to these questions, the all-affected principle cannot be said to offer a realistic model for global democracy.

Discursive representation

In democratic theory there is a deliberative tradition claiming that it is not sufficient that citizens are given the right to rule, whether directly or indirectly. In addition, there has to be free and open discussion, based on information from independent sources, before they go to the polls. What distinguishes discursive representation from other varieties of deliberative democracy is that it sidesteps the decision-making moment of the people. Citizens do not first deliberate and then cast their vote. In discursive representation deliberation *replaces* voting as the democratic mechanism of authorisation.

Discursive representation is based on the idea that representatives should represent discourses – written or spoken exchanges of political ideas or debates – rather than peoples. The point of departure is that citizens are not distinct wholes. What is actually represented in a democracy are not the individuals themselves but their varying values and interests. Modern individuals are divided and they take part in a number of discourses which, in turn, take place at different institutional and geographical levels. When citizens vote they are able to represent only some of the discourses, but have to exclude others. Rather than treating individuals as 'unproblematic wholes', we should therefore make sure that the multiple discourses individuals engage in will be represented. All relevant discourses ought to be represented, regardless of how many people subscribe to each one (see Dryzek and Niemeyer, 2008).

But how can discourses be represented in practice? Proponents of discursive representation suggest that a global Chamber of Discourses be created, but its members should not be elected as that would presume constituencies of individuals, which is precisely what discursive representation is meant to eschew. How, then, is one to select the 'relevant' discourses and the persons able to represent them? One answer that has been suggested is that 'science' replace the people as the proper source of authorisation in global politics. Arguably it would be possible for social scientists to select and identify both the relevant discourses and the people who could represent them. For example, they would point out that the only discourses 'represented' in the field of global finance until the recent crisis have been the specialised discourses of a numerically limited cabal of experts. By various methods they might then identify other relevant discourses that ought to be represented in the global Chamber of Discourses.

The all-affected principle and discursive representation both seek to account for the excluded, the voiceless and the poor in global politics. Both claim that in order to speak for the people, we need to construct a theory of democracy without authorisation vested in the people. Both call attention to the limits of the nation-state system and explain why we need to go beyond it in order to give the excluded and the silenced a political voice.

However, the solutions they suggest appear unrealistic and challenge deeply ingrained conceptions of democracy. Rather than working for the numerous and voiceless, they end up abolishing the authority of the people in elections, which makes politics indeterminable rather than pre-determined.. The democratic principle of counting each individual equally is replaced by either counting each differently or not counting anybody at all.

Conclusions

To recap, the present crisis has to do with flows rather than territory, and it involves transnational actors in addition to states. This makes the contemporary situation different from previous attempts to create a new world order. The global flow of money beyond adequate government control is the result of national deregulation in the 1990s. Today national efforts to re-regulate are insufficient; the crisis calls for measures on a global scale. Thus when the global market fails, politicians have turned to international organisations and networks for solutions. The financial crisis has entailed a certain degree of democratisation: the G20 is more inclusive than its predecessors, and the World Bank and the IMF have yielded to pressures for broader representation.

Global finance is exemplary of transnational actors and processes. However, networks in this field tend to be exclusive. The present crisis has illustrated graphically that affected groups, such as home owners unable to pay their mortgages or other borrowers, are not organised or mobilized transnationally. Therefore they remain unrepresented in international organisations and networks. The absence of civil society organisations in deliberations concerning the financial crisis is conspicuous.

The link between civil society and democracy, highlighted by many scholars in local settings, is less self-evident in the global context. Civil society organisations may provide a foundation for democratic states, but they are not the representative or electoral institutions of democracy. Yet the term global civil society is often used by social movements and NGOs to inflate and legitimise their roles. Their claims to represent and speak on behalf of the people of the world in global governance go far beyond the more modest role of civil society organisations in national democratic settings.

One could make a distinction between interest articulation and interest aggregation (Almond and Powell, 1966). Interest articulation refers to the process by which individuals and groups make demands upon political decision-makers. Interest aggregation involves the conversion of these demands into general policy alternatives. In domestic settings political parties aggregate interests articulated by various interest groups. In the global setting there are no specific agencies for interest aggregation, with the possible exception of the secretariats of international organisations. Whereas transnational actors legitimately articulate interests in global governance, their claim to be aggregating interests lacks legitimacy.

There are two specific problems in the field of global finance. First, only a limited subset of interests is being articulated, and second, there is no forum in which these interests are weighed against others. In other words, interest articulation is truncated and there is a relative lack of interest aggregation.

As we have seen, there is no perfect formula for global democracy either in practice or in theory. Global governance arrangements in general, and those in global finance in particular, rate low on basic democratic criteria. The best we can hope for in the short to medium run seems to be incremental steps in a democratising direction. In the field of finance even small steps in that direction would constitute a significant improvement.

ReferencesAlmond, G.A. and Powell, G.B. (1966). *Comparative politics: a developmental approach*. Boston: Little, Brown.

Annan, K. (2002). Address at ceremony of adherence to the Global Compact, Madrid, 9 April. Available on-line at: www.unglobalcompact.org/NewsAndEvents/speeches_and_statements/sg_adherence_to_gc.html.

Bexell, M. and Mörth, U. (eds) (2010). *Democracy and public-private partnerships in global governance*. Basingstoke: Palgrave Macmillan.

Castells, M. (1996). *The rise of the network society*. Oxford: Blackwell.

Claude, I.L. (1964). *Swords into plowshares: the problems and progress of international organization*. New York: Random House.

Dahl, R.A. (1999). Can international organizations be democratic? A skeptic's view. In Shapiro, I. and Hacker-Cordón, C. (eds). *Democracy's edges*. Cambridge: Cambridge University Press.

Dryzek, J, and Niemeyer, S. (2008). Discursive representation. *American Political Science Review*, 102(4). Available on-line at: http://www.democraciaparticipativa.org/bellagio/arquivos/Dryzek-DISCREP%20APSR08%20FINAL.pdf

Germain, R.D. (2002). Reforming the international financial architecture: the new political agenda. In Wilkinson, R. and Hughes, S (eds). *Global governance: critical perspectives*. London and New York: Routledge.

Global Accountability Report by One World Trust. Available on-line at: www.oneworldtrust.org.

Held, D. (1995). *Democracy and the global order: from the modern state to cosmopolitan governance*. Cambridge: Polity Press.

Jönsson, C. and Tallberg, J. (eds) (2010). *Transnational actors in global governance: patterns, explanations and implications*. Basingstoke: Palgrave Macmillan.

Kahler, M. (2005). Defining accountability up: the global economic multilaterals. In Held, D. and Koenig-Archibugi, M.(eds). *Global governance and public accountability*. Oxford: Blackwell.

Lall, R. (2010). Reforming global banking rules: back to the future? *DIIS Working Paper* 2010: 16. Copenhagen: Danish Institute for International Studies.

Mörth, U. (ed.) (2004). *Soft law in governance and regulation*. Cheltenham, UK: Edward Elgar.

Näsström, S. (2010). Democracy counts: problems of equality in transnational democracy. In Jönsson, C. and Tallberg, J. (eds). *Transnational actors in global governance: patterns, explanations and implications*. Basingstoke: Palgrave Macmillan.

Reuter (2010). Reining in the banks. Available on-line at: http://graphics.thomsonreuters.com/AS/pdf/baselIII.pdf (accessed 24 November, 2010).

Schlesinger, S.C. (2003). *Act of creation: the founding of the United Nations*. Cambridge (MA) : Westview.

Shapiro, I. (1999). *Democratic justice*. New Haven and London: Yale University Press.

Sorkin, A.R. (2009). *Too big to fail: inside the battle to save Wall Street*. London: Allen Lane.

Stiglitz, J. (2006). *Making globalization work*. London: Penguin.

Tallberg, J. and Jönsson, C. (2010). Transnational actor participation in international institutions: where, why, and with what consequences? In Jönsson, C. and Tallberg, J. (eds). *Transnational actors in global governance: patterns, explanations and implications*. Basingstoke: Palgrave Macmillan.

Thompson, G., Frances, J., Levačič, R. and Mitchell, J. (eds) (1991). *Markets, hierarchies and networks: the coordination of social life*. London: Sage.

Wapner, P. (2007). Civil society. In Weiss, T.G. and Daws, S. (eds). *The Oxford Handbook on the United Nations*. Oxford and New York: Oxford University Press.

Weiss, T.G., Carayannis, T. and Jolly, R. (2009). The "third" United Nations. *Global Governance*, 15(1): 123-142.

Values, interests, power and democracy at a time of crisis

Bernard Lategan

Introduction

In the wake of the momentous events of 1989 and the subsequent collapse of the Soviet Union, the free-market system and a capitalist economy seemed to be 'the only game in town'. But less than two decades later, with the onset of the sub-prime mortgage delinquencies and the subsequent financial crisis of 2008-2009, the free-market system has come in for criticism. And as fears about the effects of the crisis on the stability of democracy began to mount, so the values underlying capitalism were placed under the spotlight. At the same time the question of how to deal with crises of this nature and with the conflicts they produce has come to the fore.

The recent crisis has been inevitably also a crisis of values, above all about values that underpin financial systems. But given the nature of democracy, or any other type of government for that matter, the issue is never about values in the abstract, but about their *interplay* with power and interests. While in a pure sense values express norms such as freedom, truth or equality, the business of government consists of making choices, of prioritising, of balancing conflicting interests and often also of a pragmatic opting for less than ideal solutions.

The tension arising from the need for order and governance, on the one hand, and the desires, interests and wellbeing of people, on the other, is inherent to democracy in any setting, but is exacerbated in contexts of plurality and complexity, especially at times of economic stress. The following analysis focuses on the *role* of values in situations of diversity to explore the possibility of developing common values across cultural boundaries.

From conflict to values

One approach to the study of the close correlation that exists between power, interests, values and rights is conflict theory. This theory sees democracy not as a means by which to eradicate conflict, but rather as a way in which to channel or structure it. Exponents of this theory[1] proceed from the realistic,

---

1   They include, among others, Coser, 1956; Dahrendorf, 1959; Diamond & Marks,1992; Allan, 2007.

some might even say cynical, perception of reality that conflict is a natural state of human affairs and does not necessarily rip a society apart, but might in fact be one of the most important ways by which to hold it together. They claim that conflict is instinctive in human beings and therefore an essential element of group formation and group life. Jointly they make an important contribution to our understanding of the formation of social dynamics and social movements. This in turn, helps to anticipate social change, as Randall Collins, one of the leading conflict theorists, famously did when he foresaw the impending demise of Soviet Russia some years before the event (Collins, 1986). A more recent example is the growing tension within the European Union as a direct consequence of the economic crisis that is threatening the existence of the once highly prized ideal of European unity.

Conflict theory is based on the principle of binary opposition, which can be very productive in some fields, as demonstrated, for example, by the astonishing expansion of the digital world. This world relies on the simple binary opposition of positive and negative electronic impulses. But in the case of social theory, the scope of a binary approach is simply too limited to deal with the growing complexity of our world. Collins (1993) himself was aware of this concern when he defended conflict theory against the criticism that it was one-sided and did not take social solidarity seriously. Yet he still preferred to explain solidarity in terms of conflict as a fundamental starting point.

The binary approach is also unhelpful for dealing with the complex social reality of today in the area of international law. In an era where the nation state is under growing threat, legal boundaries are becoming increasingly problematic. Lindahl (2010) talks in this regard of the emergence of 'a-legality', by which he means that law has become more global, more local and more transversal than the nation-state. Legal orders increasingly overlap. The World Trade Organisation claims to be global in scope; the informal legal orders of squatter settlements develop without recourse to the state order; and multinationals act as if there is a transnational legal order. The same fragmentation is evident in the *content* of legal orders. We are witnessing the emergence of a variety of more or less autonomous cross-border legal orders which claim to address specific kinds of human activity: self-regulation by various professional bodies, technical standardisation, indigenous law inside and across countries, laws pertaining to migration and various stages of political integration.

The oppositional framework of conflict theory pays little heed to the forms of communality, solidarity and cross-cutting relations that arise from the fact that individuals belong to more than one group, which results in their participating in multiple group conflicts. One of the most prominent social scientists of our era, Seymour Martin Lipset, stressed the role of cross-cutting cleavages in reducing the intensity of political conflicts. He also foreshadowed the idea of multiple identities and their role in ameliorating conflict. Quoting empirical studies, Lipset maintained that isolated communities who did not readily develop such cross-cutting relations were more prone to extremist behaviour. In his book *Political Man* (1960), he popularised the notion that cross-cutting cleavages contribute to promoting democratic stability. In his view the chances for stable democracy were enhanced when groups and individuals had cross-cutting political affiliations. Although Lipset acknowledged the *role* of cross-cutting cleavages, or multiple identities, he paid little attention to the *content* of these commonalities. Nonetheless, he ended the fixation on conflict and opened the way to move beyond it to also study communalities, shared values and common goals.

The need to broaden the understanding of the interrelatedness of values, power, interests and democracy was dramatically illustrated by a series of developments during the past two decades which substantially changed the context in which modern-day democracies have to function. Three such interrelated phenomena are of interest: culture, religion and economy.

Culture

The growing effect of globalisation has spawned a series of social movements as a reaction against the new global order. Religious fundamentalism, cultural nationalism and territorially defined communities can basically be interpreted as defensive strategies. These counter-movements take the form of local identities, which rely for their specific identity on distinct markers, most of them of a cultural nature. These movements against the global order range from small, often extremist, groups to nation states, which are reluctant to relinquish their national sovereignty. In the early 21st century a growing disjunction can be observed between the "globalization of issues, the self-identification of people, and the affirmation of national interests in the reluctantly shared ground of the informal network state" (Castells 2004: 364).

The point of interest here is the role that cultural values can play in the process of differentiation even within one and the same state. A case in point was the reunification of Germany. The single unifying Basic Law was different from the lived reality in the two former states; life experience in the former DDR in particular was far removed from its tenets. In the minds of the citizens the Basic Law is the 'explicit constitution' that exists alongside the 'implicit constitution', which is based on the opinions, feelings and values of ordinary people, whatever the legal order prescribes. To achieve reunification in the full sense of the word, these value systems have to be taken into account (Meulemann, 1996).

At a national level the integration of Europe provides another example. The difficulties posed by the political integration of new member states are directly related to real or perceived cultural diversity. The same applies to the integration of migrant populations into existing societies. The furore surrounding the book by Thilo Sarrazin (2010), the remarks of the Turkish

Prime Minster during his recent visit to Germany (Andrews, 2011), and the influence of Wilders in the Netherlands are just random examples of how the question of European unity is perceived as, and expressed in terms of, cultural differences. The difficulties experienced in these basically mono-cultural environments are even more complex in multicultural societies.

As far as the field of economic activity is concerned, the role of corporate culture is of particular significance, especially in transnational companies. When these companies begin to trade in countries other than their home country, or when mergers between companies from different countries take place, paying attention to corporate culture can be crucial for the success of the undertaking. In many of the unsuccessful cases the inability to adapt the existing corporate culture or to merge two different cultures plays a significant role. One such high-profile example was the Daimler-Chrysler merger, where the apparent inattention to proactively combining the Stuttgart way of doing things with the corporate culture of Detroit contributed towards the poor results that in the end led to the disintegration of the merger.

At the global level there is homogenisation whereby consumer products, fashion, music, films and art are aimed at a global audience. But this masks the differences in culture and value systems that exist and even thrive below the radar of global culture. The new environment is characterised by complexity and turbulence. This makes it imperative to pay renewed attention to organisational values, as these are bound to be out of sync with the changed context. A value system based on the premise of stability cannot support strategies that are designed to deal with turbulence and complexity. This involves at least four types of values discourse: business ethics related to behaviour in the workplace but also in the wider social context; the values that individuals bring to an organisation by virtue of their cultural and social identities; the values of the organisation as a whole, expressed in its mission and reason for existence; and finally the values that flow from the political and economic system within which these organisations operate, be that of a capitalist or socialist nature (Castells, 2004; Müller, 2010).

Religion[2]

One of the surprising developments in recent years has been the return of religion in various forms, despite the predictions of so-called secularisation theory. According to this theory, the need for religion would diminish and would eventually cease altogether as the process of modernisation unfolded. The theory provided a convincing explanation of some aspects of the process

---

2   The main sources consulted for this section include: Berger, 1969; Berger & Luckmann, 1966; Norris & Inglehart, 2004; Graf, 2004; Micklethwait & Wooldridge, 2009; Müller 2009; Meulemann, 2009.

of modernisation, especially in its more sophisticated form that recognises differences in the role of religion in advanced industrial societies and societies where traditional religious views are dominant. But the situation has become much more differentiated and complex. While both the influence and public role of organised religion have indeed declined, during the last decade there has also been a concurrent and dramatic rise in religiosity in both developed and developing societies. Although the picture differs considerably from country to country, with Europe and the United States representing two contrasting stories, the tenacity of religion has been clearly underestimated. Secularisation theory has therefore come under pressure. On the one hand, the adequacy of using church attendance and prayer, the traditional forms of religious expression, as indicators of religiosity can be questioned in postmodern societies where the quest for normativity and meaning takes different forms. On the other hand, the link between religion and economic prosperity in rising Asian communities needs further investigation.

Values are of course a fundamental aspect of religion – in terms of worldview, morality, commitment, action and the like – and the 'return of God' has placed the issue of values squarely back on the agenda. This does not imply that the matter has become easier. If anything, it has become more complicated. Just two examples will illustrate the point.

The power of religious beliefs was demonstrated dramatically in the attacks of September 2001. The global audience witnessed through their own eyes that beliefs can have consequences and that these consequences can be destructive in the extreme. The counter-reaction from America was likewise couched in religious imagery and terminology. Not only was there an outcry of moral indignation, but the response to terrorism was understood as a 'calling', or a 'mission' against the forces of evil. Despite the fact that technocrats such as Dick Cheney and Donald Rumsfeld ran the war, it was religious rhetoric that dominated the discourse. This was as much a war of beliefs and values as it was a military operation. Apart from the actual struggle, the events raised much more fundamental issues about war and peace, violence and the response to violence, the implications of a multi-religious world and the possibility (or impossibility) of ever finding a common ground.

The second example of the growth of religion is the remarkable expansion of Christianity in Africa, Latin-America and especially Asia. Driven mainly by American evangelical/pentecostal energy, Christianity in the 'new' world is now outstripping Christianity in the 'old' world. America has always engaged in exporting religion, starting with the wild lands of the American West and eventually expanding to all the corners of the earth to the extent that the export of religion has assumed global dimensions. The main carriers of the religious message have been 'pastorpreneurs', philanthropists as well as Christian media and missionaries. Whereas in 1950 only 2.4 percent of the population in South Korea was Protestant, the figure now is close to 20 percent, while Christians as a whole amount to 30 percent of the population. The latest focus of missionary efforts is China, where house-churches, especially among the upwardly mobile, are on the increase. Often, in the true spirit of the American gospel of prosperity, Christianity is 'sold' as a necessary precondition for personal and professional success. While official figures show an increase from fourteen million Christians in 1997 to twenty-one million in 2006, some estimates put the figure as high as seventy-seven million (Micklethwait and Wooldrige 2009).

The export of Christianity is driven by powerful values. One of these values is religious freedom. For the first generation of pilgrims to America the lack of religious freedom in their home countries was one of the major reasons why they plunged into an uncertain world, looking for a place where they would be free of restraint and could practice their beliefs unhindered. The recent discovery by Americans that religious persecution still exists in many countries became an important motivating factor and a central issue on the agenda for the missionary effort.

However, religion always comes in a specific cultural guise and brings with it a mixture of religious and cultural values. As with the spread of Christianity in Africa during the nineteenth century, the more recent expansion of American Christianity brings with it not only the gospel, but also a very specific way of life. Central to this life is the symbiosis between religion and capitalism and their mutual reinforcement flowing from this relationship. Micklethwait and Wooldridge (2009: 244) come to the harsh conclusion: "America is thus contributing not once but twice to the global revival of religion – as the world's leading exporter of religion and as the world's leading supplier of the capitalism that increases demand for religion. In Marx's terms, they are both exporting opium and stoking the demand for opiates."

Economy

One of the remarkable features of the debate following the 2008-2009 financial crisis was the moralistic discourse that accompanied the more technical analyses of the debacle. Popular discourse abounded in emotive treatments of the issue. The anger of disillusioned investors and ordinary members of the public whose financial position was directly affected by the crisis was often expressed in the form of moral indignation. This indignation was directed at the *greed* of Wall Street investors; the *irresponsible* agencies who receive fees but are unable to give an unbiased assessment of risk; the *reckless behaviour* of homebuyers making aggressive purchases at high risk; the *unethical conduct* of auditors by not disclosing the real situation of companies; the *unjustifiably* high salaries of top executives and the *immoral* practice of continuing to give bonuses to the management of failing or bailed-out companies (Petroff, 2011).

Whether the blame allocated in each of these cases is justified or not is an open question. What is clear is the moral tone of the discourse, which points to the underlying value substratum of any economic system. The *economy,* whether of an individual or a collective such as the state, is after all about the regulation and the ordering of domestic arrangements. Economy is in essence about *priorities,* about *choices* and about the *allocation* of (scarce) resources. All of these inevitably involve value judgements. The setting and implementation of economic measures by definition presuppose values and ethical decisions.

In a democracy the value dimension of the economic system with which it is associated is even more prominent. This prominence is largely due to the convergence of the moral and the rational trajectories of the post-1948 humanist tradition. The embracing of basic human rights, including economic rights, meant that the values of liberty and equality became the common currency in economic discourse from both a capitalist and socialist perspective, giving rise to the obligation not only to do what is right but also what is good (Joas, 2000).

In the corporate sphere the increasing emphasis on values took the form of explicit codes of conduct for companies. In South Africa, for example, the three reports of the King Commission (King 1994, King 2002, King 2009) covered all possible aspects of corporate and governance behaviour. The values discourse has been explicit in the insistence on fairness, responsibility, transparency and accountability.

More than the accountable conduct of role players, the respective merits and demerits of financial systems themselves came under the spotlight. One such issue has been the 'moral hazard', discussed in this volume by Stan du Plessis, which was engendered by the custom of bailing out failing banks, with the result that banks became less prudent than they should have been, while creditors became less concerned about the imprudence of the banks to which they were lending. And there were other incentives working in the same direction, not least among them the culture of high salaries and bonuses on Wall Street, which seem to continue despite the crisis (Morgenson, 2011).

The debate about the most equitable and responsible economic system is of course an old one. It dates back to Adam Smith and has undergone countless iterations, including Marxist and capitalist versions. In the current economic climate informed by the crisis the debate has assumed a new urgency. The traditional approach is in turmoil as new uncertainties emerge, a situation in which value considerations again play, or at least should play, an important role so as to open up new possibilities.

How realistic is the quest for *common* values?

The present circumstances, in short, demand that more attention be accorded to the role of values and, more specifically, to the ways and means by which to move towards shared values. But is the quest for common values attainable? It seems that plurality, the increasing complexity of society, the ongoing processes of fragmentation and the appearance of new types of conflicts rule out any form of communality across cultures on convictions, beliefs and values.

This pessimistic conclusion, however, can be qualified by saying that it holds only as long as there is no change in thinking about values. The basic problem is the common assumption that diverse values cannot be bridged. But what is usually perceived as a conflict of *values* as such is actually a conflict at the level of their *application,* which has to do with needs that embody values. It is in the application of values where a measure of communality can be found and can help solve problems, especially in societies that are culturally diverse and are under considerable economic stress.

Two examples illustrate the point, one at the macro the other at the micro level. In the first instance, one can look at constitutions as an expression of common values, helpful especially at a time of consolidating a democracy. Constitutions are historical documents that carry the scars of their own genesis. They disclose some of the tensions surrounding their conception and birth, and they often reflect the *Zeitgeist* in which they had come into being. In this sense they serve as memorials to the past. But they also act as compasses by which to steer the ship of state through troubled waters. This is especially true in their description of the basic values on which the particular democracy rests, often expressed in the form of a bill of human rights. One cannot but be struck by the obvious similarities in formulation in the constitutions of democracies that came into being after 1989. The influence of the 1948 *Universal Declaration of Human Rights* of the United Nations is evident, but there is also a certain amount of 'borrowing' among the constitutions. This is indicative of a communality of values shared by a diverse group of democracies, and of a certain standardisation of what a democratic state entails.

Of course, the values encapsulated in a constitution are the result of negotiations, compromises and unresolved problems. In this sense, despite their foundational appearance, they are work in progress. Often they are phrased in an idealist and poetic language far removed from the realities of everyday life. Nonetheless, they symbolise a workable consensus that is supported by often deeply divided sectors of the population. A striking example is the constitution of Poland, where the set of basic values is explicitly underwritten both by "those who believe in God as the source of truth, justice, good and beauty, as well as those not sharing such faith but respecting those universal values as arising from other sources".

Everything depends on how these lofty ideals are implemented. In this regard constitutional courts carry a heavy responsibility to apply the agreed upon values in an independent and even-handed way, regardless of who the parties involved are. Overall, the record of constitutional courts across various democratic nations has been encouraging. One instructive example is the judgement by the South African Constitutional Court that declared as unconstitutional the legislation enabling the establishment of the 'Hawks', a specialised investigation unit of the police. In a detailed and precedence-setting verdict the Court argued on the basis of the separation of powers, the independence of the juridical process and the obligation to combat corruption, reaching the conclusion that the act seriously undermined respect for human rights. This shows that despite a very diverse society, fractured by deeply conflicting interests, it is possible to implement an agreed set of common values in a way that strengthens a given society. Extrapolating this point, it is not unreasonable to suggest that a similar mechanism could work not only within but also across nations.

But can what happens at the macro level also hold for processes at the micro level? Is it really possible to *generate* common values through a participative process in situations of intense conflict?

One positive example was the successful consultative process developed for a large South African mining company. The process was initiated at a time of high levels of political volatility that had intensified just before the release of Nelson Mandela. The period was characterised by deep fears among the white citizens and the unrealistically high expectations of their black counterparts. There was also financial uncertainty ensuing from diminishing production and a falling gold price, as well as cultural diversity of the many racial groups, many languages and contrasting political affiliations, labour unrest due to disputes between management and union, all of which were further compounded by pressure from the international community.

Initially, the probability of achieving common values in such a situation seemed remote. However, the level at which conflict manifested itself was an important guiding factor. One vignette: a white mine manager enters his office where a black miner is waiting for him, sitting in a chair. The miner does not stand up, does not greet the manager and averts his eyes. The manager, who comes from a culture where one greets one's superior first, stands up in their presence and looks them straight in the eye, regards this behaviour as very disrespectful. The miner, who comes from a culture where one tries to appear smaller than a superior, does not speak until spoken to, and considers looking somebody straight in the eye as disrespectful, is only trying to show his respect. For both, respect is a very important value, but they show and perceive it in very different ways. Not knowing any better, they take offence where respect was intended. Such cultural differences are of course commonplace. The important point is that underneath the differences there may be more communality than we normally assume.

An idea helpful for bridging diverse values was developed by Manfred Max-Neef (1991), a Chilean developmental economist. Intended as an 'alternative' theory of development, his hypothesis has important implications for thinking about and dealing with diversity. The main objective is to broaden and deepen the conventional growth-centred approach to development, which restricts human needs to the desire for objects, particularly material goods and services. This is a narrow view that fails to include such vital non-material features as the need for an identity, participation and freedom. In the theory a critical distinction is made between 'needs' and 'satisfiers'. A fundamental need, such as the need for freedom, can be satisfied in a variety of ways. These satisfiers can be either positive or negative in their effect on the quality of life. Examples of negative satisfiers for freedom would be inhibiting satisfiers, such as paternalism, which is rooted in customs and habits; persuasion-induced pseudo-satisfiers such as indoctrination; or destructive satisfiers imposed on people such as authoritarianism or censorship. Positive satisfiers can be either singular like the right to freedom of expression, or synergetic, satisfying more than one need at the same time, for example, participating in democratic structures and processes.

The distinction between positive and negative satisfiers was very important for the process followed at the gold mine. The distinction made clear that there are a number of ways in which the same basic need can be satisfied. It is immaterial whether members of a diverse group satisfy their need for leisure by playing or watching soccer or rugby. These positive forms of diversity are not only admissible; they should in fact be encouraged. In the same vein members of a team need not sacrifice their identities in order to complete a task successfully. But alongside the harmless satisfiers, there are also the destructive satisfiers, and these are the ones that require attention. A destructive satisfier is one where a person's own need is met at the expense of another's; stealing the week's wages from a team member, for example, may be a very effective way to satisfy one's own need for subsistence, but it is destructive for the other person.

The concept of needs and satisfiers was used as the framework for more than a hundred representative workshops stretching over a period of four years. The workshops were designed to take participants through specific phases. The first step was to create a climate where people were willing to share their perceptions of the country, the company and of the 'other' in their direct work environment. From the perspective of diversity, this was potentially the most explosive phase. Careful facilitation was required to create a climate of openness, and it was crucial that stereotypes were articulated and experienced in the presence of the 'other'. In this way, submerged tensions, 'hidden transcripts' and the stereotypes people have of each other were brought into the open.

The second step was to shift attention from present perceptions to the future. By asking about hopes and fears, it usually became clear that the same fears (increased violence, crime) and the same hopes (economic security, good education, stability) were shared across the lines of diversity. Some sense of communality started to emerge at this stage. To reinforce this tendency, participants were asked in the next phase what they expected of their supervisors, colleagues and subordinates. Starting with the role of supervisors, it was not difficult to compile a long list of desiderata: fairness, empathy, decisiveness, respect, good communication, leadership. When the lists of expectations for colleagues and for subordinates were compiled, the commonalties also immediately became evident.

It was critical, first, to translate these expectations into needs, for example, the need for respect and safety, and then to recognise these needs as values. In this way the dynamic nature of values was accentuated in the spirit of the beatitude: 'Blessed are those who *hunger and thirst* for righteousness'. In this way a list of shared values emerged, whatever other diversities existed within the group. A typical set would include values such as teamwork, communication, respect, trust and honesty, fairness, education and training, responsibility, leadership, safety and health, profitability. These became the building blocks from which a final set of values was compiled for the mine as a whole.

It is important to keep in mind that these were values and satisfiers applicable to a specific work situation. The teams were not trying to solve the county's problems as a whole. The object was to find a workable code and a set of practices that would enable people to operate constructively and effectively in their specific context. This 'piecemeal approach' made the task more achievable. Of course, wider issues did impact on their thinking and their 'local' solutions no doubt had wider ramifications for society at large, but in order to get a very complicated and difficult process off the ground, this initial narrower focus proved to be a productive strategy.

Apart from being dynamic, this type of discourse is also self-regulating. One of the practical results of the values process was the establishment of representative work place forums at the various shafts, which used the common values as basis for their planning and operations. It also became the framework for decisions on future developments and for the solving of new problems. The success of the forums as examples of effective worker participation and joint decision-making was such that it subsequently affected labour legislation. It so happened that one of the participants in the process was the regional representative of the National Mineworkers Union, who was later elected Member of Parliament for the African National Congress (ANC) and subsequently became a member of the drafting committee for the new Labour Relations Act. The Act made the formation of workplace forums a legal requirement. The process of developing shared values was then applied in a wide variety of companies and organisations – noticeably in the field of agriculture and forestry, state and semi-state departments, institutions of higher education, community organisations and other institutions as part of the much wider process of social transformation.

The process of developing common values at the micro level has since been implemented not only in a variety of contexts but also at other levels. For example, the approach proved useful as part of a critical re-examination at the national level of the state of human society in South Africa, and for re-defining the contours of an inclusive and participating democracy. A similar approach is now also being implemented as part of the UN programme 'Alliance of Civilizations' as a conscious alternative to the 'Clash of Civilizations' paradigm.

Conclusion

Four conclusions flow from the preceding discussion.

First, the debate about values cannot but intensify in the foreseeable future. This is not only because of the uncertainty of the present harsh economic climate, but also because of the growing complexity of relations at the individual, national and international levels. It is likely that there will be an increase in the appeal to values in all kinds of discourses, as we are already witnessing in the condemnation of individual and corporate greed in the financial crisis; in the calls for freedom echoing in the streets of Cairo and Tripoli and in the rest of the Arab world; in the astonishingly composed attitude of the victims of the earthquake in Japan and its aftermath; and in the reconfiguration of international relations. The ability to deal with values and the conflicting claims based on values is likely to be in high demand.

Secondly, despite this growing plurality and complexity at all levels of society, the prospect of finding common ground has increased. The disintegration of monolithic power blocks, the new forms of cross-cutting cleavages, the embracing of multiple identities, the discovery that in both the West and in the Arab world the urge for freedom and the determination to achieve it are unstoppable – these have all contributed to a new atmosphere where communality has once again become a possibility. However, the precondition for any success in this regard is the willingness to move deeper than the obvious conflict at the level of satisfiers and to make the underlying communality of universal needs or values the point of departure. The proposal for the alliance of civilisations as an alternative to the paradigm of a clash of civilisations will only be feasible if this basic precondition is met.

Thirdly, opportunities for participation and representation should be exploited to the maximum in all spheres of society (cultural, political, economic). The concept of consensus democracy proposed by Lijphart (1999) has retained its relevance. Whether in the form of electoral systems aimed at proportional representation, bipartisan parliamentary and public committees, coalitions, governments of national unity, structures for enabling and sanctioning negotiation, arbitration and reconciliation – all practical possibilities should be harnessed. This is needed not only to ensure that the 'other side' is being heard, but to create a context in which it becomes possible to penetrate the secondary level of conflict in order to discover underlying communality. The gold mine experience proved that this is not merely an idealistic dream, but a concrete and practical way to arrive at common values in extremely adverse conditions.

Finally, the situation arising from the Great Recession offers a unique opportunity to move beyond the stalemate of sterile and outdated oppositions. Both the West and the East are experiencing a crisis of their embedded value systems. Paradoxically, this is generated by contrasting considerations. The West is experiencing a crisis of many of its liberal values; the East has mounted the tiger of the market system, while it wants to retain its nationalistic ethic. As China, severely constricted by its domestic society, is trying to adapt to the liberal world order, this very order is undergoing serious re-examination. The uneven record of liberal foreign policies in delivering a more secure and just world order has challenged the key liberal values of freedom and prevented the liberal world order from living up to expectations. As a result, that world is experiencing a crisis of legitimacy. In looking for ways to re-gain legitimacy, values and their bridging power need to be taken into serious consideration.

Sources

Archer, R. (1995). *Economic democracy. The politics of feasible socialism.* Oxford: Oxford University Press.

Allan, K. D. (2007). *The Social Lens. An invitation to social and sociological theory.* Thousand Oaks: Sage Publications.

Andrews, J. (2011). Mr Erdoğan goes to Germany. *The Economist.* 1 March.

Berger, P.L. and Luckmann, T. (1966) . Secularization and Pluralism. *International Yearbook for the Sociology of Religion.* 2: 73-84.

Berger, P.L. (1969). *The sacred canopy. Elements of a sociological theory of religion.* New York: Anchor Books.

Campus, D. and Pasquino, G. (eds.) (2009). *Masters of political science.* Colchester: ECPR Press.

Castells, M. (1998). *End of Millennium.* Oxford: Blackwell.

Castells, M. (2004). *The Power of Identity.* Oxford: Blackwell. (2nd edition).

Cilliers, P. and Preisker, R (eds.) (2009). *Complexity, difference and identity.* Heidelberg: Springer.

Collins, R. (1975). *Conflict sociology. Toward an explanatory science.* New York: Academic Press.

Collins, R. (1986).*The future decline of the Russian Empire.* Cambridge: Cambridge University Press.

Collins, R. (1993). What does conflict theory predict about America's future? 1993 Presidential Address. *Sociological Perspectives* 36: 289-313.

Coser, L. (1956). *The functions of social conflict*. New York: The Free Press.

Dahl, R. A. (1985). *A preface to economic democracy*. Berkeley: UCLA Press.

Dahrendorf, R. (1959). *Class and class conflict in an industrial society*. Stanford: Stanford University Press

De Gruchy, J.W. (ed.) (2011). *The humanist imperative in South Africa*. Stellenbosch: SUN Media.

Diamond, L. and Marks, G. (eds.) (1992).*Reexamining democracy*. Thousand Oaks: Sage Publishers.

Du Toit, P. and Kotze, H. (2010). *Liberal democracy and peace in South Africa. The pursuit of freedom as dignity*. Basingstoke: Palgrave Macmillan.

Du Toit, S. J. 2011. Interview on social justice. Accessible on-line at: http://www.unesco.org/new/en/unesco/news/interview_with_fanie_du_toit. Consulted on 18.03.2011.

Ginsberg, T. (2003). *Juridical review in new democracies. Constitutional courts in Asian cases*. Cambridge: Cambridge University Press.

Godsell, B. (2011). At this time and at this place. In De Gruchy, J.W. (ed.). *The humanist imperative in South Africa*. Stellenbosch: SUN Press.

Graf, F. (2004). *Die Wiederkehr der Götter. Religion in der modernen Kultur*. München: Beck.

Hoffmann-Lange, U. (2009). Seymour Martin Lipset: Modernization, social structures and political culture as factors in democratic development, in: Campus, D. and Pasquino, G. (eds.) Masters of political science. Colchester: ECPR Press, pp. 145-165.

Holgate, R. G. (2002). Liberty and democracy as economic systems. *Independent Review* VI . 3: 407-425.

Huntington, S. P. (1991). *The Third Wave. Democratization in the late twentieth century*. Norman: Oklahoma University Press.

Kotze, H. and Steenekamp, C. L. (2009). *Values and democracy in South Africa. Comparing elite and public values*. Johannesburg: Conrad-Adenhauer-Stiftung.

Lategan, B. C. (2011). Developing common values in situations of plurality and social transformation. In: *Festschrift* for Dirkie Smit (in press).

Lijphart, A. (1999). *Patterns of democracy. Government forms and performance in thirty-six countries*. New Haven: Yale University Press.

Lindahl, H. (2010). A-legality: Postnationalism and the question of legal boundaries, *The Modern Law Review*. 73 (1): 30-56.

Lipset, S. M. (1960). *Political Man*. London: Heinemann.

Max-Neef, M. (1991). *Human scale development: conception, application and further reflections*. New York: Apex Press.

Meulemann, H. (1996). *Werte und Wertewandel.ZurIdentiäteinergeteilten und wiedervereinte Nation*.Weuiheim: JuventaVerlag.

Meulemann, H. (2009). Secularisation or the revival of religion? In: Rieger, M (ed.). *What the world believes*. Gütersloh: Verlag Bertelsmann Stiftung

Micklethwait, J. and Wooldridge, A. (2009). *God is back. How the global rise of faith is changing the world*. London: Penguin.

Müller, H. (2010). Business ethics from below: rethinking organisational values, strategy and trust, in: Cilliers, P. and Preisker, R (eds.). *Complexity, difference and Identity*. Heidelberg: Springer.

Müller, T. (2009). Religiosity and attitudes towards the involvement of religious leaders in politics: A multilevel-analysis of 55 societies. *World Values Research*. 2(1):1-29.

Norris, P. & Inglehart, R. 2004. *Sacred and secular. Religion and politics worldwide.* Cambridge: Cambridge University Press.

Petroff, E. 2011. Who is to blame for the subprime crisis? Available on-line at: http://www.investopedia.com/articles/07/subprime-blame.asp.

Rieger, M. (ed.) 2009. *What the world believes. Analyses and commentary on the Religion Monitor. 2008.*Gütersloh: Bertelsmann.

Sarrazin, T. (2010). *Deutschland schafft sich ab.* München: Deutsche Verlagsanstalt.

Universal Declaration of Human Rights 1948. New York: United Nations. Available on-line at: http://www.un.org/en/documents/udhr/index.shtml

Van Beek, U. (ed.) (2005). *Democracy under construction: Patterns from four continents.* Bloomfield Hills: Barbara Budrich Publishers.

Van Beek, U. (ed.) (2010). *Democracy under scrutiny: Elites, citizens, cultures.* Opladen: Barabara Budrich Publishers.

Woodhead, L. (ed). (2001). *Peter Berger and the study of religion.* London: Routledge.

The consequences of the Great Recession: hypotheses and scenarios

Edmund Wnuk-Lipinski

Over eighty years ago the world was shattered by the Great Depression. When the recent crisis hit the US economy, and later the rest of the world, the spectre of the Great Depression immediately returned as a relevant point of reference to help us grasp the magnitude and the range of the unfolding turbulence. Analysts and politicians were concerned not only with the grim implications for the global economy, but also with the social and political consequences of protracted negative trends in the financial and industrial sectors of the global market. Following the Great Depression a number of parliamentary democracies suffered serious legitimacy problems and some were replaced by autocratic regimes. The most spectacular collapse was that of the Weimar Republic, with consequences for the world that we all know only too well. No wonder then that this time round much of the attention was focused on the remedies that would not only limit the damage to the world market, but that would also safeguard the stability of democratic regimes, particularly those of the young democracies that emerged over two decades ago.

However, a comparison between the Great Recession and the Great Depression reveals a number of significant differences, as highlighted by Dirk Berg-Schlosser in this opus. To begin with, the recent crisis was not nearly as severe as the crisis of the 1930s if one compares the GDP, industrial production, exports and unemployment rates. And even though the range and magnitude of the 2008-2009 financial crunch were considerable and there are indications that some countries, such as Greece for example, are facing a rather painful process of cuts in public spending with the associated local social unrest, the term 'recession' rather than 'depression' seems more accurate and has been used throughout this volume. Secondly, the Great Depression was basically limited to the Western world. Today, owing to the advanced stage of globalisation, the world is incomparably more interlinked than it was in the 1930s, particularly in the economic sector. Two other important differences in comparison to the Great Depression can be noted. The one is that national egotisms, though certainly in evidence, have been far more tempered this time round, and the coordination at the supranational level in search of remedies that would limit the damage was much more efficient; the G8 and

G20 summits as well as EU internal policies are among the most striking examples.

Additionally, and in contrast to the 1930s, the Great Recession has not
produced any significant extremist political responses as was the case during
in the 1930s and as Dirk Berg-Schlosser has explained in his chapter. As he
noted, "there are now better informed insights into the causes and mechanisms of the crisis; neo-Keynesianism has been accepted again on a much
greater international scale. Nevertheless, effective international controls to
avoid similar bubbles and excesses are still lacking". Social unrest, visible
here and there, has been induced not so much by the crisis as by austerity
measures implemented to limit the adverse economic consequences. And so
far the Third Wave of democratisation has not been reversed as an immediate
consequence of the crisis. Meanwhile, the ongoing 'Arab Spring' creates
hope for the democratisation of the Islamic world, although the final outcome
is far from clear. The young democracies that have emerged from the ruins of
the Soviet bloc have not been seriously shaken by the crisis. Even in countries where severe counter-measures were implemented, including cuts in salaries as was the case in Estonia, for example, the democratic order has not
shown any symptoms of destabilisation, nor has it been challenged by anti-
democratic forces,

In short, at least so far the Great Recession has not had any fundamental
political consequences on the global scale. However, as noted by Stan du
Plessis and Philip Mohr in this volume, for a variety of reasons large emerging markets have been visibly less affected by the crisis than the old well-
established capitalist democracies were. Brazil, India and especially authoritarian China managed to cope surprisingly well, implying that the crisis could
undermine the trend-setting role that the developed capitalist democracies
had played in the past.

The crisis also brought into sharp focus the issue of global governance,
and above all, the issue of accountability, or more precisely the severe deficit
in democratic accountability of policymakers whose decisions have global
consequences. Christer Jönsson argued in his chapter that in the globalised
world "we are all affected by decisions taken elsewhere". The Great Recession revealed this truth with striking clarity. And most of these decisions
"taken elsewhere" suffer not only from the deficit of democratic legitimacy,
but also from the lack of transparency, especially in the financial and military
arenas. Jönsson writes that "the all-affected principle calls attention to how
the ideal of 'one person, one vote' has become perverted under present political conditions where national borders do not coincide with existing power
structures". This view is shared here along with the pessimistic assessment of
the various attempts to introduce more democratic control over decisions that
have global consequences. Giddens, Held, McGrew and many others noticed
the problem years ago, but their proposed remedies were rather utopian.

Democratic control over global governance is impossible without a global polity, and global polity needs a common normative basis as a foundation. Our world, however, is multicultural and to create a common set of global values is truly a Herculean task, which brings us back to the starting point. Bernard Lategan notes that "on one level there is homogenisation in the way consumer products, fashion, music, films and art are aimed at a global audience. But this masks the differences in culture and value systems that exist and even thrive below the radar of global culture". This dialectics of the homogenising effect of globally distributed goods and services, and the diversifying effect of local cultures and value systems, which shape local identities of individuals and give them a sense of belonging and security, is not only a source of growing tensions, but sometimes also diffuse violence.

Even if we refer only to the superficial press coverage of the crisis, one fact remains beyond question: some countries have been more affected than others. Philip Mohr, in his review of the various economic models that operate on the global market, formulated the following explanation: "the level of financial development and integration in the more advanced economies made them much more vulnerable to the crisis than developing countries with less developed financial sectors. As a result, the crisis has been labelled a rich world's crisis." China and India (and to some extent Brazil) may serve here as model examples of countries able to maintain a relatively high economic growth in the face of the global crisis. Contrastingly, China is an authoritarian country, whereas India is often labelled the largest democracy in the world. And they reacted to the crisis in different ways. As Sang-jin Han and Peng Lu put it: "as the international financial crisis spread from developed countries to emerging economies and as it spilled over from the financial sector to the real economy, China has not remained immune to the recession in the West, but neither has the exogenous financial crisis caused an endogenous economic meltdown and/or social turmoil in the country. In some respects: "the crisis has actually turned out to be a blessing in that it relieved the Chinese leaders' previous concern of an over-heating economy and encouraged a reorientation of production to the domestic market". Heavy state intervention and, particularly, extensive investments in infrastructure and hidden subsidies of export, maintain high economic growth in spite of the external crisis. Philip Mohr argues that "a key factor in Chinese economic growth has been, and remains, the massive amount of unemployed, underemployed or unproductive labour in the rural areas available for productive employment at low wages in the cities. The Chinese miracle is first and foremost a labour story. Without the availability of unlimited supplies of labour it would not have occurred". The so-called 'Chinese model' is in fact, says Mohr, "a unique combination of state control and rampant free-market capitalism" that can hardly be imitated elsewhere.

India, on the other hand, has chosen the opposite strategy: deregulation and market-oriented economic reforms. Yet both the Chinese and Indian strategies proved effective in combating the possibly negative consequences of the global financial crisis. The logical conclusion one can draw is that the determinants of success are located elsewhere and reside in the relative backwardness of the financial system, a massive population with an extensive reservoir of cheap labour and a huge domestic market that can play the role of a buffer in case of turbulences on the global market. In short, both democratic India and autocratic China proved relatively immune to the Great Recession. But this was not necessarily the case with poor Third Wave democracies or authoritarian systems showing poor economic performance.

In the first case, as Ursula Hoffmann-Lange observed, "those Third Wave democracies that have been hardest hit by the global recession have shown a remarkable resilience. Rather than turning against democracy, voters in these countries have instead tended to punish incumbent governments and to vote new – and frequently even rightist rather than leftist – governments into power". In the case of autocracies with poor economic performance, the already weak political legitimacy has been weakened even further. Hoffman-Lange argues that the recent massive unrest in the Arab world strongly supports this thesis. The unrest may be interpreted as a withdrawal of legitimacy from authoritarian regimes as a result of the fall in economic output, which had acted as a substitute for procedural democratic legitimacy.

Does this mean that all democratic regimes are flexible enough to absorb the shockwaves of the Great Recession without any threat to their system's stability? Much depends on the level of systemic consolidation and the efficiency of democratic procedures. As Laurence Whitehead observes in this volume: "democratic procedures have offered a safety valve for citizen discontent, an opportunity for the peaceful renewal of political authorities, and perhaps even some scope for the termination of failed strategies of economic management, and their replacement by more promising approaches. National democracies seem to provide some structural opportunities for collective deliberation and lesson-learning that might be harder to achieve under alternative political dispensations". In his view democracies in general and consolidated democracies in particular work as relatively effective "error-correction" mechanisms. And indeed, such an "error-correction" mechanism apparently worked in the United States, where in November 2008 the Americans transferred legislative and executive power from the Republicans to the Democrats; some two years later this mechanism also worked in the United Kingdom, where a Conservative-Liberal coalition replaced the Labour Party and formed a government united around the idea of repairing the damage, predominantly in an economic arena. Whitehead concludes that "at least in the core established democracies most responsible for the crisis, democratic alternation intervened as a powerful mechanism of political accountability and (perhaps even) 'error correction'."

The problem, however, remains in young and peripheral democracies, where the consolidation of the regime is rather weak and where democratic institutions and habits are not rooted deeply enough in all the segments of the society. In this particular context the recent crisis may be interpreted as the "broken promise" of democracy, to use Bobbio's (1987) expression, where there is uncertainty instead of stability, regression instead of development, chaos instead of order, and marginalisation instead of civic emancipation. For weakly consolidated democracies the crisis and its consequences have been a demanding test. Under trying circumstances it is natural for people to look for political alternation so as to ease economic hardships. The habitual attitude in well-established democracies, as Whitehead indicates, is the search for alternation within the democratic order. In young democracies, however, the search for alternation may also include an authoritarian alternative, which could be seen be as a radical exit from an unbearable situation.

As mentioned, we have not yet seen any indication of a reversal of the Third Wave of democratisation. Quite the opposite: the 'Arab Spring' illustrates a search for alternatives under authoritarian regimes that include popular demands for the liberalisation of the regime and for civic emancipation. Nonetheless, the search for alternatives at present represents rather a general sentiment, both in the democratic and authoritarian parts of the world. The global crisis revealed the simple truth that a serious economic downturn affecting one of the major global players exposes other global players to a similar threat, while actors along the periphery also suffer but have little say in global economic affairs.

One may formulate the hypothesis that in order to deal with the consequences of a crisis, global economic players implement both short-term and long-term strategies that fit in with the logic of their own particular sociopolitical system. As Laurence Whitehead observes, democracies put into motion corrective procedures, of which the most common is a democratic alternation that allows for the electoral ousting of a national political leadership held responsible for the economic debacle. But major authoritarian players do not remain passive either. They switch priorities in their centralised resource redistribution system to areas that require intervention and where these resources are most needed.

However, the expectation is that the less consolidated the system, whether authoritarian or democratic, and at the same time the greater its economic distance from the major players of the global core, the more likely it is that the array of alternatives that exists within a given system will not suffice and that anti-systemic alternatives might be contemplated for implementation. The likely scenario for peripheral autocracies would include more liberalisation of the rules of the game, more accountability from those in power and more civic emancipation. Young peripheral democracies, on the other hand, might well entertain radical authoritarian solutions, which in the popular perception would be the better way to restore order and stability.

In other words, the hypothesis assumes that the Great Recession will impact on the global balance of power, especially if the global economy is headed for a second dip. The consequent shifts may run both ways, either from authoritarian regimes to democracy, or from 'defective' democracies to autocracy. The next decade or so will show the direction of the change. For the moment the Third Wave of democracy is at a crossroads. It might actually gain new momentum should the 'Arab Spring' place the countries of the region on a path leading to a transition to democracy; should the 'Arab Spring' fail to initiate such a transition in the region, the Third Wave will regress. The latter option cannot be dismissed lightly and has been pondered in this volume by a number of authors. Dirk Berg-Schlosser pointed out that "for some countries China might possibly serve as a new model combining a controlled market economy with authoritarian rule. This also provides more leeway for other authoritarian or rogue states, such as Angola or Sudan. Similarly, a new national-authoritarian model in Russia and other CIS and neighbouring countries may follow this route".

The arguments presented in this volume by Pierre du Toit and Edmund Wnuk-Lipinski run along similar lines. Du Toit focuses attention on some additional aspects of the expected shifts in the global balance of power. He argues that both authoritarian and democratic global players are deeply interested in maintaining a global peace, because only in such a context will they be able to pursue their main goals, which are modernisation and technological progress. Of course, this does not mean that local military conflicts will have been eradicated and that mankind will have reached Kant's famous eternal peace. What it means is that global military confrontations will be unlikely and that violent conflicts will be diffused and will not accumulate along the territorial borders of nation-states. Conflicts will be less territorially based than value-based, and while rivalry between global players will still exist, it will take place elsewhere, namely in the arenas of economic growth, technological innovation and cyberspace domination.

During the first phase of the Third Wave up until about the collapse of the Soviet bloc, the unassailable assumption held that the best and most efficient – if not the only – route to economic development and technological advancement was through a combination of liberal democracy and a capitalist economy. The assumption was consistently supported by empirical studies in different regions of the world and the disintegration of the communist system further reinforced this widespread conviction.

Since then the stunning economic and technological progress of authoritarian China coupled with the relatively rapid eradication of poverty for hundreds of millions of people has made the proposition more problematic. Moreover, the effectual eradication of poverty among vast segments of Chinese society did not evoke – at least not yet – any popular aspirations for more liberty and human rights, as might have been expected. Instead it whet the appetite for greater consumption. As Han and Lu noted, the liberalisation and democratisation of the system is more a subject of discussion among Chinese intellectual elites than a focus for the public demands of the masses. In other words, economic growth did not convert ordinary people into citizens demanding their rights, but rather turned them into consumers, or 'acquiescent subjects', who are predominantly interested in social stability and the improvement of their individual wellbeing.

Is this only because China happened to be organised as an authoritarian state? A positive answer to such a question would be superficial for, as our analyses show, the reasons run deeper. The specific Chinese culture and philosophy that inform everyday relations between the Chinese people is what makes a significant difference. As Ursula van Beek observes, the recent work of the ruling elite and many Chinese intellectuals has been "to weave the threads of Confucian tradition into the fabric of Marxism by emphasising elements the two are said to have in common, such as strong leadership, social justice and harmony.... The core values of thrift, diligence and an ethic of hard work encourage dedication and commitment as a way to contribute by the individual to the development of a harmonious society". The normative code specific to China is also shared by the majority of the intellectual elite, who for pragmatic reasons tend to choose adaptation over nonconformism, and cooperation with the power elite over conflict, and who favour meritocracy over democracy. According to Han and Lu, "Since the 1990s talented intellectuals, scientists and technocrats are lured increasingly into the existing system as 'interested shareholders' with offers of abundant government funding, affluent living conditions and prestigious political/academic titles". In consequence, in China the Great Recession confirmed rather than undermined the significance of patronage by officials of the vast number of private entrepreneurs who believe that harmonious relations with the power elite and the institutions of the centralised state are the more efficient strategy to secure their group interest than any other alternative, and especially a democratic transition. The two authors conclude that "as long as most entrepreneurs still think the system generally works for them (via personal or institutional conduits) there seems little chance they will support democratisation". In short, the Chinese economic elite will probably be satisfied with their status of producers and consumers, and will most likely not seek the conversion of this status into free citizenship, as this is understood in the West.

China must undoubtedly be seen as a key factor in developing any global scenarios for the next decade or two – not because of the massive size of its population, but because of its successful pursuit of economic and technological leadership on the world scene. In the coming years China may enter a transition to democracy, however specifically defined this might be in the Chinese cultural context, or it may remain an economically and technologically successful authoritarian capitalist state. In the first case the Third Wave would get a tremendous new impetus, and in the latter and more likely case, China may become a trendsetter for the less successful authoritarian systems and 'defective democracies' on the world's periphery.

The Great Recession proved that the present-day world is not immune to severe economic crises, which put a question mark over the steady improvement of life conditions for people in different corners of the globe. It has also shown that economic difficulties in one area are quickly felt in other parts of the world. And the spill-over effect is nowadays not only faster but also deeper, if compared with the time of the Great Depression. This is simply because the world is now more globalised than ever before. There are two possible responses to the global spill-over effect. The one calls for an equally global solution; the other for a retreat to the idea of 'beggar-thy-neighbour' to salvage whatever possible at the local level of the nation-state. Of course, there is an obvious implication to the latter response: the stronger nation-states survive at the expense of the weaker nation-states, which ultimately pay the price for the crisis. The first option needs stronger cooperation in the global economic arena and the establishment of binding rules of the game that would increase the accountability of the economic policymakers towards those who may potentially be affected by their decisions. However, this is hardly viable without a deep reform of global institutions, including the UN. What these institutions need is more executive power and having at their disposal effective law-enforcement instruments. In the absence of reform, even the commonly agreed upon rules of the game will be devoid of meaning. But executive power and law-enforcement instruments need democratic control over the process of decision-making. Democratic control, in turn, needs commonly adopted procedures and, above all, the development of a civil society that transcends the traditional boundaries of the nation-state.

In order to prevent further economic turmoil global players, such as the G20, will have to choose from the whole range of possible alternatives and their choices will determine the most likely short-term scenario for the world order. It will be of crucial importance whether the choices made by the most powerful nation-states will be aimed at universal or particular solutions, and whether the choices will be inclusive or exclusive on the global scale.

Theoretically, one can distinguish four possible scenarios that may be the outcome of the choices made, as shown in the Table below.

Table 1

Actions taken by the global players	Universal	Particular
Inclusive	Multi-polar world order based on a global social contract	Bi-polar world: competition between democratic and authoritarian capitalisms
Exclusive	Multi- polar world order based on the isolation of poor peripheries	Return to the Westphalian type of world order: national egotisms prevail over supra-national regulations

Universal and inclusive solutions would entail at least two fundamental changes in comparison to the past. First, liberal democracy and the observance of human rights cease to play a role as the entry ticket to the core of globalisation since authoritarian China has to be included. Secondly, the new world order has several 'centres of gravity'. In theory the centres are competing with each other by means of commonly agreed upon rules of the game, but in practice the giant emerging markets of Brazil, India and China have a much stronger voice in global affairs than ever before. In this model everybody is included, but economically the strongest players set up the rules of the game that the weaker ones have to follow.

Particular and inclusive solutions produce an entirely different world order. Liberal democracy and the preservation of human rights are retained as a specific ideological criterion, which block access to the core of globalisation by undemocratic economic global players as long as these economic giants (first of all China, but also Russia and some Arab countries with rich oil resources) remain authoritarian or even not fully democratic. In this scenario one may expect the gradual re-emergence of a bi-polar world order with aggregate economic and technological competition between authoritarian and democratic capitalisms.

Exclusive and universal solutions would result in the emergence of a multi-polar world of successful economies, which isolate themselves from poor and inefficient economies. This model implies an increase in global inequalities and the isolation of the world's enclaves of poverty executed by means of strict anti-immigration laws which protect the enclaves of wealth.

Exclusive and particular solutions would mean that consensus at the global level is not possible and the particular nation-states adopt individual strategies to cope with possible threats to their economic growth. In this model competition and conflict prevail (including various military conflicts over access to scarce resources) and co-operation according to common rules of the game is reduced to a minimum.

Which of these scenarios is the most likely to be realised? Probably none, since international relations at the global level are far too complex and diversified to fit any single one of the above four simple models. Nonetheless, ex-

clusive and particular solutions seem rather unlikely, given the fact that globalisation is so far advanced that a retreat to the Westphalian model would
produce even more serious troubles than another global recession. The most
likely projection is a mixture of inclusive universal and particular solutions,
which would secure the interests of the major global players and would create
an international context conducive to their further economic and technological development. The lesson learnt from the Great Recession leads to the
conclusion that neither the Washington Consensus nor the Beijing Consensus
is likely to play the role of the new global contract, which should be both
universal and inclusive. The advancement of globalisation calls for new initiatives which would adjust obsolete institutional arrangements to the needs of
the interconnected world of today.

Sources

Bobbio, N. (1987): *The future of democracy. A defence of the rules of the game.* Ox-
ford: Polity Press.
Giddens, A. (2000): *Runaway world. How globalization is reshaping our lives.* New
York: Routledge.
Held, D. (1997). *Democracy and the global order. From modern state to cosmopoli-
tan governance.* Oxford: Polity Press.
McGrew, A. G. (1999). Democratising global governance. Democratic theory and
democracy beyond borders. *Theoria. A Journal of Social and Political Theory.*
December. 94: 30-47.

Bibliography

Adrian, T. and H. S. Shin (2009). Financial intermediaries and monetary economics. New York, Federal Reserve Bank of New York Staff Report. No. 398.

Ahrend, R. *et al.* (2008). Monetary policy, market excesses and financial turmoil. Paris, OECD Economics Department working paper No. 597.

Allan, K. D. (2007). *The social lens. An invitation to social and sociological theory.* Thousand Oaks: Sage Publications.

Almond, G.A. and Powell, G.B. (1966). *Comparative politics: a developmental approach.* Boston: Little Brown.

Almunia, M. *et al* (2009). From Great Depression to great credit crisis: similarities, differences and lessons. Cambridge (Ma). NBER working paper No. 15524.

Amsden, A. (1989). *Asia's next giant: South Korea and late industrialization.* Oxford: Oxford University Press.

Andrews, J. (2011). Mr Erdoğan goes to Germany. *The Economist* . 1 March.

Annan, K. (2002). Address: The Global Compact, Madrid, 9 April. Available on-line at: www.unglobalcompact.org/NewsAndEvents/

Archer, R. (1995). *Economic democracy. The politics of feasible socialism.* Oxford: Oxford University Press.

Awdry, Ch. (2010). *China cements status as world growth leader.* Available on-line at: http://www.ftchinaconfidential.com/MacroEconomy/CapitalMarkets/Features.

Baumohl, B. (2008). *The secrets of economic indicators* (second edition). Upper Saddle River (NJ): Wharton School Publishing.

BBC World Service, GlobScan (2011) survey. Accessible on-line at: http://www.bbc.co.uk/pressoffice/pressreleases/stories/2011/03_march/28/china.shtml

Beattie, A. (2009). *False economy. A surprising economic history of the world.* London: Viking.

Beattie, A., J. Chaffin, *et al.* (2010). China defends its currency policy. *Financial Times.* London. 7 October.

Beetham, D. (2009). Democracy: universality and diversity. *Ethics & Global Politics.* 2 (4): 281-296.

Bell, D. (2010). The Chinese Confucian Party. *Globe and Mail.* 19 February.

Berger, P.L. (1969). *The sacred canopy. Elements of a sociological theory of religion.* New York: Anchor Books.

Berger, P.L. and Luckmann, T. (1966). Secularization and pluralism. *International Yearbook for the Sociology of Religion.* 2: 73-84.

Berg-Schlosser, D. and Mitchell, J. (eds) (2000). *Conditions of democracy in Europe, 1919-39: systematic case-studies.* London: MacMillan.

Berg-Schlosser, D and Mitchell, J. (eds) (2002). *Authoritarianism and democracy in Europe, 1919-39: comparative analyses.* London: Palgrave.

Bernanke, B. and Gertler, M. (1999). Monetary policy and asset price volatility. Federal Reserve Bank of Kansas City Economic Review (4th quarter): 17-51.

Bernhagen, P. (2009). Democracy, business, and the economy. In: Haerpfer, C, Bernhagen,P., Inglehart, R.F., Welzel, C. (eds.). (2009). *Democratization.* Oxford: Oxford University Press.

Bexell, M. and Mörth, U. (eds) (2010) *Democracy and public-private partnerships in global governance.* Basingstoke: Palgrave Macmillan.

Blanchard, O. J. (2009). The crisis: basic mechanisms and appropriate policies. Washington, IMF. Working paper, WP/09/80.

Blinder, A. S. (2008). Two bubbles, two paths. *New York Times,* 15 June 2008.

Blinder, A. S. (2005). Understanding the Greenspan standard. Paper presented at the Federal Reserve Bank of Kansan City symposium. The Greenspan era: lessons for the future. Jackson Hole, Wyoming, 25-27 August 2005.

Board of Governors of the Federal Reserve System (2003). Minutes of the Federal Open Market Committee. 24-25 June , 2003. Washington.

Bobbio, N. (1987). *The future of democracy. A defence of the rules of the game,* Polity Press: Oxford.

Borio, C. and Disyatat, P. (2009). Unconventional monetary policies: an appraisal. Basel, BIc. Working paper No. 292.

Borio, C. and Zhu, H. (2008). Capital regulation, risk-taking and monetary policy: a missing link in the transmission mechanism. Basel, BIS. Working paper No. 268.

Bracher, K. D. (1953). Die Auflösung der Weimarer Republik. Villingen: Ring Verlag.

Buzan , B (2010) . China in international society: Is 'Peaceful Rise' possible? *Chinese Journal of International Politics.*3(1): 5-36.

Cai, F. and Chan, K. (2009). The global economic crisis and unemployment in China. *Eurasian Geography and Economics.* 50(5):513–531.

Callahan, W.A. (2004). Historical legacies and non/traditional security: commemorating National Humiliation Day. Paper presented at Renmin University, Beijing. April.

Campus, D. and Pasquino, G. (eds.) (2009). *Masters of political science.* Colchester: ECPR Press.

Castells, M. (1996). *The rise of the network society.* Oxford: Blackwell.

Castells, M. (1998). *End of millennium.* Oxford: Blackwell.

Castells, M. (2004). *The power of identity.* Oxford: Blackwell. (Second edition).

Cecchetti, S. G. (2009). Crisis and responses: The Federal Reserve in the early stages of the Financial Crisis. *Journal of Economic Perspectives.* 23(1): 51-75.

Cecchetti, S. G., Mohanty, M.S. and F. Zampolli (2010). The future of public debt: prospects and implications. Basel, BIS Working paper No. 300.

Chan, E. (2009). China's stimulus package and its effect on China's SOEs: bad for the economy and bad for the prospect of democracy. Available on-line at: http://chinaelectionsblog.net/?p=12852

Charron, N. and Lapuente,V. (2010). Does democracy produce quality of government? *European Journal of Political Research.* 49 (4): 443-470.

Chomsisengphet, S. and Pennington-Cross, A. (2006). The evolution of the subprime mortgage market. Federal Reserve Bank of St Louis Economic Review January/February: 31-56.

Chou Yu-sun (1996). Nationalism and patriotism in China. *Issues and Studies.* 32 (11): 67-86.

Cilliers, P. and Preisker, R (eds.) (2009). *Complexity, difference and identity.* Heidelberg: Springer.

Clarida, R. *et al.* (1997). Monetary policy rules in practice: some international evidence. New York, New York University, C.V. Starr Centre for Applied Economics. Economic research report No. 97-32.

Claude, I.L. (1964). *Swords into plowshares: the problems and progress of international organization.* New York: Random House.

Coase, R. H. (1991 [1994]). The institutional structure of production. Essays on economics and economists. Chicago: Chicago University Press.

Coase, R. H. (1937).The Nature of the Firm. *Economica.* 4: 386-405.

Collins, R. (1975). *Conflict sociology. Toward an explanatory science.* New York: Academic Press.

Collins, R. (1986).*The future decline of the Russian Empire.* Cambridge: Cambridge University Press.

Collins, R. (1993). What does conflict theory predict about America's future? 1993 Presidential Address. *Sociological Perspectives.* 36: 289-313.

Contessi, N. P. (2009). Experiments in soft balancing: China-led multilateralism in Africa and the Arab world, *Caucasian Review of International Affairs.* 3 (4):404-434.

Coser, L. (1956). *The functions of social conflict.* New York: The Free Press.

Coval, J., Jurek, J. and Stafford, E. (2009). The economics of structured finance. *Journal of Economic Perspectives.* 23(1): 3-25.

Dahl, R.A. (1971). *Polyarchy. Participation and opposition.* New Haven: Yale University Press.

Dahl, R. A. (1982). *Dilemmas of pluralist democracy.* New Haven: Yale University Press.

Dahl, R. A. (1985). *A preface to economic democracy.* Berkeley: UCLA Press.

Dahl, R.A. (1998). *On democracy.* New Haven: Yale University Press.

Dahl, R.A. (1999). Can international organizations be democratic? A sceptic's view. In Shapiro, I. and Hacker-Cordón, C. (eds). *Democracy's edges.* Cambridge: Cambridge University Press.

Dahrendorf, R. (1959). *Class and class conflict in an industrial society.* Stanford: Stanford University Press

Dahrendorf, R. (1967). *Society and democracy in Germany.* New York: W.W.Norton.

De Gruchy, J.W. (ed.) (2011). *The humanist imperative in South Africa.* Stellenbosch: SUN Media.

Department of Defense (2007). Annual report to Congress. Military power of the People's Republic of China 2007, Washington D.C.

Diamond, L. (1992). Economic development and democracy revisited, *American Behavioural Scientist.* 35: 450-499.

Diamond, L. and Marks, G. (eds.) (1992). *Reexamining democracy. Essays in honour of Seymour Martin Lipset.* Thousand Oaks: Sage Publishers.

Diamond, L. (1996). Is the Third Wave over? *Journal of Democracy.* 7(3): 20-37.

Diamond, L. (2008). The democratic rollback. *Foreign Affairs.* March/April: 36-48.
Diamond, L.(2011). Why democracies survive. *Journal of Democracy.* 22 (1):17-30.
Dickson, B. (2003). *Red capitalists in China: the party, private entrepreneurs, and prospects for political change.* Cambridge: Cambridge University Press.
Di Xu, (1992). *A Comparison of the educational ideas and practices of John Dewey and MaoZedong in China.* San Francisco: Mellen Research University Press.
Dryzek, J, and Niemeyer, S. (2008). Discursive representation. *American Political Science Review.* 102(4). Available on-line at: http://www.democraciaparticipativa. org/bellagio/arquivos/Dryzek-DISCREP%20APSR08%20FINAL.pdf
Du Toit, P. and Kotze, H. (2010). *Liberal democracy and peace in South Africa. The pursuit of freedom as dignity.* Basingstoke: Palgrave Macmillan.
Du Toit, S. J. 2011. Interview on social justice. Available on-line at: http://www. unesco.org/new/en/unesco/news/interview_with_fanie_du_toit.
Esping-Andersen, G. (1990). *The three worlds of welfare capitalism.* New York: Polity Press.
Fraenkel, E. (1991). *Deutschland und die westlichen Demokratien.* Enlarged edition. Frankfurt/Main: Suhrkamp (first published in 1964).
Freedom House (2010). *Freedom in the world 2010: erosion of freedom intensifies.* Available on-line at: (http://www.freedomhouse.org/uploads/fiw10/FIW_2010_ Tables_and_Graphs.pdf)
Friedman, M. and Schwartz, A.J. (1963). *A monetary history of the United States 1867 to 1960.* Princeton, Princeton University Press.
Fukuyama, F. (1989). The end of history? *The National Interest.* 16: 3-18.
Gambacorta, L. (2009). Monetary policy and the risk-taking channel. *BIS Quarterly Review* (December): 43-53.
Gat, A. (2006). *War and civilization.* Oxford University Press: Oxford.
Gawlikowski, K. 2005. From false "Western universalism" towards true "universal universalism". *Dialog and Universalism* No. 5.
Geithner, T. F. (2008). Reducing systemic risk in a dynamic financial system. Remarks at the economic club of New York, New York City.
Germain, R. (2002). Reforming the international financial architecture: the new political agenda. In Wilkinson, R. and Hughes, S. (eds). *Global governance: critical perspectives.* London and New York: Routledge.
Germain, R. (2009). Financial order and world politics: crisis, change, and continuity. *International Affairs.* 85(4).
Giddens, A. (2000). *Runaway world. How globalization is reshaping our lives.* Routledge: New York.
Gilley, B. (2004). *China's democratic future: how it will happen and where it will it will lead?* New York: Columbia University Press.
Ginsberg, T. (2003). *Juridical review in new democracies. Constitutional courts in Asian cases.* Cambridge: Cambridge University Press.
Globescan, 2011: *Sharp drop in American enthusiasm for free market, poll shows.* Accessible on-line at: www.globescan.com/news_archives/radar10w2_free_market/.
Global FirePower.com. Accessible on-line at: http://www.globalfirepower.com/.
Godsell, B. (2011). At this time and at this place. In: De Gruchy, J.W. (ed.). *The humanist imperative in South Africa.* Stellenbosch: SUN Press.
Goldstone, J. A. (2010). The new population bomb. *Foreign Affairs,* (January/February): 31-43.

Goodfriend, M. (2005). The monetary policy debate since October 1979: lessons for theory and practice. Federal Reserve Bank of St Louis Economic Review 2005(March/April): 243-261.

Goodhart, C. A. E. (2010). The emerging new architecture of financial regulation. Paper prepared for the conference: Monetary policy and financial stability in the post-crisis era. Pretoria. South African Reserve Bank (SARB). 4-5 November 2010.

Gorton, G. B. (2010). Questions and answers about the financial crisis. Cambridge (Ma).NBER. Working paper No. 15787.

Graf, F. (2004). Die Wiederkehr der Götter. Religion in der modernen Kultur. München: Beck.

Greenspan, A. (2004). Risk and uncertainty in monetary policy. *American Economic Review* (Papers and Proceedings). 94(2): 33-40.

Habermas, J. (1973). *Legitimation crisis.* Boston: Beacon Press.

Hall, P. A. and Soskice, D. (200). An Introduction to varieties of capitalism. In: Hall P. and Soskice, D. (eds.): *Varieties of capitalism. The institutional foundations of comparative advantage.* Oxford: Oxford University Press.

Hall, R. E. (2010). Why does the economy fall to pieces after a financial crisis? *Journal of Economic Perspectives.* 24(4): 3-20.

Han, S-Jin (2009). The dynamics of the middle class politics in Korea: why and how do the middling grassroots differ from the propertied mainstream? *Korean Journal of Sociology.* 43(3): 1-19.

Han, S-J. (2010a). The grassroots identity of the middle class and participation in citizen initiatives, China and South Korea. In Cheng Li (ed.) *China's emerging middle class: beyond economic transformation.* Washington (DC): Brookings Institution Press (forthcoming).

Han, S-J. (2010b). Redefining second modernity for East Asia: a critical assessment. *British Journal of Sociology.* 61(3): 465-489.

Hays, J. C. (2009). *Globalization & the new politics of embedded liberalism.* Oxford: Oxford University Press.

Held, D. (1995). *Democracy and the global order: from the modern state to cosmopolitan governance.* Cambridge: Polity Press.

Helimann, S (2008). From local experiments to national policy: The origins of China's distinctive policy process. *The China Journal* (January). 59: 1-30.

Hitchcock, D.I. (1994). Asian values and the United States: How much conflict? Washington, D. C. Centre for Strategic and International Studies.

Hoffmann-Lange, U. (2009). Seymour Martin Lipset: Modernization, social structures and political culture as factors in democratic development, in: Campus, D. and Pasquino, G. (eds.) Masters of political science. Colchester: ECPR Press.

Holbig, H. (2000). Remaking the CCP's ideology: determinants, progress and limits under Hu Jintao. *Journal of current Chinese affairs.* 38 (3): 35-61.

Holgate, R. G. (2002). Liberty and democracy as economic systems. *Independent Review.* VI (3): 407-425.

Hsu, S., Shiyin, J. and Heyward, H. (2010). The global crisis' impact upon China's rural migrants. *Journal of Current Chinese Affairs.* 39 (2):167-185.

Huntington, S.P. (1991) Democracy's Third Wave. *Journal of Democracy.* 2 (2): 12-34.

Huntington, S. P. (1991). *The Third Wave. Democratization in the late twentieth century.* Norman: Oklahoma University Press.

Inglehart, R. and Welzel, C. (2005). *Modernization, cultural change, and democracy. The human development sequence*. Cambridge: Cambridge University Press.

IMF (2009). World economic outlook. Washington, D.C. April 2009.

Jönsson, C. and Tallberg, J. (eds) (2010). *Transnational actors in global governance: patterns, explanations and implications*. Basingstoke: Palgrave Macmillan.

Kaletsky, A. (2010). *Capitalism 4.0: The birth of a new economy in the aftermath of crisis*. London: Bloomsbury.

Kahler, M. (2005). Defining accountability: the global economic multilaterals. In Held, D. and Koenig-Archibugi, M. (eds). *Global governance and public accountability*. Oxford: Blackwell.

Kang, Xiaoguang (2006). Confucianisation: a future in the tradition. *Social Research.* 7(1): 77–120.

Kasper, W. and Streit, M. (1998). *Institutional economics: social order and public policy*. Cheltenham: Edward Elgar.

Keefer, P. (2007). The poor performance of poor democracies. In: Boix, C. and Stokes, S.C. (eds.): *The Oxford handbook of comparative politics*. Oxford: Oxford University Press.

Kennedy, S. (2005). *The business of lobbying in China*. Cambridge: Harvard University Press.

Keynes, J. M. (1936). *The general theory of employment, interest and money*. Cambridge: Cambridge University Press.

Kielmansegg, P. G. (1988). *Das Experiment der Freiheit*. Stuttgart: Klett/Cotta.

Kindleberger, C. P. (1973). *The world in depression 1929-1939*. London: Allan Lane.

Kling, A. (2009). *Not what they had in mind: a history of policies that produced the financial crisis of 2008*. Arlington (VA). Mercatus Centre: George Mason University.

Klingemann, H-D and Welzel, C. (2007). Theories of the development of democracy. In: Hettne, B. (ed). *Human values and global governance*. Vol. 2. Houndmills: Palgrave Macmillan.

Kotze, H. and Steenekamp, C. L. (2009). Values and democracy in South Africa. Comparing elite and public values. Johannesburg: Conrad-Adenhauer-Stiftung.

Kunzig, R. (2011). Population 7 billion. *National Geographic*. 219(1): 32-69.

Lall, R. (2010). Reforming global banking rules: back to the future? *DIIS Working Paper* 2010: 16. Copenhagen: Danish Institute for International Studies.

Lam, W. (2009). Jintao unveils major foreign policy initiative. *China Brief* (December). 9 (24): 2-4.

Lane, D. (2010). Post-socialist states and the world economy: the impact of global economic crisis. *Historical Social Research.* 35 (2): 218-241.

Lategan, B. C. (2011). Developing common values in situations of plurality and social transformation. In: *Festschrift* for Dirkie Smit (in press).

Leamer, E. E. (2007). Housing in the business cycle. Paper presented at the Federal Reserve Bank of Kansas City. Jackson Hole symposium: Housing, housing finance, monetary policy. Wyoming, 30 August to 1 September, 2007.

Lee, J. (2009). Global financial crisis makes it more difficult for China to pursue political reform. *Executive Highlights*. 29 June. No. 859.

Lijphart, A. (1999). *Patterns of democracy. Government forms and performance in thirty-six countries*. New Haven: Yale University Press.

Lin, J. and Chang, H. (2009). Should industrial policy in developing countries conform to comparative advantage or defy it? A debate between Justin Lin and Ha-Joon Chang. *Development Policy Review*. 27(5): 483-502

Lindahl, H. (2010). A-legality: Postnationalism and the question of legal boundaries, *The Modern Law Review*. 73 (1): 30-56.

Lipset, S.M (1959). Some social requisites of democracy: economic development and political legitimacy. *American Political Science Review*. 53: 69-105.

Lipset, S. M. (1960). *Political man - the social bases of politics*. New York: Doubleday.

Lipset, S.M. (1994). The social requisites of democracy revisited. *American Sociological Review*. 59: 1-22.

Liu Li, Ruan, V. and Batson, A. (2010). China's economic policies face dilemmas, says Premier Wen. *The Wall Street Journal*. 5 July.

Liu, Z. *et al.* (2009). Private business sidelined by China's stimulus. *Economic Observer* (Jingji Guancha Bao). 16 March. 409.

Lo, B. (2010). China and the global financial crisis. Available on-line at: www.cer.org.uk/pdf/essay_974.pdf

Lubman, S. (2010). Are strikes the beginning of a new challenge? Available on-line at: http://blogs.wsj.com/chinarealtime/2010/06/25/stanley-lubman-are-strikes-the-beginning-of-a-new-challenge/

Lockhart, D. P. (2008). Thoughts on the subprime mortgage crisis. Paper presented at the Atlanta Commerce Club in a panel discussion entitled: The subprime crisis: is it contagious? 29 February, 2008.

Lu, Xiaobo (2000). Booty socialism, bureau-preneurs, and the state in transition. *Comparative Politics*. 32(3): 273-295.

Marquand, R. and Arnoldy, B. (2007). China emerges as leader in cyberwarfare. *Christian Science Monitor* (14 September). Accessible on-line: http://www.dtic.mil/cgi-bin/GetTRDoc?Location=U2&doc=GetTRDoc.pdf&AD=ADA508213

Max-Neef, M. (1991). *Human scale development: conception, application and further reflections*. New York: Apex Press.

McGrew, A. G. (1999). Democratising global governance. Democratic theory and democracy beyond borders. *Theoria. A Journal of Social and Political Theory*. December. 94: 30-47.

Merkel, W. (2010). *Systemtransformation*. 2. Auflage. Wiesbaden: VS Verlag für Sozialwissenschaften.

Meulemann, H. (1996). *Werte und Wertewandel.ZurIdentiäteinergeteilten und wiedervereinte Nation*.Weuiheim: JuventaVerlag.

Meulemann, H. (2009). Secularisation or the revival of religion? In: Rieger, M (ed.). *What the world believes*. Gütersloh: Verlag Bertelsmann Stiftung

Michael, D. (2009). China's stimulus package: opportunities and roadblocks. A report of Boston Consulting Group.

Micklethwait, J. and Wooldridge, A. (2009). *God is back. How the global rise of faith is changing the world*. London: Penguin.

Mills, C. W. (1956). *The power elite*. Oxford University Press: New York.

Mishkin, F. S. (2007). *Monetary policy strategy*. Cambridge (Ma): MIT Press.

Mishkin, F. S. (2008). How should we respond to asset price bubbles? Speech at the Wharton Financial Institutions Centre and Oliver Wyman Institute's Annual Financial Risk Roundtable, Philadelphia, Pennsylvania, 15 May 2008.

Mörth, U. (ed.) (2004). *Soft law in governance and regulation*. Cheltenham, UK: Edward Elgar.

Müller, H. (2010). Business ethics from below: rethinking organisational values, strategy and trust, in: Cilliers, P. and Preisker, R (eds.). *Complexity, difference and Identity*. Heidelberg: Springer.

Müller, T. (2009). Religiosity and attitudes towards the involvement of religious leaders in politics: A multilevel-analysis of 55 societies. World Values Research 2(1):1-29.

Morlino, L. (2009). Are there hybrid regimes? Or are they just an optical illusion? *European Political Science Review*. 1(2): 273-296.

Naisbitt, J. & Naisbitt,D. (2010). *China's megatrends. The 8 pillars of a new society.* New York: Harper.

Näsström, S. (2010). Democracy counts: problems of equality in transnational democracy. In Jönsson, C. and Tallberg, J. (eds). *Transnational actors in global governance: patterns, explanations and implications*. Basingstoke: Palgrave Macmillan.

Ngo, Tak-Wing (2008). Rent-seeking and economic governance in the structural nexus of corruption in China. *Crime, Law and Social Change*. 49 (1): 27-42.

Norris, P. & Inglehart, R. (2004). *Sacred and secular. Religion and politics worldwide*. Cambridge: Cambridge University Press.

North, D. C. (1990). *Institutions, institutional change, and economic performance*. Cambridge (Ma): Harvard University Press.

Obstfeld, M. and K. Rogoff (2005). Global current account imbalances and exchange rate adjustments. Brookings papers on economic activity. 1: 67-122.

O'Donnell, G. and Schmitter, P. (1986). *Transitions from authoritarian rules: tentative conclusions about uncertain democracies*. Baltimore: Johns Hopkins University Press.

O'Donnell, G. (2004). Why the rule of law matters. *Journal of Democracy*. 15 (4), 32-46.

Offe, C. (1984). *Contradictions of the welfare state*. Cambridge: MIT Press.

Offe, C. (2006). *Strukturprobleme des kapitalistischen Staates*, Frankfurt: Campus Verlag.

Pearson, M. (1997). *China's new business elite: the political consequences of economic reform*. Berkeley: University of California Press.

Pei, M. (2006*). China's trapped transition: The limits of developmental autocracy*. Cambridge (MA): Harvard University Press.

Pei, M. (2010). China's political awakening? The diplomat. Available on-line at: www. http://the-diplomat.com/ 2010/07/14/china

Perry, E. J. (2001). Challenging the Mandate of Heaven: Social protest and state power in China. Watertown (Ma): East Gate Books.

Perry, E.J. (2007). Studying Chinese politics: farewell to revolution? *The China Journal* .(January). 57: 1-22.

Petroff, E. (2011). Who is to blame for the subprime crisis? Available on-line at: http://www.investopedia.com/articles/07/subprime-blame.asp.

Petrou, M. (2010). Europe's war against Islam. *Maclean's*. 123(1): not paginated.

Plattner, M. F. (2011). From the G-8 to the G-20. *Journal of Democracy*. 22(1): 31-38.

Poole, W. (2007). Understanding the Fed. Federal Reserve Bank of St. Louis Economic Review 2007(January/February): 3-13.

Przeworski, A. (1991). *Democracy and the market. Political and economic reforms in Eastern Europe and Latin America.* Cambridge: Cambridge University Press.

Przeworski, A. *et.al.* (1996). What makes democracies endure? *Journal of Democracy.* 7 (1): 39-55.

Puddington, A. (2008). The 2007 Freedom House Survey: Is the tide turning? *Journal of Democracy.* 19(2): 61-73.

Puddington, A. (2010). The Freedom House survey for 2009: the erosion accelerates. *Journal of Democracy.* 21(2): 136-150.

Pye, L. and Pye, M. (1985). *Asian power and politics. The cultural dimensions of authority.* Cambridge (Ma): Harvard University and London: The Belknap Press.

Read, B. (2003). Democratising the neighbourhood? New private housing and home-owner self-organisation in urban China. *The China Journal.* 49(1):31-59.

Ramo, J. (2004). *The Beijing Consensus.* London: Foreign Policy Centre.

Reinhart, C. and Rogoff, K. (2010). From financial crash to debt crisis. Boston(Ma). NBER Working paper No. 15795.

Reinhart, C. and K. Rogoff (2004). The modern history of exchange rate arrangements: a reinterpretation. *Quarterly Journal of Economics* (February). 119: 1-48.

Reuter (2010). Reining in the banks. Available on-line at: http://graphics.thomsonreuters.com/AS/pdf/baselIII.pdf

Rieger, M. (ed.) (2009). *What the world believes. Analyses and commentary on the Religion Monitor 2008.* Gütersloh: Bertelsmann.

Roberts, R. (2010). *Gambling with other people's money. How perverted incentives caused the financial crisis.* Arlington, (Va). Mercatus Centre: George Mason University.

Romer, C. D. (1992). What ended the Great Depression? *Journal of Economic History.* 52: 757-784.

Rose, A. K. (2006). A stable international monetary system emerges: inflation targeting is Bretton Woods reversed. *Journal of International Money and Finance.* 26: 663-681.

Rummel, R.J. (1997). *Power kills. Democracy as a method of non-violence.* Brunswick (NJ): Transaction Publishers.

Russett, B. M. (1993). *Grasping the democratic peace. Principles for a post-Cold War world.* Princeton (NJ): Princeton University Press.

Rustow, D.A. (1970). Transitions to democracy: toward a dynamic model. *Comparative Politics.* 2: 337-364.

Sarrazin, T. (2010). Deutschland schafft sich ab. München: Deutsche Verlagsanstalt.

Universal Declaration of Human Rights 1948. New York: United Nations. Available on-line at: http://www.un.org/en/documents/udhr/index.shtml .

Sartori, G. (1987). *The theory of democracy revisited. The classical issues.* Vol.2. Chatham: Chatham House Publishers.

Schlesinger, S.C. (2003). *Act of creation: the founding of the United Nations.* Cambridge (MA): Westview.

Schmitter, P. C. and Karl, T.L. (1991). What democracy is ... and is not. *Journal of Democracy.* 2 (3):75-88.

Schram, S.R. (1984). Economics in command? Ideology and policy since the Third Plenum, 1978-84. *The China Quarterly* (September). 99: 417-461.

Schwartz, P. and Randall, D. (2003). *An abrupt climate change scenario and its implications for United States national security,* mimeo.

Sen, A. (1999). Democracy as a universal value. *Journal of Democracy.* 10 (3): 3-17.
Shapiro, I. (1999). *Democratic justice.* New Haven and London: Yale University Press.
Sharma, R. (2010). The post-China world. *Newsweek,* 20 June.
Shih, V. (2009). *Factions and finance in China: elite conflict and inflation.* Cambridge: Cambridge University Press.
Smith, A. (1776 [1981]). *An inquiry into the nature and causes of the wealth of nations.* Vol. 1. Indianapolis: Liberty Fund.
Sorkin, A.R. (2009). *Too big to fail: inside the battle to save Wall Street.* London: Allen Lane.
South China Morning Post. (2010). Don't be so panicked about raising wage. 9 June.
Stern, G. and Felman, R. (2004). Too big to fail: the hazards of bank bailouts. Washington (DC): Brookings Institution.
Svensson, L. E. O. (2009). Flexible inflation targeting: lessons from the financial crisis. Speech given at the workshop: Towards a new framework for monetary policy? De Nederlandsche Bank, Amsterdam, 21 September, 2009.
Stiglitz, J. (2006). *Making globalization work.* London: Penguin.
Sun, L. (2009). The logic of financial crisis and its social consequences. *The Chinese Journal of Sociology.* 2: 1-15.
Sun, L. et al. (2010). New thinking on stability maintenance: long-term social stability via institutionalized expression of interests. *South Weekly.* 14 April.
Sunday Times Business Times, 1 November 2009: 12.
Tallberg, J. and Jönsson, C. (2010). Transnational actor participation in international institutions: where, why, and with what consequences? In Jönsson, C. and Tallberg, J. (eds). *Transnational actors in global governance: patterns, explanations and implications.* Basingstoke: Palgrave Macmillan.
Tanzi, V. and Hamid, D. (2001). Corruption, growth, and public finances. In: Arvind K. Jain (Hrsg.): *The political economy of corruption.* London: Routledge.
Taylor, J. B. (1993). Discretion versus policy rules in practice. Carnegie-Rochester conference series on public policy. 39(2): 195-214.
Taylor, J. B. (1998). Applying academic research on monetary policy rules: an exercise in translational economics. The Harry G. Johnson Lecture, Stanford University.
Taylor, J. B. (2007). Housing and monetary policy. Federal Reserve Bank of Kansas City's 2007 symposium: Housing, housing finance, monetary policy. Jackson Hole, Wyoming, 30 August to 1 September 2007.
Taylor, J. B. (2009). *Getting off track.* Stanford: Hoover Institution Press.
The Economist *(2010). Brazil, Russia, India and China matter individually. But does it make sense to treat the BRICs – or any other combination of emerging powers – as a block? 15 April.*
The Economist Intelligence Unit (EIU) (2010). The state of the state. Accessible on-line at: http://www.economist.com/node/17493405
The Economist (2011). Market of ideas: capitalism's waning popularity. 7 April. Accessible on-line at: www.economist.com/node/18527446.
Thompson, G. *et al* (eds) (1991). *Markets, hierarchies and networks: the coordination of social life.* London: Sage.
Tingyang Zhao (2006). Rethinking empire from a Chinese concept 'All-under-Heaven' (Tian-xia). *Social Identities* (January). 12 (1): 29- 41.

Toon, J. (2008), *China as global technology leader?* Accessible on-line at: http://www.ventureoutsource.com/contract-manufacturing/trends-observations/2008/china-as-global-technology-leader.

Trailokya Raj Aryal (2010). Confucianism and communism in China. *Republica Opinion*, 22 June.

Tsai. K. (2007). *Capitalism without democracy: the private sector in contemporary China*. New York: Cornell University Press.

Tsou, T. (1995). Chinese politics at the top: factionalism or informal politics? Balance-of- power politics or a game to win all? *The China Journal*. 34: 95-156.

Tuck, C. (1995). Is the party over? Political instability in post-Deng China. *Contermoarary Review* (May). Accessible on-line at: http://findarticles.com/ p/articles/ mi_m2242/is_n1552_v266/ai_17041146/

UNDP. 2010. *Human development report*. New York: United Nations Development Programme.

Van Beek, U. (ed.) 2005. *Democracy under construction: Patterns from four continents*. Bloomfield Hills: Barbara Budrich Publishers.

Van Beek, U. (ed.) 2010. *Democracy under scrutiny: Elites, citizens, cultures*. Opladen: Barbara Budrich Publishers.

Van Creveld, M. (1991). *The transformation of war*. New York: Free Press.

Van Creveld, M. (2008). *The culture of war*. New York: Ballantine Books.

Wang, K. (2010a). A China paradox: migrant labour shortages amidst rural labour supply abundance. Available on-line at: Faculty.washington.edu/kwchan/ Chan_paradox_shortages_paper.pdf

Wang, M. (2010b). Impact of the global economic crisis on China's migrant workers: a survey of 2,700 in 2009. *Eurasian Geography and Economics*. 51 (2):18-235.

Wapner, P. (2007). Civil society. In Weiss, T.G. and Daws, S. (eds). *The Oxford handbook on the United Nations*. Oxford and New York: Oxford University Press.

Wasserstrom, J. (2010). *China in the 21st century: what everyone needs to know*. Oxford: Oxford University Press

Williamson, J. (1990). What Washington means by policy reform. In J Williamson (ed). *Latin American adjustment: how much has happened?* Washington (DC). Institute for International Economics: 5-35.

Weiss, T.G., Carayannis, T. and Jolly, R. (2009). The "Third" United Nations. *Global Governance*. 15(1):123-142.

White, G (1984). Developmental states and socialist industrialisation in the Third World. *Journal of Development Studies*. 21 (1): 97: 120.

White, L. J. (2010). The credit rating agencies. *Journal of Economic Perspectives*. 24(2): 211-226.

Winkler, H.A. (1993). *Weimar 1918-1933*. München: Beck.

World Bank (2009). Available on-line at: http://data.worldbank.org

World Development Report (2010). The World Bank. Washington D.C. Accessible in-line at: www.worldbank.org/wdr2010

Worldwatch Institute (2008). *China on pace to become global leader in renewable energy*. Available on-line at: http://www.worldwatch.org/node/5497.

Wolf, M. (2010a). Currencies clash in the new age of beggar-thy-neighbour. *Financial Times*. London. 29 September.

Wolf, M. (2010b). How to fight the currency wars with a stubborn China. *Financial Times*. London. 6 October.

Wong, C. (2000). Central-local relations revisited: the 1994 tax-sharing reform and public expenditure management in China. *China Perspectives.* 31: 20-41.

Woodhead, L. (ed). (2001). *Peter Berger and the study of religion.* London: Routledge.

Xinhua News Agency, 24 November, 2009. In: Lam, W. (2009). Jintao unveils major foreign-policy initiative. *China Brief.* December. 9 (24). Accessible on-line at: http://www.jamestown.org/programs/chinabrief

Zakaria, F. (1997). The rise of illiberal democracy, *Foreign Affairs.* November/December: 22-43.

Zhan Zhongle & Su Yu (2009). Poverty eradication and human rights safeguards: China's progress and reflections. The second Beijing forum on Human Rights: Harmonious Development and Human Rights. Beijing, November.

Zhang, Z. et al. (2009). Handling the global financial crisis: Chinese strategy and policy response. Available on-line at: www.unpan1.un.org/intradoc/groups/public/documents/.../unpan038696.pdf

Zheng, Yongnian (1999). *Discovering Chinese nationalism in China. Modernisation, identity and international relations.* Hong Kong: Colocraft

Zick, A., Pettigrew, T.F and Wagner, U. (2008). Ethnic prejudice and discrimination in Europe. *Journal of Social Issues.* 64(2): 233-251.

Zoellick, R. (2010). The G20 must look beyond Bretton Woods. *Financial Times.* London. 8 November.

Index